# Southeast Asia's
# BEST RECIPES
## From Bangkok to Bali

Wendy Hutton

Foreword by Charmaine Solomon
Photography by Masano Kawana

**TUTTLE** Publishing

Tokyo | Rutland, Vermont | Singapore

# Contents

A Tropical Culinary Adventure  **6**
Fabulous Flavors From Bangkok to Bali  **8**
Essential Southeast Asian Ingredients  **12**
Tips and Techniques  **22**

**BASIC RECIPES 24**
Cucumber and Pineapple Salad  25
Vinegared Cucumber Salad  25
Tangy Tomato Dip  26
All-purpose Dippers  26
Vietnamese Fish Sauce Dip  27
Simple Thai Fish Sauce and Chili Dip  27
Cambodian Salt, Lime and Black Pepper Dip  27
Malaysian Chili and Dried Shrimp Paste Dip  28
Thai Shrimp Paste and Lime Dip  28
Red Bell Pepper Relish  29
Vietnamese Bean Sprout Pickles  29
Daikon and Carrot  30
Burmese Crispy Dried Shrimp Sprinkle  30
Salted Soybean, Pork and Peanut Sauce  31
Roasted Thai Chili Paste  31

**CHAPTER 1: STARTERS AND SNACKS 32**
Extraordinary Beef Satay  34
Tasty Thai Shrimp or Fish Cakes  35
Vietnamese Spring Rolls  36
Thai Tuna Carpaccio  37
Saigon Shrimp and Pork Pancakes  38
Northern Thai Leaf Cup Nibbles  40
Southern Thai Corn Fritters  41
Tangy Marinated Fish  42
Grilled Vietnamese Meatballs  43
Fragrant Cambodian Chicken Wings  44
Fresh Summer Rolls  45
Laotian Spiced Beef Jerky  46
Balinese Seafood Satays  47

**CHAPTER 2: SOUPS AND SALADS 48**
Javanese Tamarind Vegetable Soup  50
Spicy Thai Beef Soup  51
Southern Thai Beefball Soup  52
Clear Soup with Spinach and Corn  53
Classic Shrimp Tom Yam Soup  54
Fragrant Coconut Chicken Soup  55
Creamy Coconut Pumpkin Soup  56
Cambodian Sweet and Sour Fish Soup  57
Penang Nonya Laksa Noodle Soup  58
Thai Rice Soup with Pork or Chicken  59
Singapore-style Laksa Noodle Soup  60
Vietnamese Beef Noodle Soup  62
Madurese Chicken Noodle Soup  64
Thai Lemongrass Soup with Mushrooms  65
Sweet and Spicy Green Papaya Salad  66
Thai Green Mango Salad with Cashews  67
Tropical Fruit Salad with Palm Sugar Dressing  68
Crunchy Burmese Cabbage Salad  69
Barbecued Pork Salad with Thai Herbs  70
'Big Salad' with Chicken, Pork and Shrimp  71
Smoked Fish and Green Mango Salad  72
Vietnamese Chicken Salad  73

**CHAPTER 3: NOODLES, RICE AND BREADS 74**
Burmese Noodles in Coconut Broth  76
Nonya Rice Noodles with Toasted Coconut  77
Classic Pad Thai Rice Noodles  78
'Birthday Noodles' with Pork and Shrimp  79
Malay Rice Noodles in Sweet Tamarind Gravy  80
Singapore Hokkien Noodles  82
Vegetarian Noodles with Chinese Mushrooms  83
Thai River Noodles with Beef and Broccoli  84
Singapore Fried Kway Teow  85
Thai Rice Salad with Toasted Coconut  86
Classic Indonesian Fried Rice  88
Cambodian Rice Noodle Soup  89
Vietnamese Mixed Coconut Rice  90
Malaysian Coconut Rice  91
Thai Fried Rice with Shrimp and Pork  92
Lacy Malay Pancakes  93

## CHAPTER 4: POULTRY AND MEAT  94

Vietnamese Honey-glazed Chicken  96
Fragrant Cambodian Chicken  97
Thai Basil Chicken  98
Chicken with Green Curry Paste and Basil  99
Thai Barbecued Chicken  100
Green Curry Chicken  101
Laotian Chicken with Onions and Tomatoes  102
Mild Javanese Chicken Bathed in Coconut Milk 103
Indonesian Grilled Chicken  104
Roast Duck on a Bed of Crispy Noodles  105
Chicken with Mango and Cashews  106
Spicy Tamarind Chicken with Lemongrass  107
Cambodian Garlic Pork  108
Lemongrass Beef with Peanuts  109
Thai Grilled Beef Salad  110
Malaysian Lamb Curry  111
Nonya Soy Braised Pork  112
Simple Thai Pork Omelet  113
Sweet Soy Balinese Pork  114
Thai Red Beef Curry  115
Scrambled Eggs with Chinese Sausages  116
Green Mango Pork  117
Laotian Beef Stew with Asian Herbs  118
Spicy Laotian Ground Beef  119

## CHAPTER 5: SEAFOOD AND FISH  120

Crunchy Thai Stuffed Shrimp  122
Marinated Shrimp Skewers  123
Squid with Garlic and Black Pepper  124
Delicate Squid with Thai Herbs  125
Fragrant Steamed Mussels  126
Famous Singapore Chili Crab  127
Fish Mousse with Basil and Red Curry  128
Thai Fried Fish with Ginger Sauce  129
Fish with Sweet Tamarind Sauce  130
Grilled Whole Sambal Fish  131
Fragrant Grilled Fish Cakes  132
Grilled Fish with Sweet Soy Dip  133

## CHAPTER 6: VEGETABLES AND TOFU  134

Stir-fried Vegetables with Oyster Sauce  136
Cabbage Braised in Creamy Coconut Milk  137
Spicy Sambal Eggplant  138
Stir-fried Pumpkin and Snowpeas  139
Fragrant Spiced Pineapple  140
Laotian Grilled Eggplant  141
Stir-fried Tofu and Bean Sprouts  142
Red Curry and Tofu  143
Silken Tofu with Chinese Vegetables  144
Fried Tofu with Tomato Sambal  145

## CHAPTER 7: DESSERTS  146

Sweet New Year's Rice Cakes  148
Rice Flour Crêpes with Sweet Cinnamon and Peanut  150
Mangoes with Sweet Sesame Coconut Rice  151
Water Chestnut and Sweet Corn Pudding  152
Sago Pearls with Sweet Coconut Cream  153
Coconut Pancakes  154
Thai Red Rubies in Sweet Coconut Milk  155
Banana and Sago Pudding  156
Balinese Black Rice Pudding  157

Index  **158**

photo by Fred Kroh

# A Tropical Culinary Adventure

At last, here is the book I have long awaited from a food writer I really trust. Wendy Hutton is one of the too few Western food writers on Asian food who knows her subject inside out. She takes the trouble to research painstakingly and then conveys her knowledge and enthusiasm for Southeast Asian food with recipes that really work.

I have known Wendy for almost 30 years and from the moment we met, recognized in each other a kindred spirit. She was half the editing team who worked on my *Complete Asian Cookbook*, making an onerous task one of great satisfaction.

Her *Singapore Food* is the only other cookbook (besides mine) that I keep in my kitchen and actually cook from. We consult each other on matters culinary and track down elusive ingredients with the enthusiasm of bloodhounds. Wendy has a much more adventurous attitude to food than I have and often sends me jottings from the wild, as it were, where her descriptions of dishes she has tried during her travels in Asia fill me with awe.

While we might not all live in a tropical country with mangoes dropping from the trees and lemongrass growing happily in the garden, thanks to immigration, a wide range of Asian ingredients is now readily available in most Western countries. This book will open the door to those exciting hot, sweet, sour, salty, spicy and sometimes bitter flavors which make the food of Southeast Asia such a palate awakening experience. Even for those whose culinary aspirations are limited, this book is an inspiring read as Wendy Hutton shares her experiences and her recipes.

*Charmaine Solomon*

# Fabulous Flavors from Bangkok to Bali

Southeast Asia is my adopted home. I came intending to stay two or three years. More than forty years later, I'm still here. How could I possibly tear myself away from such a fascinating region which also—or could this be the real reason?—offers some of the world's most sublime food.

When I first arrived in the Malaysian capital, Kuala Lumpur, towards the end of 1967, I was overwhelmed by the astonishing variety of food created by the three major ethnic groups: Malay, Chinese and Indian. It was a revelation to someone who previously had only ever eaten Chinese food, considerably adapted to what were perceived to be Western tastes; several rather indiffer-

ent Indian curries and just one Southeast Asia dish, Nasi Goreng or Indonesian-style fried rice prepared by a Dutchman who'd left Indonesia and migrated to Australia after Independence.

I felt almost inebriated by the sheer exuberance of Malaysia's lush tropical surroundings, the almost bewildering range of faces, styles of dress, incomprehensible languages and above all, food. I went on a non-stop voyage of discovery, eating in coffee shops, roadside stalls, restaurants and in the homes of friends, all the time trying to find out how to reproduce some of these amazing dishes myself.

Today, with cookbooks and TV shows telling you how to make just about anything from just about anywhere, it's strange to recall that back in the late 1960s, there were virtually no English-language cookbooks on Malaysian or Singaporean food. I eventually found my first cookbook, which I still have today and which is probably now a collector's piece: the 9th edition, published in 1962, of *The YWCA of Malaya's Cookery Book: A Book of Culinary Information and Recipes Compiled in Malaya.*

Armed with a list of ingredients and their local names, I was able to start buying what I needed to try to some of the recipes in this treasure of a cookbook. Thanks to Aminah, our *amah* who didn't speak a word of English, I had a crash course in Malay and was soon able to ask for ingredients by their local name in the markets. I must confess, though, that when I read of curry leaves, a popular southern India herb, I thought it must have been a joke (the Indian counterpart to the "spaghetti tree"). But once I learned that the curry leaf was *daun kari* in Malay (easier to pronounce than the Tamil *karuvapilai*), I was able to ask for it without feeling I'd provoke a burst of laughter.

This was the beginning of a process which continues even today, asking how unfamiliar ingredients are used, begging to be allowed to watch how the food is prepared in kitchens around Asia, asking friends or their cooks for their recipes and comparing these with recipes in cookbooks I was able to find. Whenever I travel, I look for locally written cookbooks and have a wonderful collection including gems such as *The East Indian Women's As-*

**Famous Singapore Chili Crab**

*sociation Cookbook*; a book on Indonesian regional cooking, *Resep Masakan Daerah* and *Cook and Entertain the Burmese Way*.

Following recipes as I've scribbled them down while watching a cook, or starting with recipes from a local cookbook, I then tweak or modify the recipe until it produce the flavors that I remember and may even adjust them to suit my palate. It may sound presumptuous to change recipes from someone who belongs to the particular culture that produced the cuisine, but I soon learned that is just what cooks do around Asia. Written recipes are rarely used. Most dishes made from memory, the cook tasting and adding a pinch of this or that, a splash more coconut milk, a spoonful of Chinese rice wine or a small amount of sugar to bring together all the flavors of a dish.

When I lived in Singapore, our home-base for forays into the rest of Asia for many years, I was delighted that a similar ethnic mix there meant that much of the food was similar to what I'd fallen in love with in Malaysia. As time went on, however, I discovered a number of uniquely Singaporean and Malaysian dishes that you won't find anywhere else, such as Indian Fried Noodles, Fish-head Curry (neither of which you'll find in India), Famous Singapore Chili Crab and Roti John (perhaps best thought of as a Malay-style hamburger).

In addition to these local specialties, both Singapore and Malaysia have a distinct cuisine which has evolved over the years: Eurasian food, an original East-West blend created by cooks with both Asian and European ancestry. Eurasian cooks are notorious for not sharing their recipes, or if they do tell you their secrets, you can be almost certain they've left out a vital ingredient or a special twist that makes their recipe unique. Nonetheless, thanks to the generosity of Eurasian friends (including being lent a handwritten recipe book dating back at least 50 years), I was able to build up a collection of Eurasian recipes.

Even more to my taste—because of its liberal use of fresh herbs and clever blending of Chinese and Malay ingredients and cooking methods—Nonya cuisine was once found only in private homes in Singapore and Malaysia (particularly in Malacca and Penang). Over the past two to three decades, this exquisite cuisine is now found in a number of restaurants, receiving the recognition it deserves.

A year spent in Java in the early 1970s was my introduction to the variety and complexity of the Indonesian archipelago. We lived below an active volcano in the royal city of Jogjakarta, where the Sultan still occupied his palace and where I went either by bicycle or pony cart to the central market to shop. At this time,

**Delicate Squid with Thai Herbs**

Indonesia was still very poor and undeveloped, but that didn't mean that there wasn't exciting food around. Once I learned to speak Indonesian (luckily very similar to Malay), I could use Indonesian-language cookbooks and try to cook a dazzling number of regional favorites.

Like most Southeast Asians, Indonesians are warm and generous and usually amused to meet a Western woman who is so curious about their food. Lots of time in kitchens taught me a great deal more than the cookbooks I used, which assumed you were already familiar with the food. For example, one of my Indonesian-language cookbooks gives a recipe for a sauce, listing ginger, chilies, green onions, vinegar and so on. The amounts for each ingredient? *Secukupnya*, was all that was written, which simply means "enough" or "to taste". Not very helpful for someone relatively new to the cuisine.

Over the years, my collection of recipes grew and when I leaf through them, many bring back memories of the person who gave them to me. There was the lovely Malay pancake, *roti jala*, which my Malay amah in Singapore taught me to make, using it

**Marinated Shrimp Skewers**

**Chicken with Mango and Cashews**

**Fragrant Coconut Chicken Soup**

to mop up the delicious sauce of her curries. I used a metal cup with four spouts in the bottom to get the conventional lacey effect as the batter hit the skillet. Fatimah laughed at such modern affectations, telling me that back in the *kampung*, the village women put their hand in the batter and let it trickle down their fingers into the skillet.

In the late 1970s, my two young children and I spent 6 months back-packing right across Indonesia, from Irian Jaya (the Indonesian portion of New Guinea, now known as Papua) through countless incredibly beautiful islands all the way to Sumatra in the west. We were very fortunate to be passed from one family to the next as we traveled, staying in local homes all the way. While my children played with the inevitable horde of children in the village or fed the ducks as they learned impolite words in the local dialect, I was busy going to markets and helping out in the kitchen. Many of the Indonesian recipes I still use today—such as Extraordinary Beef Satay (page 34), Madurese Chicken Noodle Soup (page 64) and Menado-style Indonesian Grilled Chicken (page 104)—date from this period.

Thailand is almost next door if you're living in Singapore and it was easy to make fairly frequent trips there, both with and without my children. Luckily, both my children are discerning eaters and were happy when I set them tasks such as deciding which was the best grilled chicken in Thailand, or the yummiest dessert-like cakes sold by mobile vendors or in the markets. Wherever we went, scribbled recipes went into my notebook. Trekking in northern Thailand with a Thai guide gave me a crash

course in edible wayside plants; staying the night in a tribal village gave me a look at the way fresh soybean milk was made; buying snacks for breakfast with Thai friends in Nahkorn Si Thammarat helped me discover yet more new foods.

My trips to dynamic Vietnam, to lovely Laos and to Cambodia have been less frequent than those to other parts of Asia and travel restrictions in Burma curtailed the length of time I've been able to stay there. But I learned that one of the best ways to discover interesting recipes anywhere in Asia—especially if you don't speak much of the language—is to travel with a local.

Many years ago, during a visit to Burma, my young son and I decided to put ourselves in the hands of an English-speaking Burmese with the improbable name of Sweet. He came into our carriage as the train arrived from Rangoon, begging to be our guide. It seemed like a good idea so off we went in Sweet's trishaw. He not only found us an inexpensive hotel (where supposedly rich foreigners weren't supposed to stay) but for the next few days, pedaled us all around Mandalay.

One evening, he kindly invited us to a sort of "pot luck" dinner given in his district. Guests went from house to house, each family offering a different dish, such as fermented tea leaf salad at one home, an amazing soup with shredded banana stem and unidentifiable herbs in another. After my son gorged himself on sweetmeats at the last house, we were taken to see a special show held to raise funds for the local temple. Once again, thanks to the generosity of people I'd never met before, I managed to get recipe tips along with a large dose of Burmese culture.

Burmese Noodles in Coconut Broth

Spicy Laotian Ground Beef

Balinese Black Rice Pudding

In Siam Reap, Cambodia, I hired a young man with a motorcycle to be my transport and guide for the few days I stayed there. We met early each morning. The first task of the day for my guide is to pick me up early in the morning to take me a local market where I was introduced to the sort of breakfast he would normally ate. Then it was off to the temples of Angkor and surrounding villages, lunch in a local restaurant, followed by early afternoon nap to avoid the hottest part of the day, then in the evening, off to explore more Cambodian cuisine. Now that's my idea of a blissful holiday.

I am still overwhelmed by the generosity of cooks, both in private homes and restaurants. I cannot recall ever having been refused to watch cooks as they prepared their food, jotting down notes so I could try to reproduce these dishes when I was back home.

After many years of eating my way around Asia, I admit that much and all as I love Chinese, Malay and Indian food, my palate responds even more to the incredible fragrance of much of the food found in Thailand, Vietnam, Laos, Cambodia and, to a lesser extent in Bali. Unlike some of the excellent spicy food of Sumatra in Indonesia and the more subtle seasonings of Javanese cuisine, the food created in what was once called Indochina is drenched in herbal flavors that never fail to delight me. All kinds of herbs (leaves, roots and even flower buds), the tang of fresh lime juice, the bite of chili and above all, a fishy aroma combine to make the sort of food I love best.

This fishy aroma comes in the form of a dried shrimp paste in much of Southeast Asia, from the coastal regions of Burma all the way to Bali. Thai and Vietnamese food cuisines are unthinkable with the more delicate salty fish sauce. An even more pungent fishy seasoning found in parts of Thailand, Vietnam, Cambodia and Laos, fermented fish in a thick grayish sauce (*padek* or *prahok*). When I realized it was an essential ingredient for a number of Cambodian dishes, I hunted for it in the markets of Phnom Penh, only to be told everyone makes their own or has a regular supplier.

The English friends with whom I was staying suggested I try to buy it from one of the Vietnamese families living aboard their boats in the large Tonle Sap, the lake near Siem Reap which is the jumping off point for the magnificent ruins of the 12th-century kingdom of Angkor. So off I went with a swanky empty jar (coincidentally from the swanky British emporium, Fortnum and Mason). The Vietnamese woman whom I eventually approached to ask for some of the fermented fish from the large glazed jar on the back deck of the boat seem absolutely astonished, but filled my jar and took a few riels in exchange.

Perhaps you are fortunate enough to already have food memories from various parts of Southeast Asia. If not, I hope that cooking some of these recipes will start you on your own voyage of discovery and remembrance.

Wendy Hutton

# Essential Southeast Asian Ingredients

**Anchovies,** commonly know as "whitebait" in the West, are available dried, either whole or cleaned and range in size from about ¼ in to 2½ in (0.5 cm to 6 cm). They are salted and sun-dried to make a seasoning and snack item. They are particularly popular in Malaysia and Indonesia (where they're known as *ikan bilis* and *ikan teri* respectively). Dried anchovies are often cooked in a little oil to flavor vegetable dishes and soups; instant stock powder made from dried anchovies is now available. If possible, buy cleaned anchovies which have had the head and dark intestinal tract removed; otherwise, you'll need to snap off the heads and flick out the intestinal tract of each tiny fish with the point of a sharp knife. Check that packets of dried anchovies do not look powdery or stale before buying. Store in a tightly closed container on the shelf.

Asian basil

Lemon basil

**Basil, Asian** (*bai horapa* in Thai, *rau que* in Vietnamese) is the most common type of basil used in Southeast Asia, generally known outside the region as Asian or Thai basil. It has a wonderful aniseed aroma, making it quite different to the common Mediterranean or sweet basil and has medium to dark green leaves with a purple tinge to the upper stems and purplish flower heads. Use regular sweet basil as a substitute if unavailable. **Lemon basil,** (known in Thai as *bai manglak*) has smaller, soft pale green leaves and is usually cooked (when the flavor intensifies) rather than eaten raw; unfortunately it is not widely found outside the region. It is not difficult to strike Asian or lemon basil for growing at home; put a few stems in ½ in (1 cm) of water in a glass and keep in a sunny spot until rootlets appear from the bottom of the stem. Transfer to a pot of well-dug soil or plant in the garden in a sunny place. You could also plant Asian basil seeds, which are sometimes available in Asian food shops or nurseries.

**Bamboo shoots** of several types of bamboo are inexpensive and readily available in most of Southeast Asia, very often gathered wild by villagers. Although deep-frozen and dried bamboo shoots are usually available elsewhere, I recommend using canned bamboo shoots if fresh ones are not available. Provided canned shoots are briefly boiled in fresh water before being added to recipes, they have an acceptable flavor and texture.

**Banana leaves** are indispensable as food wrappers, used to wrap food for steaming or grilling, to provide little trays to hold food for steaming and as a kind of cookie cup for sweetmeats. The moisture within the banana leaf makes a difference to the texture and flavor of the food, but if you can't find fresh or frozen banana leaf, use aluminum foil. For how to prepare banana leaf, see page 22.

**Bean sprouts** are made by soaking small, round, green mung beans, then keeping them moist in a warm place until the crisp white shoots emerge 3 to 4 days later. One of the most important vegetables in the region, they are eaten raw, briefly blanched, stir-fried, or made into a pickle. Buy crisp shoots with no sign of green leaves appearing at the seed end. Refrigerate covered in water for up to one week, changing the water each day. Pinch off the straggly tails before using the sprouts and discard any loose black skins, but do not remove the seed heads.

**Black Chinese mushrooms** (often known by their Japanese name, *shiitake*) are cultivated in most of Southeast Asia and enjoyed for their firm texture and meaty flavor when fresh. The dried mushroom, often imported from China, is even more widely used and is often preferred for its more intense flavor and keeping ability. Buy dried black mushrooms that do not show any signs of powder under their gills, which would indicate they are deteriorating. Store in a dry place in a closed container. Before using, soak in hot water until they soften; this will range from about 15 minutes to 1 hour, depending on the thickness of the cap; "flower mushrooms," which have creamy white streaks making them look a bit like a chrysanthemum, are particularly tough and need a full hour to soften. Discard the stem before using the cap.

Napa cabbage      Bok choy      Chinese flowering cabbage

**Cabbage** is found in several varieties in Southeast Asia. The round white cabbage common in temperate climates is grown in cooler areas around the region and eaten both raw and cooked. More frequently found in local markets is Chinese celery cabbage or **Napa cabbage**, with very long, pale green to almost white overlapping leaves, used both raw and cooked. Another type popular for stir-frying is Chinese white cabbage. This name is somewhat misleading because although the stems are usually bright white, the leaves are either pale or mid-green. This delicately flavored cabbage is widely known abroad as **bok choy**. Another variety of this cabbage, with green instead of white stems, is often called Shanghai *bok choy*. **Chinese flowering cabbage** (*choy sam* or *cai xin*) is one of the most delicious members of the cabbage family, with soft mid-green leaves and stems, sometimes sold with delicate yellow flowers visible.

**Calamansi lime** is medium-sized and round, with a thin green skin that ripens to a pale yellow color. These are commonly used to provide lime juice for countless sauces and other dishes in Southeast Asia. Tahitian or other varieties of lime, or even lemon, can be used as a substitute, although the flavor and fragrance are not identical. Small round green limes (as pictured), are 1 to 1¹/₂ in (2.5–4 cm) in diameter and called *limau kesturi* in Malaysia and *lemo* in Bali and have a mild and very fragrant juice. They are often sold as calamondin outside Asia, or may be known by their Filipino name, *kalamansi*. Substitute with regular lime juice, adding, if you like, a few drops of orange juice.

**Candlenuts** are waxy, cream-colored nuts related to the macadamia. Sold raw, they must be cooked (generally crushed and fried in seasoning pastes) before being eaten. They add texture and a faint flavor to food. Choose candlenuts that are light cream in color, not golden brown, as the latter may be rancid. Candlenuts have a high oil content, so are best refrigerated. Substitute one unsalted macadamia or two cashew nuts for each candlenut.

**Cardamom** is a Southwest Indian spice used to flavor some curries and sweet dishes. Whole cardamom pods have a fibrous straw-colored bark that encloses about 12 to 16 intensely fragrant black seeds. Generally, whole pods—slit with a knife and bruised to help release their fragrance—are used. You could substitute a pinch of cardamom seeds for one whole cardamom; ready-ground cardamom is not recommended as it loses its fragrance very quickly.

**Chayote**, originated in Central America, is also known as choko, christophene, custard marrow and vegetable pear. The last name describes its size and shape perfectly. Chayote has a delicate flavor and, when young and raw, a pleasant crisp texture. In most of Southeast Asia, however, the vegetable is cooked. Be sure to peel off the wrinkled, somewhat prickly skin; the central seed is edible.

**Chinese celery** is a small pungent plant, with leaves resembling large, dark green coriander leaves (cilantro). It is used as a flavoring herb and not as a vegetable, particularly in Malaysia and Indonesia. The leaves are often used as a garnish for soups (in fact, the Malay name for this translates as "soup leaf") and for noodles. Chinese celery plants can be refrigerated for up to one week with the roots in a jar containing a little water; cover the plant and jar with a large plastic bag.

**Chinese rice wine** is used in Chinese-inspired recipes and sometimes added to marinades in other local dishes. The best Chinese rice wine is from Shaoxing in China; use dry sherry as a substitute.

**Cinnamon** may have been specified in these recipes, but the flavoring bark used in Southeast Asia is in fact from the cassia tree, a related species with a thicker, darker and more pungently flavored bark than true Ceylon cinnamon. Since cassia is generally labeled "cinnamon"

| Dried red chilies | Green and red finger-length chilies | Bird's-eye chilies | Sriracha chili sauce |

when sold, I've used this name throughout the recipes, but cassia is what you should be using.

**Chili** is a Central American native and available in Southeast Asia in many different varieties of varying heat and flavor. The heat comes from an enzyme known as capsaicin, which is present in the seeds and membranes. Take care to wash your hands carefully after dealing with chilies, as the juice will sting—don't ever rub your eyes or nose when working with chilies. **Fresh finger-length chilies** are used either green or red. The most common type are about finger length and of moderate intensity. Fresh chilies are often crushed to use as a seasoning; one finger-length chili is roughly equal to one teaspoon of crushed chili. It is possible to buy jars of crushed chili (generally mixed with a little salt), which can be kept refrigerated and these are an acceptable substitute for finger-length chilies. Crushed chili is sometimes sold under the Dutch-Indonesian name, *sambal oelek* or *ulek*. Generally speaking, the smaller and thinner the chili, the greater the heat. Small bird's-eye chilies are much hotter and also have a different flavor and aroma to finger-length chilies. **Bird's-eye chilies** can range in size from the aptly (if indelicately) named "rat's-dropping chili" which can be as tiny as

1/2 in (1 cm), up to 1 1/4 to 1 3/4 in (3–4.5 cm) in length. Green, orange and red bird's-eye chilies are all used, generally in spicy dips and relishes. Fresh chilies can be stored whole in a plastic bag in the freezer; remove them and slice or chop while they are still frozen. If you want the full flavor of chilies, but less heat, discard some of the seeds before using. Dried chilies give a much deeper red color to food and lack the smell of fresh chilies. They are usually cut into short lengths and soaked in hot water until soften, 10 to 15 minutes depending on the thickness of the chili. **Dried chilies** vary in intensity; the hottest I have tasted come, surprisingly, from China; Thai dried chilies are hot but not unbearably so, while some Indian varieties are actually quite mild. When buying dried chilies, make sure they still have a good deep color; any which are fading in color or breaking up will be passing their use-by date pretty soon. Dried chilies should keep a few months on the shelf, or almost indefinitely refrigerated. Toasted or dry-roasted dried chilies are coarsely crushed to make crushed **dried chili flakes**, sometimes sold as "chili flakes." These are always served on the table in Thailand

as a condiment. Dried red chilies ground to a very fine powder are sold as **ground red pepper (cayenne)**; do not confuse this with American ground red pepper which contains black pepper and oregano and is used in Mexican dishes. Ground red pepper (cayenne) is sometimes added during cooking to provide heat when other types of chili are not used. A final tip for when someone has eaten a fiery chili and is suffering: don't drink water, eat a spoonful of sugar instead. This is remarkably effective. **Chili sauce** is widely used in South-east Asia as a condiment. Many manufactured chili sauces have added garlic or ginger; some are sweet, others quite acidic and the chili content (read heat factor) differs considerably. One of the most widely exported chili sauces is a Thai blend of chili, garlic and vinegar sold as **Sriracha chili sauce**. Perhaps the most versatile dipping sauce is the mild combination of chilies, ginger and sugar often labeled **"sweet Thai chili sauce;"** this is particularly good with grilled chicken and fish. Most brands of chili sauce can be kept on the shelf, although you might like to refrigerate it if you want to store it for many months.

**Coconut** is one of the most useful plants in the region, although not found everywhere in Southeast Asia. The flesh of the mature coconut is grated and squeezed to make coconut milk. The water from inside the young coconuts (often sold abroad in cans as "coconut juice") is sometimes used to simmer meat (it has a tenderizing effect) and also enjoyed as a cooling drink. Although nothing matches fresh coconut milk for use in cakes and desserts, adequate substitutes are available. If I can't get fresh coconut milk, I prefer to use small packets of concentrated **coconut cream** (the one I use is reduced from two whole coconuts to make 3/4 cup/185 ml of liquid). This can be used straight from the packet as coconut cream; diluted with two parts of water to make **thick coconut milk** and diluted with three parts of water to make **coconut milk**. Some brands of concentrated canned coconut milk are also quite good, although I've come across some very mediocre products that I've had to throw away. Experiment with what you can find locally, buying products labeled "coconut cream" or those which are clearly concentrated to give you the flexibility to create the type of coconut milk you require. Packets of powdered coconut milk are a useful standby when you need just a few spoons of coconut milk, but I do not recommend this product for general use. Once you've opened a packet, store it in the refrigerator.

**Coriander leaves, seeds & roots (cilantro)** is the world's most widely used herb and perhaps even more popular in Southeast Asia than in Central and South America and the Middle East. **Coriander leaves** have a distinctive smell and attractive appearance and are the most important flavoring herb and garnish throughout the region. **Coriander seeds** are the most popular spice; for maximum freshness, local cooks prefer to use whole coriander seeds, heating them slightly to help release their volatile oils and make them easier to pound or grind whenever required. Each time you have finished using the leaves of whole fresh **coriander plants,** cut off the roots, wash well, dry and slice very thinly. Store in a small airtight container in the freezer; do this each time you use coriander and you will soon have a stock of **coriander roots** for use in Thai recipes. If you do not have enough roots when these are required in a recipe, you could use finely chopped **coriander stem** to make up the amount. Fresh coriander plants can be stored for about one week by putting them in a jar with the stems ends standing in about 1/2 in (1 cm) of water. Enclose the coriander and the jar with a large clear plastic bag and stand in the refrigerator.

**Curry powder** is a mixture of ready ground spices, used particularly in Malaysia and Singapore. Different mixtures are available, prepared from a range of spices depending on the type of dish which is required and are generally labeled accordingly. Curry powders labeled "for fish" or "for meat and poultry" are best bought in small quantities and stored in an airtight container in the refrigerator for maximum flavor.

**Daikon radish** has a very thin skin, which can be scraped off with a knife. It is normally eaten raw in Southeast Asia, generally after salting to remove some of the bitterness and is frequently partnered with carrot. Use the smaller radishes around 6 to 7 in (16–18 cm) if possible, as these will generally have a milder flavor and finer texture than the larger ones.

**Dried Chinese sausage** (*lap cheong*) is particularly popular among the Vietnamese. Perfumed with rose-flavored wine, they are never eaten alone, but cooked with rice or other food. They keep well in a dry place, although if you live in a humid climate, you may prefer to refrigerate them.

**Dried Shrimp** are used in countless ways throughout the region. They are an important flavoring in their own right and not used as a replacement for fresh shrimp. Although various sizes are available, the most common ones are around 3/4-in (2-cm) long. They should look orangey-pink and plump; avoid any with a grayish appearance or with an unpleasant ammonia smell. It is possible to buy packets of powdered dried shrimp (generally labeled "floss" or "powder"), but it is better to buy the whole shrimp so you can check the quality. Dried shrimp will keep for several months if refrigerated. Before use, dried shrimp are usually soaked to soften slightly; 5 minutes in warm water should be sufficient. If dried shrimp powder is to be used as a garnish or flavoring, the dried shrimp have a better flavor if dry-roasted in a wok or saucepan for about 4 to 5 minutes (rather than being soaked) before being processed to a fine powder or floss.

**Eggplant** (also known as aubergine) comes in many different shapes, sizes and colors, ranging from tiny pea-sized eggplants (generally lightly pounded and added raw to dips), to egg-shaped vegetables and short or long slender eggplants. The color ranges from white through bright orange to pale green, pale purple and deep purple and there are even streaked green and purple varieties. Apart from the bitter **pea-sized eggplant** and a round, tough-skinned orange variety which is very sour, most Asian eggplants have the same mild flavor, which lends itself well to all types of seasoning. Try to use **slender Asian eggplants,** which are less bitter than their Western counterparts and do not need pre-salting; they also have tender, edible skins. Some eggplants, especially Japanese varieties, are very short, about 5 to 6 in (12.5 to 15 cm) in length, while others can be up to 10 in (25 cm). The length is not important, so long as you can obtain slender Asian varieties, you'll find them much more palatable than the Western type.

**Fish, preserved** is preferred to dried shrimp paste in Cambodia and Laos, where it is known as *prahok* and *padek* respectively. The Vietnamese call it *mam ca sac* and use both this and fermented anchovy sauce (*mam nem*) as a flavoring. Chunks of fresh fish are salted and packed in barrels with a little cooked rice to aid the fermentation. Preserved fish is available in glass jars, often exported from Thailand. The English names vary, from Pure Pickled Gouramy Fish, to Pickled Grey Featherback Fish, to Preserved Mudfish, or something similar; the brand I am currently using also bears the French name *poisson en saumure.* You can recognize it by the pale beige or grey color of the thick paste, which has a few chunks of fish visible. This should be used sparingly. A jar will keep in the cupboard for at least a couple of years. Anchovy sauce or even fish sauce can be used a substitute.

**Fish sauce** is to most of Southeast Asia what soy sauce is to the Chinese and Japanese, the most widely used salty seasoning. Fish sauce has a unique fragrance which gives so much of the regional food its characteristic flavor and aroma. Made from the liquid poured off salted and fermented fish, fish sauce is a clear golden brown color. Thai and Vietnamese brands are usually readily available abroad; in general, Vietnamese fish sauce is slightly stronger in flavor than Thai brands. Keep fish sauce in the cupboard; it lasts almost indefinitely.

**Five spice powder** is a Chinese seasoning sometimes used in Thai and Vietnamese cooking. This finely ground mixture of cassia, cloves, fennel, Sichuan pepper and star anise has a warm fragrance and flavor and is commonly used in braised dishes, or a pinch added to pork sausages or paté. To keep its freshness as long as possible, store in the refrigerator.

**Galangal** is preferred to common ginger in much of Southeast Asia. It is pale cream with delicate pink tips while still young and becomes quite tough and fibrous as it ages. The fragrance of this rhizome seems to embody the smell of the tropics: warm, exciting and faintly spicy with a hint of camphor. Just the aroma alone is enough to get the taste buds going. If you can obtain fresh galangal, scrub it well, peel off any thick papery skin (but don't worry about the tender skin, which can be left on). Cut the galangal in thin slices and store in a sealed bag in the freezer; use the slices as required while still frozen. Dried galangal slices are sometimes available and can be soaked in hot water for about 30 minutes to reconstitute, but a better alternative to the fresh product is galangal packed in brine, usually sold in jars. This may be labeled with the Thai name, *kha*, or simply referred to as "rhizome." (Do not confuse it with Chinese keys or *krachai*). Avoid ground galangal, which does not have anywhere near the same flavor as other substitutes.

**Garlic chives,** also known as Chinese chives, resemble coarse flat blades of dark green grass. When raw, they have a strong flavor, which becomes more delicate after brief cooking. Sometimes, the flowering heads of this are sold as a vegetable and are considered a delicacy by the Chinese. They are also very decorative; a spray or two transforms any dish. Green onions (scallions) are the best substitute.

**Ginger buds** are the unopened flowers the of pink torch ginger, known as *bunga kantan* or *bunga siantan* in Malaysia and *kaalaa* in Thailand. It is eaten raw with a dip, added to salads or cooked in soups and curries. When cooked with fish, it has a flavor and fragrance somewhat reminiscent of Vietnamese mint. There is no substitute; if you are able to obtain the fresh buds, freeze whole for future use.

**Green mango** is universally loved throughout the region for its sour tang. It is eaten with dips, made into salads and pickles, or stir-fried with other ingredients. The mango should be peeled with a vegetable peeler and the flesh cut away from the central oval stone. Green mangoes should be stored in the fridge and peeled only just before they are needed. **Ripe mangoes** are generally eaten as they come from the tree, without any attempts to improve them. One exception is the favorite Thai dessert, where slices of ripe mango are partnered with glutinous rice drenched in coconut milk.

**Green onions (scallions)** are also known as spring onions or some-times as shallots. Green onions have slender stalks with dark green leaves and white bases. They are sprinkled generously on soups and as a garnish.

**Jicama** is sometimes confusingly called a turnip in Malaysia and Singapore. It is a roughly globe-shaped tuber, tapering slightly like a top, with papery beige skin covering crisp white flesh. Slightly sweet and juicy when small and young, jicama tends to become fibrous with age. They are eaten raw (usually with a dip) when young, or cooked when mature.

**Kaffir lime** has an unattractive knobbly skin, which earns it the unappealing alternative name of leprous lime. It has very little juice but the fragrance of the **grated kaffir lime rind** is incomparable. If you can ever lay your hands on fresh kaffir limes, put them whole in your freezer and pull them out to grate (while still frozen) whenever kaffir lime rind is needed. **Kaffir lime leaf** is one of the region's most popular herbs, recognized by its double leaf that looks like a figure eight. The intense and inimitable fragrance of the kaffir lime leaf is essential in many Southeast Asian dishes. If you can buy the fresh leaves, store them in a bag in the freezer. The dried leaves are a poor substitute, but you can sometimes find frozen leaves in Asian stores. In most recipes, you could substitute 1/4 teaspoon grated lime or lemon rind for 1 kaffir lime leaf. Fresh kaffir lime leaves are often finely shredded for adding to salads and other dishes. Fold the leaf in half and cut out the tough central rib. Roll up the leaves from the tip to stem, like a cigar, then lay on a board and use a sharp knife to cut into hair-like shreds.

**Lemongrass** is one of the most important herbs in Southeast Asia, a type of grass that grows up to 32 in (80 cm) in height. The bottom portion (about 8 in/20 cm) is a tightly packed bulb, a little like a miniature leek, while the top part of the lemongrass has coarse, broad leaves which are not used in cooking. The flavor and fragrance are concentrated in the bulb, which is either bruised and added whole (or cut into manageable lengths), or thinly sliced and often pounded or processed. Usually only the tender inner part of the bottom 3 in (7.5 cm) is used for slicing and pounding; peel off two or three of the tough outer leaves to get to the inner portion. As even the inner stem is fibrous, it must be sliced as finely as possible, or else processed, before being used. Lemongrass is added raw to

Fresh round rice flour (laksa) noodles     Fresh egg noodles     Rice-stick noodles     Dried rice vermicelli     Transparent (bean thread) noodles

**Noodles** were introduced by the Chinese and have, over the centuries, become a firmly entrenched part of Southeast Asian cuisine, although they have never replaced rice as the staple food. Noodles made from rice flour predominate, although wheat flour noodles are also eaten, especially in the towns and cities where Southeast Asians of Chinese ethnic origin tend to congregate. Both fresh and dried noodles are used. Fresh noodles should be refrigerated until used; dried noodles will keep almost indefinitely in a cupboard. **Fresh rice flour noodles** are generally cut into flat strands about 1/2 in (1 cm) in width and are usually thin and light in texture. These are known as *sen men* in Thailand and *bahn pho* in Vietnam. Fresh rice flour noodles tend to be thicker and heavier in Singapore and Malaysia, where they are known as *kway teow* or *sa hor fun*. Spaghetti-like fresh **round rice flour (laksa) noodles** are also found and generally used in noodle soups. It is also possible to buy flat sheets of rice flour dough, which can be cut to the desired size. Very thin fresh rice vermicelli is also available in the region, but seldom seen abroad. All fresh rice noodles have been steamed before being sold; before using, they should be blanched in hot water for about 1 minute to remove any oil which has been used to stop them sticking together, then drained and used as

directed in recipes. Dried rice flour noodles come in several forms. **Dried rice vermicelli** is very fine threads of rice noodle, rather like angel hair pasta. **Rice-stick noodles** (or rice-ribbon noodles) are flat and vary in width from about 1/8 to 1/2 in (3 mm–1 cm). (Some brands of rice vermicelli are confusingly labeled rice-stick noodles.) Dried rice-stick noodles should be soaked in hot water for about 10 minutes to soften. They are then generally boiled until cooked, which will take 30 to 60 seconds for rice vermicelli and about 3 to 5 minutes for rice-stick noodles, depending on their thickness. **Transparent (bean thread) noodles,** made from green mung bean starch, are also known as jelly noodles, glass noodles, cellophane noodles and green bean threads. The dried noodles are very fine and white and difficult to cut before soaking, even using kitchen scissors. For this reason, try to choose very small packets so that you will not have to fight to separate as little as 1 oz (30 g), which a number of recipes require. Before using the noodles, put the required amount in a bowl and add warm water to cover. They should be soft after 10 minutes, when they can be drained and cut to size. Packets keep almost indefinitely on the shelf. **Wheat noodles** in their fresh form are sold in flat ribbons of varying widths, or are round and vary

in size from very thin noodles to fat, heavy yellow noodles looking like spaghetti. Wheat noodles are often called "egg noodles," even though most do not actually contain eggs and get their yellow color from food dye. Fresh wheat noodles can be kept refrigerated for 2 to 3 days. Wheat and **egg noodles** are also available dried, although the thickest variety is sometimes difficult to find. Before using fine or medium fresh wheat or "egg" noodles, shake them to dislodge any starch (used to stop them sticking together) and blanch in boiling water for up to 1 minute to cook. Rinse under cold water (this is important) and drain. **Thick fresh wheat noodles** (often known as Hokkien noodles) should be put into a bowl and blanched in boiling water for about 1 minute, to remove any oil or impurities. Drain and use as directed in the recipe. Dried wheat noodles are normally added to boiling water to cook, without any pre-soaking; the cooking time will depend upon the thickness, but is usually around 3 minutes (check the time stated on the package). The noodles should be separated with a long fork or chopsticks during cooking and once cooked, rinsed in cold water and drained. If this last step is omitted, the noodles may become gluey.

salads and also cooked. If you can buy fresh lemongrass, trim off the leaves and keep about 5 in (12.5 cm) of the stem. Stand the ends in 1/2 in (1 cm) of water in a glass and keep in a warm place (a bench or window sill) for up to about 2 weeks for use when required. Alternatively, trim the lemongrass and store in the fridge for 2 to 3 weeks, or for several months in the freezer; slice while still frozen. Small packets of thinly sliced, deep-frozen lemongrass are often available in Asian stores abroad; 2 tablespoons of sliced lemongrass are roughly equivalent to the inner part of the bottom 3 in (7.5 cm) of a stem of fresh lemongrass. If you live in a moderately warm climate and would like to grow lemongrass, leave the cut stems of fresh lemongrass in water until they start to send out roots. Transfer to a large pot or a sunny spot in the garden and keep well watered. They should multiply during the summer.

**Oyster sauce** is a Chinese seasoning sauce that does not actually taste of oysters (and often doesn't even contain them; check the label to see if you're buying real oyster sauce and not "oyster-flavored" sauce) and has the ability to intensify the flavor of food. It is often splashed on to cooked vegetables, or added to marinades; it is more popular in areas with a large Chinese community.

**Palm sugar** is made from the boiled sap of several different types of palm, including the coconut and

palmyra. The flavor can be like a mild butterscotch, similar to maple syrup, or quite strong, while the texture varies from soft palm sugar sold in jars and spooned out, to hard round cylinders and wide oval cakes. (The oval shape comes from the coconut shell into which the sugar syrup is poured to set.) Palm sugar is not as sweet as regular cane sugar and has a very pleasant aroma. Use soft brown sugar as a substitute, or if making palm sugar syrup, add a little maple syrup to the brown sugar syrup.

**Pandanus leaf** is a long wide blade; it is also called fragrant screwpine. The leaves grow up to about 20 in (50 cm) in length, but are often sold trimmed. Cooks throughout the region often rake a pandanus leaf with a fork, then tie it into a knot and add it to the pot when cooking rice; it adds a subtle fragrance that makes the rice taste like prized newly-harvested rice. Pandanus leaves are also used in some curries, but mainly in cakes and desserts. They can be deep-frozen. Pandanus essence is the best substitute.

**Pickled ginger** comprises slices of ginger pickled with salt and vinegar, either prepared at home, or bought in small amounts scooped out of big jars in local markets. Chinese and Japanese brands are usually readily available in Asian stores abroad. Pickled ginger is often shredded and added to sauces or salads.

**Rice flour,** made from plain rice and glutinous rice (sometimes labeled "sweet" or "sticky" rice flour, made

from white glutinous rice) are both used in cakes and savories; they are not interchangeable.

**Rice paddy herb,** known as *ngo om* in Vietnam and *ma om* in Cambodia, is a distinctive herb with a fleshy pale stem with narrow light green leaves. It tastes a bit like very strong fresh coriander leaves (cilantro), which can be used as a substitute. Rice paddy herb is sometimes added to soups, served as part of a herb platter and also eaten with dips.

**Rice paper wrappers** is a wafer-thin disc made from a rice and water dough spread on woven bamboo trays to sun-dry (the disc retains the distinctive pattern of the tray when dried). Known in Vietnam as *bahn trang*, these discs are very brittle and need to be moistened in water to soften slightly before being used to roll up just about anything and everything Vietnamese. They are also filled and deep-fried to make the famous Vietnamese spring rolls. Packets of rice papers (often made in Thailand) are available in three forms: large discs about 8 in (20 cm) in diameter; smaller discs 5 to 6 in (12.5 to 15 cm) in diameter and

wedges which have been cut from a large round rice paper. The last are preferable for making tiny deep-fried spring rolls. Advice on handling rice papers is given in recipes where these are required. They can be stored in a covered container in the cupboard for several months.

**Rice vinegar** is mild and faintly fragrant and is the preferred vinegar throughout Southeast Asia. Inexpensive brands from China are usually readily available in the West (as well as in Southeast Asia). If buying a Japanese rice vinegar, make sure you do not buy what is labeled "sushi vinegar" as this has sweet rice wine, sugar and salt added. If you cannot obtain rice vinegar, use distilled white vinegar.

**Sago,** a starch extracted from the trunk of the sago palm, is sometimes eaten as a gluey staple in a few remote parts of Southeast Asia. However, it is more commonly dried to make tiny white balls known as **dried pearl sago**. These are not much bigger than a pin head and are mainly used in desserts and in a few soups. The balls soften and turn transparent when cooked and help thicken coconut milk or water with their gluey texture. Tapioca balls, made from the starch of the cassava root, are virtually indistinguishable in taste (there isn't any!) and can be substituted for pearl sago. Some tapioca balls are the same size as pearl sago, although it is usually found in larger balls about the size of a tear drop.

**Salam leaf** is popular in Indonesian cooking. It is quite different to the Western bay leaf (or laurel), which is often incorrectly suggested as a substitute. *Salam* leaf grows on a large tree that is a member of the cassia family; it adds a distinctive aroma to food, even when used dried. If you can obtain fresh *salam* leaves, keep them in a bag in the freezer; otherwise, store dried leaves in an airtight container in the fridge for long keeping. There is no substitute for *salam* leaves.

**Salted fish** is a standby in many Southeast Asian homes. The type used in recipes in this book is thick fillets of salted fish, often sold as Mergui fish (named after the region in southern Burma reputed to produce some of the finest salted fish). Salted fish is not normally soaked before use; when thinly sliced and fried to a crisp, it makes a wonderful garnish (and, incidentally, a good substitute for crumbled bacon in Western salads).

**Salted soybeans** is richly flavored fermented soybean, known in Thailand by its Chinese name, *dau jiao* and in Vietnam as *tuong cu da* or *tuong bac.* The beans are ferment-

ed in thick liquid and sold in jars; they vary from dark brown to light golden in color and are sometimes labeled "yellow bean sauce." The basic salted soybean paste contains only soybeans, water and salt. It is possible also to buy slightly sweetened versions, or those with added chili. The beans are usually mashed with the back of a spoon before being used.

**Saw-tooth coriander,** a long pungent blade with saw-tooth edges, tastes like a cross between coriander, mint and basil. It is known in Cambodia as *chi bonla* or *chi barang, prik chee farang* in Thailand and *ngo gai* in Vietnam (elsewhere, it is sometimes referred to by its botanical name, *eryngo*). Saw-tooth coriander is generally added to soups and served as part of a platter of fresh herbs with Vietnamese food. Fresh coriander leaves (cilantro) is the best substitute.

**Sesame oil** is made by extracting the oil from toasted sesame seeds, giving it a rich flavor and aroma that is lacking in Middle Eastern sesame oils, extracted from raw seeds. Sesame oil is used sparingly as a seasoning, not as a cooking medium. Look for a Chinese brand if possible.

**Sesame seeds** are tiny tear-drop shaped seeds, creamy white in color and rich in oil. In Southeast Asia (particularly Vietnam), they are generally toasted and used as a sprinkle on food, including desserts.

**Shallots** are small and purplish, each weighing about 1/3 oz (10 g) and often preferred to larger onions for their sweetness and texture. If these are not available, the brown-skinned or "French" shallot (eschalot) can be substituted, taking into account any significant difference in size when measuring the quantity required for a recipe. Alternatively, use a red or brown skinned onion; a 3 to 3 1/2 oz (85–100 g) onion is roughly equivalent to eight shallots. In Vietnamese recipes, it's fine to use the white portion of green onions (scallions) if shallots are not available. Shallots are frequently pounded and used to flavor

and thicken sauces and curries, added raw to many salads and also deep-fried until crisp as a popular garnish. Packets of crisp-fried shallots are normally available in Asian stores, but it is easy to make your own (see page 22).

**Shrimp crackers** are dried wafers made from shrimp and starch (generally tapioca flour) and are very popular as a garnish or snack, especially in Indonesia, where they are known as *krupuk.* Similar wafers are made with fish, vegetables, or the *melinjo* nut. All wafers should be stored in an airtight container and must be thoroughly dry before be-

Dried shrimp paste

Thick black shrimp paste

**Shrimp paste** is common everywhere from Burma (where it's called *nagpi*) through to Bali (where the local name is *terasi*) and some form of dried shrimp paste is an important part of Southeast Asian cuisine. Made from fermented salted shrimp pressed into a paste (which can range in texture from moist to firm and dry), **dried shrimp paste** varies in color from very dark brown through to a purplish pink. This paste is very strong smelling when raw and must be cooked before being eaten (see page 22). It can be stored almost indefinitely in a firmly covered container in a store cupboard. **Thick black shrimp paste** should not be confused with dried shrimp paste, as it has a different flavor and texture (although it still declares its origin in terms of smell). This black, treacle-like paste is sold in jars, sometimes labeled "black shrimp paste" or "*petis.*" It is used in Malaysia and Singapore, particularly by Nonya cooks and also in Indonesia, usually in sauces. The Chinese name is *hay koh.*

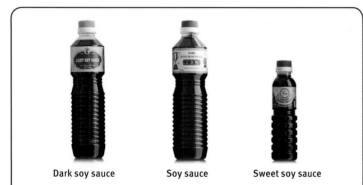

Dark soy sauce     Soy sauce     Sweet soy sauce

**Soy sauce,** introduced by the Chinese, is made from salted and fermented soybeans. Widely used in Southeast Asia, the most common type is regular soy sauce, which is a clear medium brown liquid with a salty taste. **Dark soy sauce** (Chinese brands are often labeled "Superior soy sauce") is dense black and thicker, somewhat less salty and with a malty tang. In Indonesia, **sweet soy sauce** (*kicup manis*) is the most widely used variety. If you can't obtain this, add 1 teaspoon soft brown sugar to 1 tablespoon of dark soy sauce. If using soy sauce which is naturally fermented (check the label, the best Japanese brands are made in this way), it is best refrigerated after opening. Other types of soy sauce can be kept in a cupboard for many months.

ing dropped in very hot oil for a few seconds, until they puff up. (Some local cooks sun-dry them before frying, but you can also use a very low oven.)

**Star anise** is native to Southern China and looks like a small dried brown flower with shiny brown seeds within each of its eight petals. Sometimes some of the "petals" of this aniseed-flavored spice get broken; if a whole star anise is required, add more petals to make up the required number. Star anise is particularly popular with braised pork dishes and is essential in Vietnamese beef stock.

**Tamarind** is a fruit from the huge and decorative tamarind tree. The pods contain flesh-covered seeds which are used either when young and green or, more commonly, picked when mature and used as a pulp. **Tamarind juice,** which adds a fruity sourness to countless dishes throughout the region, is made from tamarind pulp, soaked in a little water, then squeezed and strained to provide the juice. **Tamarind pulp** is usually sold as a dark brownish mass, pulp, seeds, fibers and all. Some brands of tamarind pulp are compressed into a very hard brick and are best avoided, as

it is concentrated tamarind paste sold in jars. Try to find Thai brands of tamarind pulp, which are usually moist and of good quality. Stored in a jar or firmly covered container on the shelf, tamarind pulp keeps almost indefinitely.

**Tapioca** is also known as cassava. The tubers of this plant and even the young leaves are sometimes eaten as a vegetable. The starch extracted from the tubers is sometimes dried and made into small balls (see Sago). **Tapioca flour** is most commonly used in desserts (and is, incidentally, used like talcum powder against prickly heat).

**Turmeric** belongs to the prolific ginger family. The plant has large soft leaves and is predominantly used for its intensely yellow rhizome. Fresh or frozen turmeric rhizome is sometimes available outside Asia; ground turmeric can be used as a substitute, but although it gives plenty of color, the flavor of ground turmeric is somewhat acrid compared to the fresh rhizome. Turmeric leaf is used as a herb in some Indonesian and Malaysian dishes; there is no substitute.

**Vietnamese mint** or **laksa leaf** is a pungent herb with dark, narrow

green leaves known by a number of names in the West: polygonum (the botanical name), Vietnamese mint, hot mint, long-stemmed mint and laksa leaf. To help avoid any confusion, here are the major local names: Vietnam, *rau ram*; Thailand, *phak phai*; Laos, *phak pheo*; Malaysia *daun kesom*; Singapore, *daun laksa*. This distinctively flavored herb is frequently part of a platter of fresh herbs served with noodle soups in Laos, Cambodia and Vietnam and is added to laksa noodle soup in Singapore and some parts of Malaysia. You can strike Vietnamese mint from plants bought in an Asian store if you live in either a hot or temperate climate. Stand a few stems in water in a glass set in a sunny spot (the window sill, perhaps); as soon as you see white roots appearing, plant it in the soil in a sunny position and water frequently.

**Water chestnuts** are Chinese vegetable grown in muddy waters. It has an almost milky sweetness and crisp white flesh that retains its delightful texture even after cooking. Rinse well to remove any dirt before peeling, then put into cold water immediately to avoid discoloring. Water chestnuts can be eaten raw or stirfried. They are minced to add texture and flavor to fillings. They are also added to desserts and sweetmeats, particularly in Thailand.

**Water spinach** is a popular and highly nutritious leafy green vegetable that grows in damp areas. It goes by a variety of names, including

Silken tofu

Pressed tofu

Salty fermented tofu

Dried deep-fried tofu

Dried tofu skin (crinkled strips)

**Tofu** (bean curd) was introduced by the Chinese and has become part of the local diet in much of Southeast Asia. The two most commonly used forms are regular or soft tofu, which is reasonably soft and sold in blocks and **pressed tofu,** which has been compressed to expel most of the moisture and form a solid cake. Soft tofu is generally used in soups and braised dishes, while pressed tofu is normally deep-fried. **Silken tofu** (Japanese in origin) is very soft; it is found in some cities in the region and either steamed or added to soups, particularly by cooks of Chinese origin. Fresh tofu should be covered with water and refrigerated; it can be kept for several days. Pasteurized tofu is sold in vacuum packs or plastic tubs outside Southeast Asia; refrigerate until the expiry date. Another type of tofu sometimes added to

braised dishes or soups is **dried deep-fried tofu,** which is generally sold in small rectangles. These are often sold on strings in Asia, but are elsewhere usually packed in plastic. They are light and spongy in texture and need to be dipped briefly in boiling water to remove the oil before being used. Dried deep-fried tofu has an almost nutty flavor and is particularly appreciated for the way it soaks up the liquid to which it is added. It can be kept refrigerated for at least two weeks. **Dried tofu skin** is the dried skin that forms on top of boiling soy milk. It is dried and sold in sheets as a wrapper or sold in thick crinkled strips about 1 1/4-in/3-cm wide. Tiny squares of **salty fermented tofu,** often reddish brown on the outside, are sold in jars and used exclusively as a seasoning (especially with pork) and as a condiment which is often served with rice porridge.

morning glory, water convolvulus and swamp cabbage. It has hollow stems with pointed, mid-green leaves, which have a soft texture and appealing mild flavor when cooked. Young shoots are frequently eaten raw as part of a salad platter or with a dip, while the leaves and tender stems are usually braised. It does not keep well; wrap in damp newspaper or a cloth and refrigerate for one to two days.

**White fungus** sometimes called silver fungus, is generally a pale ivory color and very crinkly in appearance, almost like a dried chrysanthemum. It is used mostly in soupy desserts, where it is enjoyed for its slightly chewy texture and translucent appearance. It should be soaked in warm water to reconstitute.

**Wild pepper leaves** are sometimes incorrectly called betel leaves in English (*cha plu* in Thai, *bo la lot* in Vietnamese, *pak i leut* in Lao and *daun kadok* in Malay). They have a pleasant, faintly peppery flavor and are used as a salad herb or, particularly in Thailand and Vietnam, as a food wrapper. These can sometimes be found in Vietnamese food shops and can be kept refrigerated in a cloth for a day or two.

**Winged bean** is also known as angled or Goa bean. It has a slight touch of bitterness and a pleasant crisp texture. Look for small young beans which snap rather than bend. Before cooking, pinch the tip and pull down any strings. Winged beans are either eaten raw, usually with a dip, or blanched briefly in boiling water, then sliced to make salads. They can also be stir-fried, but do not over-cook or they will lose their crisp texture.

**Woodear fungus** is used for its slightly chewy texture and dark color. Wood or cloud ear fungus literally grows on trees and has virtually no flavor but is added to soups, salads and vegetable dishes. Two varieties of **dried wood ear fungus** are available: one is small, thin, crinkly and uniformly black, while the other is larger and thicker with a pale grey or beige underside. There is no difference in flavor, but the smaller version is less chewy and reconstitutes more quickly. It keeps almost indefinitely in a covered container on the shelf. Before using, soak the wood ear fungus in warm water until it softens and swells to about five times its dried size. Small thin fungus pieces will take 5 minutes, while thicker pieces need longer. Drain and cut out any hard central portion, then slice or chop according to the recipe.

# Tips and Techniques

The preparation of various Southeast Asian ingredients (such as shallots, lemongrass, etc) is described in Essential Southeast Asian Ingredients (pages 12–21). Some other important tasks which are a little more complex or take longer to describe are discussed here in greater detail.

**Dry-roasting Grated Coconut**  This can be done using either fresh or desiccated coconut; the latter will turn golden much more quickly than freshly grated coconut. Put the coconut in a heavy dry wok and put over low heat. Cook, stirring frequently, until golden all over, about 8 to 10 minutes for fresh coconut, 3 to 4 minutes for desiccated. Remove immediately and cool completely before storing in an airtight container. Sometimes, roasted coconut is pounded while still hot until it turns into an oily paste.

**Toasting Dried Shrimp Paste**  Dried shrimp paste is almost always cooked, except in a few Thai dips. Sometimes, it is added raw to other pounded ingredients which are then fried or simmered, but more often, it is cooked on its own before being added to the dish. Even the most ardent shrimp paste lover will agree that it has an incredibly pungent smell during cooking, so to avoid having to do the job too often and to have a stock of cooked dried shrimp paste on hand, I suggest toasting 1 to 2 tablespoons and keeping it in a sealed jar (you seldom need more than 1 teaspoon per recipe). Do not, however, use ready-toasted dried shrimp paste for dips and sambals; the full flavor of freshly cooked shrimp paste is vital for these.

One of the best ways to cook dried shrimp paste without the smell forcing everyone out of the house is to put the required amount on a piece of foil, folding over a flap and pressing down to make a thin layer. Tuck the edges of the foil in loosely to make a packet, then set this on a wire grill directly over a medium gas flame, or under a broiler or grill. Cook for about 2 minutes, then turn and cook the other side for another couple of minutes. Open the packet to check that the shrimp paste has lost its wet, raw look and smells fragrant. If you don't have a grill or broiler, you can put the foil package into a wok or nonstick skillet; it may need a little longer to cook.

**Roasted Rice Powder**  Put 1/4 cup (50 g) of uncooked long-grain rice in a heavy dry wok and put over low heat. Cook, stirring frequently, until the rice is golden-brown all over, about 8 to 10 minutes. While still hot, transfer to a mortar or spice grinder and grind or process to a sandy texture; do not grind finely as it is important for it to have a crunchy texture. I prefer to use a mortar to be able to monitor closely just how fine the rice is getting; around 30 seconds of turning the pestle firmly is generally enough. When the rice powder is completely cold, store in an airtight jar.

**Using Banana Leaves**  If you are fortunate enough to have access to a whole banana plant, cut off an entire leaf. Cut down either side of the thick central rib to obtain two long leaf halves, then trim these to the required size using a pair of scissors. Most cooks will have to make do with packets of either fresh or frozen banana leaves. To prepare banana leaves for cooking, wash the leaves, then cut to the size specified in each recipe. To make banana leaf pliable for folding around food or for fashioning into little cups, it must be softened by passing it briefly through a gas flame (you can watch the moisture starting to rise and the color turn brighter), or by soaking the leaves in boiling water until they soften. When using banana leaf as a wrapper, keep the upper, more shiny side on the outside. (Aluminum foil can be used as a substitute, but it does not provide the moisture, nor the subtle flavor, that are characteristic of banana leaf.)

**Making Crisp-fried Shallots or Garlic and Flavored Oil**  Peel the shallots or garlic and slice thinly and evenly; this is important so that they will cook evenly. Heat enough oil to cover the shallots or garlic in a wok. When it is just warm, not hot, add the sliced shallots or garlic and cook over low heat, stirring frequently, until they are golden brown and crisp. It is essential to keep the temperature low otherwise the shallots or garlic will brown before they are cooked through; shallots may take around 6 to 8 minutes of slow cooking, garlic a little less. Lift out and dry on paper towels and when completely cold, store in an airtight jar; do not add salt as this will turn them limp. The flavored shallot or garlic oil is kept and used as a seasoning oil, drizzled over cooked food.

**Preparing Ground Spices and Seasoning Pastes with a Spice Grinder** If you're ever tempted to use ground spices bought in a bottle or plastic pack, just try this test. Lightly toast in a dry pan some whole spice seeds (coriander, for example) for about a minute, or until they start to smell fragrant. Transfer them to a spice grinder and process to a fine powder. Lift the lid and sniff the result, then compare this with commercially available ground coriander that was processed goodness knows how long ago and has gone from the factory to the store to your cupboard and been kept there until you're about to use it. I'm certain that after doing this test, you'll be convinced that it's best to grind your own spices. Heating spices before grinding crisps them slightly, making them easy to grind and it also helps release the fragrance and flavor in the volatile oils.

Freshly roasted and ground spices can be cooled before being stored in an airtight container in the freezer, where they keep every bit of their fresh fragrance. Since I use a lot of coriander and cumin, to save time, I prepare a batch of several tablespoons of freshly roasted and ground spices and freeze them; they do not freeze into a solid block but retain their powdery texture and when used, taste as if they have been freshly toasted and ground.

Seasoning pastes are used in countless Southeast Asian dishes. When using a spice grinder (and, indeed, if using a mortar and pestle), it is important to slice or chop the ingredients before processing. If using dry spices as part of the paste, these should be ground first, then the fresh moist ingredients such as chilies, shallots, garlic, galangal and lemongrass added.

If you are not including shallots, which give off a lot of moisture, you may need to add some liquid to the spice grinder to keep the blades turning. Process the ingredients to break them up, switch off the grinder and scrape down the sides and lid with a rubber spatula and process again. Keep repeating this, adding a little oil, water or coconut milk (each recipe suggests which is appropriate) if needed. Don't overload the jar of your spice grinder; divide the ingredients into two or even three batches if needed and process each until completely ground.

**Dry-roasting Peanuts** Roast the peanuts in a dry wok, preferably with the skins intact, in the same fashion as for coconut, for about 8 to 10 minutes. After cooking, leave the peanuts until cool enough to handle, then take outside and rub the skins vigorously to loosen the skin. Toss the peanuts a little, blowing to dislodge the skins (or let the wind do it for you).

**Basic Chicken or Pork Stock** This simple, lightly seasoned stock is the basis of countless soups and other dishes in Southeast Asia. Vietnamese cooks like to add a pinch of sugar; some cooks omit the peppercorns; others use either onion or green onion, while some use both and Lao cooks often add a whole fresh coriander plant (root, stems and leaves). This is the recipe I normally use, taking care to keep the salt content low in case I want to season it with salty fish sauce later. I find it's worth making a double quantity and deep-freezing it in 2 cups (500 ml) portions for future use.

1 teaspoon oil
1 clove garlic, minced
2 chicken carcasses, chopped in half, any skin and fatty deposits discarded, or 2 lbs (1 kg) meaty pork bones
10 cups (2.5 liters) water
1 medium onion, minced
2 green onions (scallions), minced
4 thin slices ginger
10 black peppercorns
1/2 teaspoon salt

Put the oil in a very large saucepan and heat. Add the garlic and stir-fry over low heat until it turns golden brown. Lift out the garlic and discard, leaving the garlic-flavored oil in the pan.

Add the chicken or pork and water. Bring to a boil, then simmer, uncovered, for 10 minutes, skimming off any scum that rises to the surface. Add the rest of the ingredients, cover the pan and simmer very gently for 1 hour. Remove the lid and continue simmering very gently until the stock is reduced by half, about another hour. It is important not to let the stock boil, or the result will be cloudy rather than clear.

Strain the stock into a large bowl, cool, then refrigerate for several hours. Scrape off any fat that solidifies on the surface, then transfer the stock into a covered container. Refrigerate or deep-freeze.

**NOTE:** This basic stock can be transformed into a simple soup to serve with any rice-based meal. Season it with a little fish sauce, soy sauce or salt, a sprinkle of white or black pepper, then add a little of what you fancy: a few leafy greens; bean sprouts; diced tofu; sliced fresh or soaked dried black Chinese mushrooms; a few fresh shrimp or slivers of chicken or pork. Simmer until the ingredients are cooked and serve piping hot.

# Basic Recipes

Whether you call them dips, sauces, sambals, or salsas, tangy accompaniments are an integral part of Southeast Asian food. No matter how simple the meal, there'll always be a little something on the side for extra flavor. Serve a bowl of noodle soup or some grilled chicken and you'll probably want to add Simple Thai Fish Sauce and Chili Dip, or Vietnamese Fish Sauce Dip. Malaysian and Singaporean noodle dishes just wouldn't be the same without the emphatic Malaysian Chili and Dried Shrimp Paste Dip (Sambal Belacan). Many Cambodian dishes respond instantly to Cambodian Salt, Lime and Black Pepper Dip and it's impossible to imagine a plate of deep-fried spring rolls without the famous Vietnamese Fish Sauce Dip. Although you can enjoy most of these dips as a condiment, you can also scoop many of them up with an array of ingredients called "dippers." Dips together with the dipper of your choice (such as Burmese Tangy Tomato Dip with deep-fried tofu skin or pork cracklings, for example) are often served as a between-meal snack, but they could just as well be enjoyed as the prelude to a main meal or put on the table together with the rice and other dishes. It's not just dips and sambals that add extra zing to a meal; there are various relishes, freshly-made pickles and side-salads too. The ubiqituous Vietnamese Daikon and Carrot salad, excellent Cambodian Red Bell Pepper Relish and Malay Cucumber and Pineapple Salad are just some of the side-dishes that add a refreshing note to meals based on rice.

# Cucumber and Pineapple Salad   *Kerabu timun and nenas*

I'll admit that if you're not fortunate enough to live in Southeast Asia, it's pretty hard to find the intensely fragrant wild pink ginger bud (usually called torch ginger, although botanists are still arguing whether it's Nicolaia sp or Phaemeria sp). Even without such an exotic ingredient, you can still make this refreshing salad. Its crunchy texture and sweet-sour tang make it particularly good with braised or fried food, or curries.

FRONT AND BACK: Vinegared Cucumber Salad and Cucumber and Pineapple Salad

**Serves 4–6**
**Preparation time:** 20 mins

1 cucumber (about 1 lb/500 g)
1 teaspoon salt
2 thin slices fresh pineapple (about 10 oz/300 g), peeled, cored, and diced
2 tablespoons thinly sliced ginger bud (see Note)

Dressing
4 tablespoons dried shrimp, toasted in a dry wok, 4–5 minutes
1–2 red finger-length chilies, sliced
1 teaspoon dried shrimp paste, toasted (page 22)
1–2 tablespoons lime juice, depending on sweetness of pineapple
2 tablespoons water
1 tablespoon sugar
1 teaspoon salt

1 Rake the skin of the cucumber with a fork and then rub all over with the salt. Rinse under running water, squeeze the cucumber, then cut into four lengthwise. Cut across into 1/2-in (1-cm) dice and put in a bowl with the pineapple and ginger bud, if using.
2 Make the Dressing by grinding all the ingredients to a smooth paste in a spice grinder or blender. Add to the cucumber and pineapple, toss and serve immediately.

> **NOTE:** If you can't get ginger bud, cook 1/2 cup (40 g) freshly grated or desiccated coconut in a dry wok over very low heat, stirring until it turns rich brown, taking care it does not burn. While the coconut is still hot, process or pound it to an oily paste. Cool, then add to the cucumber and pineapple together with the Dressing.

# Vinegared Cucumber Salad   *Yam tan gwa*

Variations of this easy salad—my standby for when I don't have a variety of vegetables on hand—are found throughout the region, partnering the cool crunchiness of cucumber with sweet, sour, salty and sometimes hot flavors. This Thai version add peanuts for extra crunch, though you could omit these if you prefer. This palate-cleansing salad is good at just about any meal, especially when fried food is served.

**Serves 4**
**Preparation time:** 15 mins

4 tablespoons rice vinegar
3 tablespoons water
3 tablespoons caster sugar
1 teaspoon salt
1 cucumber (about 1 lb/500 g), peeled
1 red finger-length chili, deseeded if desired, thinly sliced
2 shallots, thinly sliced
2 tablespoons coarsely crushed dry-roasted peanuts (optional)

1 Put the vinegar, water, sugar and salt in a bowl and stir until the sugar dissolves.
2 Cut the cucumber in half lengthwise and scrape out the pulpy portion only if the seeds are well formed. Cut across into 1/2-in (1-cm) slices and toss with the vinegar mixture.
3 Add the chili and shallots, mix, then cover and refrigerate for at least 30 minutes. Transfer to a serving bowl and scatter the top with the peanuts.

Tangy Tomato Dip

# Tangy Tomato Dip   *Khayan chin thi pantwe pyaw*

This roasted tomato dip is a specialty of the Shan tribe of Burma, who usually add their distinctive dried fermented soybean wafers for extra flavor; however, easily available salted soybean paste makes an adequate substitute. Roasting the tomatoes, chilies, shallots and garlic over charcoal gives this dip a wonderful flavor, but even if you have to use a grill, broiler, or a dry wok, you'll still be delighted with the result.

**Serves 4–6**
**Preparation time:** 15 mins
**Cooking time:** 10 mins

8 shallots, unpeeled
8 cloves garlic, unpeeled
4 green finger-length chilies
4–6 small tomatoes
1 tablespoon salted soybean paste
1/2–3/4 teaspoon ground red pepper (cayenne)
Salt, to taste
1 heaped tablespoon finely minced fresh
   coriander leaves (cilantro)

1 Put the shallots, garlic and chilies on a fine mesh grill over a barbecue or under a hot grill; alternatively, put them in a dry wok. Cook over medium heat, turning several times. Remove the chilies as soon as they soften, taking care the skin does not blacken, but keep cooking the shallots and garlic until the skins start to blacken and the inside is soft.

2 Slice off the stem end of the chilies. Cut each chili lengthwise and discard the seeds. Slice the chilies and put them in a mortar or spice grinder. Remove the blackened skins from the shallots. Cut the rounded end off each garlic clove, grab the skin of the other end and squeeze out the garlic. Add the shallots and garlic to the chilies.

3 Cook the tomatoes in the same way as the other ingredients, turning until they start to soften. Transfer to a plate, peel, then chop coarsely.

4 Pound or process the shallots, garlic, chilies, soybean paste and ground red pepper to make a coarse paste. Add the tomatoes and pound or process briefly, just enough to mix them well with the other ingredients but not to make a smooth paste. Add salt to taste, then stir in the coriander leaves. Serve at room temperature with dippers or as a condiment with rice. (Any left-over can be refrigerated in a covered container for up to a week.)

## All-purpose Dippers

The most interesting (and often inadvertently amusing) Burmese cookbook I've come across is Mi Mi Khiang's *Cook and Entertain the Burmese Way*. When suggesting food to enjoy with dips, she lists what she calls "dippers," and it's hard to come up with a better name for the food that you use to help scoop up a dip. Mi Mi Khiang includes in this category such exotic items as the young leaves of the acacia thorn, young mango leaves, fish bladder chips, buffalo-hide chips and dried milk sheets. You'll be happy to know you can also used somewhat more accessible ingredients such as those suggested below.

**Something crunchy**
**Deep-fried shrimp or fish crackers**
   (***krupuk***)
**Deep-fried pork skin/pork cracklings**
   (sometimes sold as ***chicharon***)
**Dried deep-fried tofu skin (use dried tofu**
   skin sold in thick, crinkled strips about
   1 1/4-in/3-cm wide)

**Raw vegetables**
**Cucumber; Daikon radish; Carrot;**
   Jicama (***bangkwang***); Celery;
   Broccoli; Cauliflower; Young winged
   beans; Baby corn; Button or oyster
   mushrooms; Bell pepper; Young long
   beans

**Leafy greens**
**Young passionfruit leaves**
**Cabbage leaves**
**Sprigs of water spinach**

**Fruit**
**Segments of pomelo**
**Sticks of unripe green mango, pineapple,**
   or half-ripe papaya
**Apple guava**
**Rose apple, wood apple, or cashew**
   apple
**Slices of star fruit**

FRONT AND BACK: Simple Thai Fish Sauce and Chili Dip and Vietnamese Fish Sauce Dip

# Simple Thai Fish Sauce and Chili Dip   *Nam pla prik ki noo*

An indispensable accompaniment to Thai food and served just as salt would be served with Western food, this dip is simplicity itself. If you can't be sure of a constant supply of bird's-eye chilies, keep some in the freezer so you're always equipped to make this dip for serving with just about anything Thai.

**Serves 4      Preparation time:** 2 mins

**1/2 cup (125 ml) fish sauce**
**1 teaspoon lime juice**
**8–10 red or green bird's-eye chilies, coarsely chopped**

**1** Combine all the ingredients in a bowl and transfer to small sauce bowls when serving.
**2** Any left-over dip can be kept in a covered container in the fridge. You can keep adding fish sauce and a squeeze of lime juice to the left-over chilies, which will keep their bite for quite some time.

# Vietnamese Fish Sauce Dip   *Nuoc mam*

This is the "serve with everything" Vietnamese dip, a clever blending of flavors, sour yet with a touch of sweetness, salty with fish sauce, fragrant with lime juice and with a judicious touch of garlic and chili. The proportions vary from one cook to the next; this recipe happens to be my favorite. Some cooks add a tablespoon or two of finely grated carrot to the sauce before serving.

**Serves 4–6**
**Preparation time:** 5 mins

**1 clove garlic, minced**
**1 red finger-length chili, minced**
**2 tablespoons caster sugar**
**2 tablespoons lime juice**
**1/4 cup (60 ml) rice vinegar**
**1/4 cup (60 ml) fish sauce**
**1/4 cup (60 ml) water**

**1** If you have a mortar and pestle, pound the garlic and chili together with a little of the sugar until coarsely ground. Stir in the rest of the sugar and the remaining ingredients, mixing until the sugar dissolves. If you prefer to use a blender, process all ingredients until the chili is fairly fine.
**2** Pour into a bowl and allow the pink froth to disappear before serving. This makes about 3/4 cup (185 ml) of dip; double the amounts if you like and refrigerate any left-over in a covered container for up to a week.

# Cambodian Salt, Lime and Black Pepper Dip   *Tik marij*

The first time I first saw this dip was in the packed lunches of workers taking a break in the shade of the stunning temples of Angkor in Cambodia. This mixture of salt and black pepper, with lime wedges for adding juice to taste, is such a universal favorite that I'm sure if I'd examined more closely the cooking and eating scenes carved into the wall of the 12th-century Bayon temple, I'd have seen it there too. It does wonders with plain rice and to just about anything you fancy to dip in it.

**Serves 4      Preparation time:** 2 mins

**1 tablespoon freshly ground black pepper**
**2 teaspoons salt**
**1 lime or lemon, quartered**

**1** Combine the pepper and salt in a small bowl.
**2** Transfer to tiny sauce bowls and put a lime or lemon piece on each bowl for squeezing in according to taste. Give the dip a stir before using.

# Malaysian Chili and Dried Shrimp Paste Dip

*Sambal belacan*

The most popular accompaniment in Malaysia and Singapore, this is a pungent mixture of red finger-length chili and toasted dried shrimp paste. It is always served with a small round green lime, its fragrant juice mixed into the *sambal* just before eating. Perfectionists claim that the ingredients should be pounded in a mortar and that the toasted dried shrimp paste should still be warm for maximum flavor. I find the sambal perfectly acceptable if processed in a spice grinder, but agree that the dried shrimp paste should be freshly toasted. The sambal keeps refrigerated in a covered jar for about two weeks, but is best freshly made.

**Serves 4**
**Preparation time:** 8 mins

5–6 red finger-length chilies, sliced
1¹/2 teaspoons dried shrimp paste, freshly
   toasted (page 22)
¹/4 teaspoon salt, or more to taste
4 small round green limes (*limau kesturi,
   kalamansi* or calamondin), top sliced off, or
   1 lime or lemon, quartered

**1** Process or pound the chilies, dried shrimp paste and salt until the chilies are finely ground, but not turned into a smooth paste.
**2** Transfer to four small sauce dishes and put a lime on each dish. Each person squeezes in the lime juice to taste, stirring it before using the dip as a condiment with rice. Any unused sambal can be refrigerated for several days in a covered container.

# Thai Shrimp Paste and Lime Dip

*Nam prik kapi*

To make this popular Thai dip, cooks start with freshly toasted dried shrimp paste, then set off on a culinary journey adding lashings of garlic, as many hot chilies as they can tolerate, a pinch of salt and fish sauce for saltiness, a squeeze of lime juice balanced with a little palm sugar. Tiny pea-sized eggplants are often lightly pounded and added and some cooks also throw in a few pounded dried shrimp. This recipe is a starting point, which you can adjust to taste. Scoop up with any of the dippers (page 26), or put a big dollop next to your rice.

**Serves 4**
**Preparation time:** 5 mins

1 tablespoon dried shrimp paste,
   freshly toasted (page 22)
4 cloves garlic
1 tablespoon shaved palm sugar
¹/4 teaspoon salt
4–8 red or green bird's-eye chilies
3–4 pea-sized eggplants (optional)
1 tablespoon lime juice
2 teaspoons fish sauce

**1** Put the warm dried shrimp paste in a mortar or spice grinder and add the garlic, palm sugar and salt. Pound or process until smooth.
**2** Add the chilies (and pea-sized eggplants, if you are using these) and pound just a few times until they are just broken up; a coarse texture is characteristic of this dip. If you are using a spice grinder, process a couple of times for a second or two.
**3** Transfer to a bowl and stir in the lime juice and fish sauce. This dip can be refrigerated in a covered container in the refrigerator for about one week, but is best enjoyed freshly made.

Thai Shrimp Paste and Lime Dip

**Red Bell Pepper Relish**

# Red Bell Pepper Relish

*Chrourk m'teh*

This is one of the most delicious relishes you'll find in anywhere and goes well with almost any food, Southeast Asian or Western. Bell peppers are grilled until the skin blackens, giving them a marvelous smoky flavor, then mixed with garlic, fish sauce and vinegar, balanced by a little sugar. This recipe is based on one from Longtein de Monteiro's *The Elephant Walk Cookbook*.

**Serves 6**
**Preparation time:** 10 mins
**Cooking time:** 10 mins

2 large red bell peppers (about ¹/₂ lb/250 g
   each)
¹/₄ cup (60 ml) rice vinegar
¹/₄ cup (60 ml) fish sauce
2 tablespoons sugar
1 teaspoon salt
4 large cloves garlic, thinly sliced
A few sprigs of Asian basil leaves (optional)

**1** Cook the bell peppers, either over charcoal, under a very hot grill, or on a rack directly over a gas flame, turning until the skin had blackened all over and the flesh is slightly softened, about 10 minutes. (You want fierce heat so that the skin will be blackened before the bell peppers become over-cooked.) Put the bell peppers in a plastic bag, close and set aside for 15 minutes to loosen the skins. Hold the bell peppers under running water and rub to remove the skin. Discard the seeds and membranes and chop the flesh into pieces roughly ³/₄-in (2-cm) square.
**2** Combine the vinegar, fish sauce, sugar and salt in a bowl, stirring to dissolve the sugar. Add the garlic, bell pepper and Asian basil, if using, stirring to mix well. Marinate for at least 30 minutes. Serve with rice and other dishes; it is particularly good with any fried food. Any left-over portion can be refrigerated for about 1 week.

# Vietnamese Bean Sprout Pickles

*Dua gia*

This lovely fresh Vietnamese pickle or relish is quickly made and goes well with just about everything. Start it before you put your rice on to cook; it takes just a couple of minutes to measure the ingredients and add the bean sprouts, then leave it all to marinate for half an hour while preparing the rest of the meal.

**Serves 4**
**Preparation time:** 10 mins

³/₄ cup (185 g) caster sugar
1 teaspoon salt
1 cup (250 ml) rice vinegar
2¹/₂ cups (125 g) bean sprouts,
   straggly tails removed

**1** Put the sugar, salt and rice vinegar in a bowl, stirring to dissolve the sugar. Add the bean sprouts and toss gently. Leave to marinate for 30 minutes, tossing once or twice during this time.
**2** Drain before serving with just about any fish, meat, or poultry dish and rice. Any left-over pickle can be refrigerated in a covered container for up to 24 hours; make sure it is well drained before storing.

Daikon and Carrot

# Daikon and Carrot

*Cu cai ca-rot chua*

This relish seems to be everywhere in Vietnam, as well as in Laos and Cambodia. Try to use an Asian vegetable shredder, which produces matchstick shreds, rather than a normal grater.

**Serves 4**
**Preparation time:** 8 mins

1 cup (150 g) finely shredded daikon radish
1 cup (100 g) finely shredded carrot
1 tablespoon salt
1 tablespoon sugar
1/4 cup (60 ml) rice vinegar
1/4 cup (60 ml) water

**1** Put the radish and carrot in a bowl and sprinkle with the salt. Rub with your hands and set aside for 10 minutes. Squeeze to remove as much moisture as possible and pour it out of the bowl. Fill the bowl with cold water, rinse, squeeze again and drain well. Put into a bowl and sprinkle with the sugar, then add the vinegar and water, stirring to mix well.
**2** Refrigerate for around 30 minutes before serving. Drain off the liquid before serving with noodle dishes, barbecued meats and also as an accompaniment to rice.

# Burmese Crispy Dried Shrimp Sprinkle

*Sambal balachaung*

Although this condiment is not well known outside Burma, it certainly deserves to be. It's crunchy, salty, full of dried shrimp, shallots and garlic, as hot as you like and normally served as accompaniment to rice-based meals. This recipe is based on one from Charmaine Solomon's classic *Complete Asian Cookbook*. Charmaine, whose grandmother lived in Burma, suggests that Balachaung addicts like myself can try it as a sandwich relish; I also sprinkle it over vegetables, salads and some soups.

**Makes about 2 cups**
**Preparation time:** 15 mins
**Cooking time:** 25 mins

1/2 cup (125 ml) oil
3 tablespoons sesame oil
10 shallots, sliced
10 cloves garlic, thinly sliced
1 cup (120 g) dried shrimp
1/4 cup (60 ml) rice or white vinegar
1–3 teaspoons crushed dried chili flakes
1 teaspoon salt
1/2 teaspoon dried shrimp paste, toasted (page 22)

**1** Heat both lots of oil in a wok. Add the sliced shallots and cook over low heat, stirring frequently, until they are golden brown and crisp. Lift out with a slotted spoon and drain on paper towels, leaving the oil in the wok. Add the sliced garlic and cook as for the shallots, making sure it does not turn dark brown. Drain and set aside.
**2** Do not soak the shrimp but put them into a food processor and process to a powder. Reheat the oil left in the wok and add the shrimp powder. Stir-fry over low heat for 5 minutes, then add the vinegar, chili flakes, salt and dried shrimp paste. Cook, stirring frequently, for 5 minutes.
**3** Remove from the wok and spread on a couple of layers of paper towels to absorb the oil. When completely cold, put the shrimp mixture in a bowl and toss with the fried shallots and garlic. Transfer to a tightly sealed jar.

**NOTE:** It is important that the shallots and garlic are sliced evenly, so that the slices will all be cooked at the same time. Ensure the temperature is kept low throughout the cooking.

Burmese Crispy Dried Shrimp Sprinkle

# Salted Soybean, Pork and Peanut Sauce

*Nuoc leo*

Traditionally served with Grilled Vietnamese Meatballs (page 43) and Saigon Shrimp and Pork Pancakes (page 39), this sauce normally contains a tiny amount of ground pork and pork liver, although I prefer to use the more readily available chicken liver. If you like, you could omit the liver altogether and increase the amount of pork to three tablespoons. It might seem like a nuisance to have to buy a tiny amount of pork for the sauce, but remember, you're going to be using pork in the accompanying dish. You could also serve this sauce as a dip.

Salted Soybean, Pork and Peanut Sauce

**Serves 4**
**Preparation time:** 8 mins
**Cooking time:** 2 mins

1 tablespoon oil
2 cloves garlic, minced
1 chicken liver, minced
1 tablespoon finely ground lean pork
3 tablespoons salted soybean paste, mashed
2 teaspoons sugar
1 tablespoon chunky peanut butter
3/4 cup (185 ml) water
2 tablespoons coarsely crushed dry-roasted peanuts
1/2–1 teaspoon lime juice

1 Heat the oil in a small saucepan and add the garlic. Stir-fry for a few seconds until it starts to smell fragrant, then add the chicken liver and pork. Stir-fry for 1 minute, then add the soybean paste and sugar, and stir-fry over medium heat for another minute.
2 Add the peanut butter, stirring until it dissolves, then add the water, bring to a boil and simmer for 3 minutes. Transfer to a bowl and stir in the peanuts. Add the lime juice, to taste, and leave to cool before serving.

# Roasted Thai Chili Paste *Nam prik pao*

Ready-made versions of this are widely available in jars outside Thailand, but you might like to try making it at home. To get the real Thai flavor, the ingredients should be roasted over hot coals, but you can get a reasonable approximation by dry-roasting the basics in a wok or under a hot grill or broiler. This paste is added to a number of dishes, including hot sour soups and can also be served as a condiment with rice.

**Makes about 1 cup**
**Preparation time:** 10 mins
**Cooking time:** 30 mins

6–8 dried red finger-length chilies, left whole, rinsed and dried
5 shallots, unpeeled
4–5 cloves garlic, unpeeled
1 tablespoon dried shrimp paste
2 tablespoons oil
1 heaped tablespoon tamarind pulp, soaked in 1/4 cup (60 ml) warm water, squeezed and strained to obtain the juice
1 tablespoon shaved palm sugar
1/2 teaspoon salt

1 If it's convenient to use a barbecue, put the chilies, shallots and garlic on a fine mesh grill and cook over a moderately hot fire or gas flame, or cook under a hot grill or broiler. Turn the chilies just until they are crisp but not blackened, taking great care as they burn very quickly.
2 Remove the chilies and continue cooking the shallots and garlic, turning until they are soft and the skin has started to blacken. Remove from the grill and leave aside until cool enough to handle. (Alternatively, you can cook the chilies, shallots, garlic and dried shrimp paste in a dry wok.)
3 Spread the dried shrimp paste into a thin layer on aluminum foil, enclose, then grill on both sides until fragrant.
4 Break the stem end off each chili, break the chilies into small pieces, then transfer to a spice grinder and grind coarsely. Remove the skins from the shallots, then cut the rounded end off each garlic clove and squeeze out the garlic. Add the shallots, garlic and dried shrimp paste to the spice grinder and process until finely ground.
5 Heat the oil in a small pan and add the ground paste. Cook over low-medium heat, stirring frequently, until fragrant and cooked, about 4 to 5 minutes. Add the tamarind juice, sugar and salt and cook over low heat until the sugar dissolves. Cool, then refrigerate in a covered jar.

# Chapter 1
# Starters and Snacks

It's often said that Asians are always eating, munching throughout the day and on into the night, stopping to buy savory nibbles or sweetmeats from itinerant vendors or roadside stalls. And why not? There are just so many irresistible goodies out there. Some of the snack and starter recipes included here are perfect for serving with drinks, such as slices of Laotian Spiced Beef Jerky (page 46). If you're looking for an impressive start to a meal, you can't do better than succulent satay made from beef (Extraordinary Beef Satay, page 34). Then again, you would consider one of the wonderful palate-tickling recipes such as Northern Thai Leaf Cup Nibbles (page 40) or Thai Tuna Carpaccio (page 37).

For party snacks, you could try various types of roll-ups, including the ever-popular Vietnamese Spring Rolls (page 36), or the refreshingly different Tangy Marinated Fish (page 42). And for a really substantial snack which makes a great lunch, you won't find anything more satisfying than Saigon Shrimp and Pork Pancakes (page 38).

Many of these snacks and starters could also be served as part of a main meal with rice, especially the various types of satay as well as Fragrant Cambodian Chicken Wings (page 44), Southern Thai Corn Fritters (page 41) and Tasty Thai Shrimp or Fish Cakes (page 35).

# Extraordinary Beef Satay  *Sate istimewa*

When I lived in Indonesia, I discovered that the best satays were invariably served in private homes. Friends from Southern Sulawesi kindly shared their family recipe; the name, *istimewa*, aptly translates as "extraordinary." Cubes of beef are marinated in sweet soy sauce, garlic, ginger, lime juice, spices and grated kaffir lime rind, with a dash of vodka or brandy (my friends are Christian, so the Muslim ban on alcohol doesn't apply). There's so much flavor in the satay that there's no need to serve it with a peanut dip.

**Serves 4–6**
**Preparation time:** 12 mins + 2 hours marinating
**Cooking time:** 6–10 mins

1/3 cup (85 ml) sweet soy sauce
3 tablespoons lime juice
3 tablespoons vodka or brandy
1 1/2 tablespoons oil
1 teaspoon ground coriander
1 teaspoon ground cumin
2 cloves garlic, minced
2 teaspoons finely grated ginger
1 teaspoon finely grated kaffir lime or lemon
    rind
1/2 teaspoon salt
1 1/2 lbs (700 g) rump steak, in 1/2-in (1-cm)
    slices, cut into bite-sized squares
Bamboo skewers, soaked in cold water for
    30 minutes

**1** Put the sweet soy sauce, lime juice, vodka or brandy, 2 teaspoons of the oil, coriander, cumin, garlic, ginger, lime rind and salt into a bowl. Add the beef, stirring to coat thoroughly. Cover and refrigerate for at least 2 hours or up to 8 hours, stirring a couple of times while marinating.
**2** Grease the grill of a barbecue or gas or electric griller with oil. Heat until very hot. Remove the beef from the marinade and thread onto the bamboo skewers. Grill over high heat, turning frequently, until the beef is cooked to your taste, about 5 minutes.

# Tasty Thai Shrimp or Fish Cakes   *Tod man kung/pla*

If you've ever visited any of the coastal areas of Thailand, you're sure to have encountered this popular street snack, fried on the spot for you at food stalls. Tod Man Kung (or Tod Man Pla, if you're using fish) has a characteristic springy texture and is wonderfully flavored with kaffir lime leaves, curry paste and fish sauce. Serve the shrimp or fish cakes with sweet Thai chili sauce, which you can buy off the shelf at most supermarkets.

**Serves 6–8**
**Makes** 8 large or 24 bite-sized cakes
**Preparation time:** 25 mins
**Cooking time:** 15 mins

2 lbs (1 kg) fresh shrimp, peeled and deveined,
   or 1¹/4 lbs (600 g) boneless white fish fillet,
   skinned and cubed
3–4 tablespoons Thai Red Curry Paste
   (page 115)
2 tablespoons cornstarch
¹/2 teaspoon bicarbonate of soda (baking soda)
2 tablespoons fish sauce
1 egg white
2–3 string beans, very finely sliced (optional)
4 kaffir lime leaves, thinly shredded, or
   2 green onions (scallions), finely minced
2 medium ripe tomatoes
¹/2 large or 1 small cucumber
Oil, for deep-frying
Sweet Thai chili sauce, to serve

1 Put the shrimp or fish into a food processor, add the curry paste, cornstarch, bicarbonate of soda, fish sauce and egg white, and process until smooth. Transfer to a bowl and stir in the string beans and kaffir lime leaves.
2 Wet your hands and shape about 3 table-spoons of the shrimp or fish mixture into a ball. Flatten it slightly to make a circle about ³/4-in (2-cm) thick. Put them on a plate and continue until all the mixture is used up.
3 Slice the tomatoes. Rake the cucumber length-wise with a fork to score the skin, then slice thinly. Arrange the tomato and cucumber in alternating slices around the edge of a serving dish.
4 Heat the oil in a wok. When it is hot, add a few shrimp or fish cakes at a time and deep-fry until cooked, turning so they turn golden brown all over, 3 to 4 minutes. Drain on paper towels and transfer to the serving dish.

# Vietnamese Spring Rolls  *Cha gio*

One of the things that makes these delightful Vietnamese spring rolls different to the Chinese variety is the delicate rice paper wrapper. The filling is a lightly seasoned combination of pork, shrimp and transparent bean thread noodles, plus some crabmeat if you like. The *coup de grâce* is the way they are eaten, tucked in a cool lettuce leaf with fragrant herbs and crunchy bean sprouts, then dipped in salty, sour, sweet and hot Vietnamese Fish Sauce Dip.

**Serves 4–6**
**Preparation time:** 45 mins
**Cooking time:** 25 mins

**30 wedge-shaped rice paper wrappers, or 20–25 small round rice paper wrappers (5–6 in/12.5–15 cm in diameter)**
**Oil, for deep-frying**

**Accompaniment**
**Lettuce leaves**
**1 cup (40 g) mint sprigs**
**1 cup (40 g) Vietnamese mint (laksa leaf) or regular mint leaves**
**1 cup (40 g) fresh coriander (cilantro) sprigs**
**1 cup (50 g) bean sprouts**
**1 cup (250 ml) Vietnamese Fish Sauce Dip (page 27)**

**Filling**
**2 shallots, minced**
**1 clove garlic, minced**
**4 oz (125 g) lean pork, diced**
**1/2 lb (250 g) small or medium fresh shrimp, peeled (or 4 oz/125 g peeled fresh shrimp)**
**1 cup (125 g) cooked crabmeat, or additional 4 oz (125 g) pork**
**1 green onion (scallion), minced**
**4 teaspoons fish sauce**
**1/2 teaspoon freshly ground black pepper**
**Handful (1 oz or 30 g) transparent (bean thread) noodles, soaked in hot water to soften, drained, cut into short lengths**

> **NOTE:** If you want to prepare the spring rolls in advance, cook them until light golden, about 3 minutes. Drain them on paper towels and keep at room temperature. Just before serving, reheat the oil until very hot, then fry the spring rolls for about 1 minute until golden brown and crisp.

**1** Prepare the Filling by processing the shallots, garlic and pork in a food processor until the pork is finely ground. Add the shrimp, crabmeat, if using, green onion, fish sauce and pepper, and process until smooth. Transfer to a bowl and stir in the transparent noodles.

**2** Put a large bowl of warm water and a clean kitchen towel on a clean work surface. Dip a rice paper wrapper in the water for 4 to 5 seconds, remove it and spread on the towel; if you are using wedge-shaped wrappers, put the pointed end facing away from you. Smooth the wrapper with your fingers until soft and pliable. Repeat until you have six to eight softened rice paper wrappers on the towel.

**3** Put about 2 teaspoons of the Filling across the wider part of a wedge rice paper wrapper, or across each round rice paper wrapper, placing it about 1 1/4 in (3 cm) from the bottom edge. Wet your fingers slightly and shape each portion of Filling into a cigarette shape about 2-in (5-cm) long. Rinse and dry your hands and then fold up the end closest to you. Tuck in both sides, squeezing gently to make sure there isn't any air trapped, then roll up firmly. Put on a plate, making sure the rolls do not touch each other. Repeat until all the rolls are prepared.

**4** Prepare the Accompaniment by washing, draining and drying the lettuce, both lots of mint leaves and coriander leaves. Divide between two large serving plates. Wash and drain the bean sprouts and add to the herbs. Put the Vietnamese Fish Sauce Dip into dipping bowls.

**5** Heat the oil in a wok until moderately hot (but not smoking). Add several of the spring rolls, one at a time, taking care not to over-crowd the wok. Fry over medium heat until golden brown and cooked, about 5 minutes, stirring occasionally to prevent them sticking together and to ensure they are golden brown all over. Drain and serve hot with the dip and Accompaniment.

**6** To eat, each person puts a spring roll on a lettuce leaf, adding some of the herbs and bean sprouts. The leaf is tucked up and dipped in the Vietnamese Fish Sauce Dip before eating.

## Thai Tuna Carpaccio

Wafer-thin slices of beef marinated in lime juice and seasonings can be found in northern Thailand but in this modern variation, fresh tuna replaces the beef and is marinated not only with lime juice but olive oil, like the well-known Italian beef carpaccio. All you need for this recipe is spanking fresh tuna, lime juice, olive oil, freshly ground black pepper and fresh coriander leaves (cilantro). It's amazingly easy to prepare and bound to be a success as a part of either a Southeast Asian or Western meal.

**Serves 4**
**Preparation time:** 8 mins

1/2 cup (125 ml) extra virgin olive oil
1/4 cup (60 ml) lime or lemon juice
2–3 teaspoons fish sauce
1/4 teaspoon freshly ground black pepper
13 oz (375 g) sashimi-quality fresh tuna, thinly sliced
3 tablespoons minced fresh coriander leaves (cilantro)

**1** Combine the olive oil, lemon juice, fish sauce and pepper in a small bowl, whisking to blend.
**2** Pour half of the dressing onto a flat plate large enough to hold the tuna slices in one layer. Arrange the tuna on top of the dressing, then spoon the remaining dressing over the top. Cover with plastic wrap and refrigerate for 20 to 30 minutes. Transfer the tuna slices to a serving plate, sprinkle with the coriander leaves before serving.

Vietnamese Spring Rolls

# Saigon Shrimp and Pork Pancakes *Bahn khoai*

This is one of several types of savory pancakes sold by street vendors and market stalls in Saigon (now Ho Chi Minh City), southern Vietnam. In line with the Vietnamese passion for fresh flavors, the pancakes are eaten with lettuce and herbs, with Salted Soybean, Pork and Peanut Sauce drizzled over (but they're just as good with the ubiquitous Vietnamese Fish Sauce Dip). The pancakes are usually prepared from scratch for each person in Vietnam, but I find it's quicker to cook all the pork and shrimp filling in advance when you're serving pancakes for several people.

**Serves 4–8**
**Makes** 8 pieces using a 8½-in (22-cm) skillet
**Preparation time:** 20 mins
**Cooking time:** 40 mins

½ lb (250 g) lean pork, shredded
1 lb (500 g) small to medium fresh shrimp,
    peeled and deveined
2 teaspoons fish sauce
2 teaspoons minced garlic
1 teaspoon Chinese rice wine (preferably
    Shaoxing) (optional)
½ teaspoon freshly ground black pepper
2 green onions (scallions), green and white
    portions separated, minced
½ cup (125 ml) oil
3 cups (150 g) bean sprouts, washed and
    drained
1 onion, halved and thinly sliced across

**Batter**
2 cups (320 g) rice flour
1 teaspoon salt
1 teaspoon caster sugar
3/4 teaspoon ground turmeric
2¼ cups (560 ml) water
3 large eggs

**Accompaniments**
2 whole butter lettuce, leaves washed
    and dried
1 cup (50 g) firmly packed mint leaves
1 cup (50 g) firmly packed fresh coriander
    leaves (cilantro)
2 small star fruit or 1 small cucumber, thinly
    sliced across
Salted Soybean, Pork and Peanut Sauce
    (page 31) or Vietnamese Fish Sauce
    Dip (page 27)

1 Put the pork and shrimp in a bowl and add the fish sauce, garlic, rice wine, pepper and the white portion of the green onions. Mix well with your fingers and set aside.

2 Prepare the Batter by combining the rice flour, salt, sugar and turmeric in a bowl and gradually stir in the water to make a very thin batter. Put the eggs in a bowl and beat lightly with a fork. Set near the stove.

3 Prepare the Accompaniments by arranging the lettuce leaves, mint leaves, coriander leaves and star fruit on a serving platter. Divide the dip between four to eight small dipping bowls.

4 Heat 2 tablespoons of the oil in a wok. When hot, add the pork and shrimp mixture and stir-fry for 3 minutes. Transfer to a plate and divide into eight portions. Put the green portion of the green onions, bean sprouts and onion in a bowl and gently toss with your fingers, then divide into eight portions and add to the portioned pork and shrimp mixture.

5 Heat 1 tablespoon of the oil in a large skillet, preferably cast-iron or non-stick, swirling it around to completely grease the base and sides. Tip out the excess oil and save it for greasing the pan next time. Reheat the pan and when very hot, stir the batter, then measure out ⅓ cup (85 ml) and pour it quickly into the skillet, tilting the pan so that it spreads over the bottom; don't worry if there are a few small gaps. Scatter over one portion of the pork, shrimp and bean sprout mixture. Cover the pan and cook over medium heat for 2 minutes.

6 Uncover the pan and drizzle over about 2 tablespoons of the beaten egg, filling in any gaps that might have been left in the pancake. Cover and cook over medium heat for 1 minute. Remove the lid and cook uncovered for about 1 minute, to make sure the bottom is crispy, then fold the pancake in half and transfer to a serving plate (see Note). Repeat, adding more oil to the pan and stirring the batter each time until you have made eight pancakes. Serve with the Accompaniments and dip. The pancakes are normally broken into pieces and tucked in a lettuce leaf with the herbs, a slice or two of star fruit or cucumber and a dollop of sauce, then rolled up and eaten.

> **NOTE:** Ideally, each pancake should be served immediately and eaten while still hot and crisp. A skillet set on a tabletop burner would be ideal, saving you from running back to the kitchen repeatedly; alternatively, you could use two skillets and cook two pancakes at the same time to speed things up.

# Northern Thai Leaf Cup Nibbles   *Miang kham*

This delightful appetizer from northern Thailand (the whole of which is definitely greater than the sum of its parts) is normally made using wild pepper leaves (*cha plu* in Thai, *bo la lot* in Vietnam). Don't worry if you have to substitute these with lettuce—the unexpectedly piquant flavors and contrasting textures of the filling still taste great. There's a fair amount of preparation, but this can be done in advance and at the last minute, all you need do is arrange the ingredients decoratively and serve.

**Serves 6–8**
**Preparation time:** 45 mins
**Cooking time:** 10 mins

6 shallots, finely minced
4-in (10-cm) young ginger, minced
1/2 cup (75 g) dry-roasted peanuts, skinned
1/2 cup (60 g) dried shrimp, soaked in water
    to soften, finely chopped
3 tablespoons Crisp-fried Garlic (page 22)
1 large lemon, skin washed and dried, skin
    and flesh finely diced, seeds discarded
8–10 red or green bird's-eye chilies,
    chopped, or 1–2 red or green finger-length
    chilies, minced
1/2 cup (50 g) freshly grated or desiccated
    coconut, toasted in a dry wok until golden
    brown
Wild pepper leaves or butter lettuce leaves

**Sauce**
3 tablespoons dry-roasted peanuts
1 tablespoons dried shrimp, soaked in water
    to soften
3 tablespoons freshly grated or desiccated
    coconut
3 shallots, minced
1 stalk lemongrass, tender inner part of
    bottom third only, thinly sliced
1 teaspoon finely minced ginger
1 teaspoon finely minced galangal
2 teaspoons dried shrimp paste, toasted
    (page 22)
1 1/4 cups (310 ml) water
1/3 cup (60 g) shaved palm sugar
1/2–1 teaspoon salt

1 Prepare the Sauce first. Process the peanuts to a fine powder in a spice grinder, then transfer to a saucepan. Do the same for the dried shrimp and then again for the coconut.

2 Combine the shallots, lemongrass, ginger, galangal and dried shrimp paste and process to a smooth paste, adding a little of the water if needed to keep the blades turning.

3 Transfer the paste to the saucepan and add the water, palm sugar and salt. Bring to a boil, stirring. Reduce the heat and simmer, uncovered, stirring frequently, until the Sauce thickens and is reduced to about 3/4 cup (185 ml), around 15 minutes. Leave to cool, then transfer to four small serving bowls.

4 Arrange separate piles of shallots, ginger, peanuts, dried shrimp, Crisp-fried Garlic, lemon, chilies and coconut on a large serving dish. (If you like, you can prepare these ingredients in advance and keep them in covered containers for about an hour, although it is best to cut the lemon just before serving.)

5 Arrange the wild pepper or lettuce leaves on a plate and serve with the filling ingredients. Everyone adds a little of the ingredients, then spoons over some of the Sauce, before tucking up the leaf and eating (usually with sighs of pleasure).

**Northern Thai Leaf Cup Nibbles**

# Southern Thai Corn Fritters  *Tod man khao phod*

I thought corn fritters were as American as apple pie until I came across an excellent Thai version in the southern city of Nakkorn Si Thammarat. Fresh corn kernels are mixed in a batter with Thai curry paste, soy sauce and fish sauce—and what a superb difference those seasonings make. If you can't get fresh sweet corn, you could use defrosted sweet corn kernels, but avoid the canned version as the texture is disappointingly limp. These tasty fritters are ideal as a snack or appetizer, or you could just as easily serve them as part of a main meal.

**Serves 4**
**Preparation time:** 7 mins
**Cooking time:** 5 mins

4 tablespoons plain flour
4 tablespoons rice flour
1½–2 tablespoons Thai Red Curry Paste
   (page 115) or curry powder
1 tablespoon fish sauce
1 tablespoon soy sauce
¼ teaspoon salt
2 large eggs
3 cups (375 g) sweet corn kernels
   (cut from 3–4 corn cobs) or defrosted
   sweet corn kernels
Oil, for shallow-frying

**1** Put both lots of flour, curry paste, fish sauce, soy sauce and salt in a bowl and stir in the eggs, mixing well. Add the corn kernels and stir; if the batter seems too dry, add 1 to 2 tablespoons of water.
**2** Heat enough oil to cover the bottom of a skillet by about ¼ in (0.5 cm). Drop in about 2 heaped tablespoons of the corn mixture, pressing lightly with a spatula to flatten it into a round cake (or make tiny fritters from about 2 teaspoons of batter if serving as finger food). Fry the fritters over medium heat, a few at a time, until golden brown on both sides and cooked through, 4 to 5 minutes.
**3** Drain on paper towels and serve warm or at room temperature. These sweet corn fritters go very well with Vinegared Cucumber Salad (page 25).

# Tangy Marinated Fish   *Goi ca*

With its intriguing balance of flavors and textures, this is one of the most refreshing appetizers I've come across. But be warned: it really gets the appetite going, so be sure you have plenty of other food to follow. Strips of fish are "cured" in vinegar, then combined with onions, herbs, crunchy peanuts and deep-fried shallots. Look for the freshest whole fish you can find (don't buy fillets unless you're absolutely sure of their freshness). If you want to try the Vietnamese version, wrap everything up in a rice paper wrapper, or go the Laotian way and use lettuce leaves.

**Serves 4–6**
**Marinating:** 1 hour
**Preparation time:** 10 mins

10–13 oz (300–375 g) fresh white fish fillets
    (grouper, whiting, or other fine-fleshed fish)
1 cup (250 ml) rice vinegar
1 onion, halved and very thinly sliced
4 teaspoons caster sugar
2 teaspoons salt
1 heaped tablespoon finely minced mint leaves
1 heaped tablespoon finely minced Vietnamese
    mint (laksa leaf) or regular mint
1 red finger-length chili, deseeded and minced
3 tablespoons crushed dry-roasted peanuts
1 tablespoon Crisp-fried Shallots (page 22)
12–16 small rice paper wrappers (6¹⁄₂ in/16.5
    cm in diameter), or 12–16 soft lettuce leaves
2 under-ripe star fruit (carambola) or 2 green
    tomatoes, thinly sliced

**1** Wash the fillets, dry thoroughly with paper towels, then cut into thin slices about ¹⁄₂ x 2 in (1 x 5 cm). Put the fish in a bowl and pour over the vinegar. Stir and leave to marinate at room temperature for 1 hour.

**2** After the fish has been marinating for 30 minutes, put the onion into a separate bowl. Sprinkle with the sugar and 1 teaspoon of the salt, massaging the onion with your fingers. Marinate for 30 minutes.

**3** When the fish has marinated 1 hour, transfer to a sieve and rinse briefly under running water. Drain well and pat the fish dry with paper towels, then put into a bowl. Squeeze the onion to remove as much liquid as possible, but do not rinse. Combine the onion, fish, remaining salt, herbs, chili, peanuts and Crisp-fried Shallots, mixing well with your hand.

**4** If using rice paper wrappers, dip them one at a time into a bowl of warm water for 3 to 4 seconds. Remove and place on a kitchen towel, smoothing them with your fingers. Add some of the fish mixture to each rice paper wrapper (or lettuce leaf), roll up to form a cigar shape and put on a serving plate. Garnish with star fruit or green tomato.

# Grilled Vietnamese Meatballs *Nem nuong*

When the wonderful fragrance of grilling meat fills the streets of Vietnam each evening, chances are that these pork balls will be among the items sizzling away. Balls of lightly seasoned ground pork threaded onto skewers are cooked over charcoal, giving off little bursts of fragrance as drops of oil hit the hot coals. The pork balls are served with fresh herbs, lettuce and bean sprouts and normally accompanied by Salted Soybean, Pork and Peanut Sauce; you could, however, serve Vietnamese Fish Sauce Dip if you prefer.

**Serves 4**
**Preparation time:** 30 mins + 1 hour marinating
**Cooking time:** 15 mins

3 1/2 oz (100 g) hard pork fat, in one piece
1 1/4 lbs (600 g) lean pork shoulder or leg,
    thinly sliced
4 shallots, finely minced
4 cloves garlic, minced
2 tablespoons fish sauce
2 teaspoons sugar
1 teaspoon freshly ground black pepper
1/2 teaspoon salt
2 tablespoons Roasted Rice Powder (page 22)
3 tablespoons oil
Salted Soybean, Pork and Peanut Sauce
    (page 31) or Vietnamese Fish Sauce
    Dip (page 27), for dipping

**Accompaniments**
2 butter lettuce, washed, leaves separated
1 1/4 cups (60 g) bean sprouts
Sliced cucumber
1 star fruit, thinly sliced crosswise (optional)
1 cup (40 g) loosely packed mint sprigs
1 cup (40 g) loosely packed Asian basil leaves
    or fresh coriander leaves (cilantro)

**1** Put the pork fat into a small saucepan with enough water to cover. Bring to a boil, simmer for 10 minutes, then drain. When cool enough to handle, chop the fat into tiny pieces the size of a rice grain then refrigerate in a covered container. Put the pork in a large bowl with the shallots, garlic, fish sauce, sugar and pepper and mix well. Cover and refrigerate for at least 1 hour, or overnight if preferred.
**2** Process the marinated mixture until it forms a paste. Add the Roasted Rice Powder and dried pork fat, pulse for 3 to 4 seconds to blend, then transfer the pork mixture to a bowl. Put the oil into a small bowl and smear some on the palms of your hands. Rub the oil onto a plate.

**3** Shape the pork paste into balls about 1 in (2.5 cm) in diameter, squeezing firmly so that the meat is firm, then put the pork balls on the oiled plate. When all the meat balls have been prepared, thread onto bamboo skewers, leaving at least 1/2 in (1 cm) between each meat ball.
**4** Put all the Accompaniments (washed and dried where relevant) on a serving plate.
**5** Heat a table top griller or barbecue until very

hot. Cook the skewers of pork, turning to brown all over, until done, about 10 minutes. Serve with the Accompaniments and individual bowls of dipping sauce. To eat the pork balls, slide them off the skewers and put 1 or 2 at a time in a lettuce leaf with some of the herbs, bean sprouts and cucumber. Spoon over a little of the dipping sauce then roll up, dunking the roll into more of the dip before eating.

# Fragrant Cambodian Chicken Wings  *Slab mouan kroeung*

The first night I investigated a cluster of food stalls in Siem Reap in Cambodia, the kerosene lighting was so dim that I wasn't quite sure what I was ordering. Luckily, I chanced upon these succulent chicken wings, marinated in a delightful blend of lemongrass, galangal, chilies, fish sauce and other seasonings. These make ideal finger food (don't forget the paper napkins as they're quite sticky) and the marinade could even be used for a whole chicken, oven-roasted in the usual Western style.

**Serves 4–6**
**Preparation time:** 10 mins
**Cooking time:** 30 mins

2 lbs (1 kg) chicken wings, pricked
    all over with a fork
1–2 tablespoons oil, for brushing

**Marinade**
2 stalks lemongrass, tender inner
    part of bottom third only, thinly
    sliced
2 shallots, minced
2 red finger-length chilies, sliced
3–4 cloves garlic, minced
1 tablespoon minced galangal
1 tablespoon oil
1/4 teaspoon ground turmeric
1 tablespoon sugar
1 teaspoon salt
3 tablespoons fish sauce

1 Make the Marinade by processing the lemongrass, shallots, chilies, garlic and galangal until finely ground, adding a little of the oil if needed to keep the blades turning. Transfer to a bowl and stir in the rest of the ingredients.
2 Add the chicken wings to the Marinade, mixing well with your hand to ensure the wings are evenly coated. Cover and marinate at least 2 hours or refrigerate overnight.
3 Brush a barbecue or gas grill or broiler with oil and heat. Grill the chicken wings over moderate heat, turning several times until they turn golden brown and crisp all over, about 15 to 20 minutes. Brush a couple of times with oil during the cooking. Drain on paper towels and serve warm. If preferred, cook the chicken wings on a rack set inside a baking dish in a hot oven (about 500°F/260°C) for 15 minutes, then turn the wings and continue cooking until they are done, another 10 to 15 minutes.

> **NOTE:** It's a good idea to prepare a double batch of these chicken wings and deep-freeze half of them after marinating. Let the wings thaw to room temperature before grilling.

**Fresh Summer Rolls**

# Fresh Summer Rolls   *Goi cuon*

The Vietnamese are famous for their superb rolls, the savory fillings wrapped in wafer-thin rice paper wrappers or tucked up in freshly steamed rice crêpes. There's no denying that you need time to prepare this recipe. I once spent over an hour making Summer Rolls for a party of about 50 in France and swore I'd never do it again. But when they were devoured in preference to other elegant French appetizers, I was ready to make them all over again for the next party. You could serve the rolls as a starter at dinner, or as finger food for parties.

**Makes 8 large or 16-20 small rolls**
**Preparation time:** 35 mins
**Cooking time:** 15–30 mins

1/2 cup (125 ml) water
1/4 cup (60 ml) rice vinegar
4 teaspoons Chinese rice wine
   (preferably Shaoxing)
1 teaspoon fish sauce
8 medium-sized fresh shrimp (about
   1/2 lb/250 g), or 16–20 if using small
   rice paper wrappers
10 oz (300 g) pork loin or fillet, in one
   piece
8 large Vietnamese rice paper wrappers
   (about 8 in/20 cm diameter), or
   16–20 small rice paper wrappers
   (6 1/2 in/16.5 cm in diameter)
8 lettuce leaves
1 cup (50 g) bean sprouts
1 1/2 oz (50 g) dried rice vermicelli,
   soaked in hot water to soften, cut
   into 2-in (5-cm) lengths
1/2 cup (20 g) loosely packed mint
   leaves
1/2 cup (20 g) loosely packed fresh
   coriander leaves (cilantro)
1/2 cup (20 g) loosely packed Asian
   basil leaves (optional)
Small bunch garlic chives or green
   onions (scallions), cut into 4–5 in
   (10–12.5 cm) lengths (optional)

**1** Bring the water, vinegar, rice wine and fish sauce to a boil in a small pan. Add the shrimp and simmer until just cooked, 2 to 3 minutes. Remove the shrimp, reserving the liquid in the pan. When the shrimp are cool, peel, devein, and cut in half lengthwise.

**2** Put the pork in the reserved liquid in the pan, adding just enough water to barely cover the meat. Bring to a boil, cover and simmer gently until tender, about 10 minutes for fillet and 25 minutes for loin. Drain, discarding the liquid. When the pork is cool, shred finely.

**3** Shortly before serving, set a bowl of warm water and a kitchen towel on a working bench. Dip a rice paper wrapper in the water for 3 to 4 seconds, remove and place on the towel. Smooth the wrapper with your fingers. Repeat with another three wrappers.

**4** Put a lettuce leaf across the center of each of the soaked rice paper wrapper and add 2 shrimp halves. Spread some of the pork, bean sprouts, vermicelli, mint, basil and coriander leaves. Lay two lengths of garlic chives across the top.

**5** Roll up the rice paper wrapper, tucking in the edges to make a cigar shape and completely enclose the filling. Alternatively, you could leave one side open, so that the garlic chives stick out and look more decorative. Repeat with the remaining wrappers. Serve whole if using small rice paper wrappers, or cut diagonally in three bite-sized portions if using large wrappers.

# Laotian Spiced Beef Jerky  *Saiko niet*

I first came across Lao-style dried beef in a simple thatch restaurant in Vientiane, where it was served with mugs of wonderfully cold beer. It's not surprising that different versions of dried beef are found in most of Southeast Asia, for in rural areas where refrigeration is non-existent, thin slices of marinated beef are sun-dried as a method of preservation. The dried beef is grilled to make a savory snack and can also be shredded and added to salads or served with rice. Don't worry if you can't sun-dry the beef—there are alternative methods.

**Serves 4**
**Preparation time:** 15 mins
**Drying time:** 4–8 hours
**Cooking time:** 4–10 mins

1 lb (500 g) striploin or topside, in one
   piece
2 tablespoons minced ginger or
   2 tablespoons very thinly sliced
   lemongrass, tender inner part of
   bottom third only
1–2 red finger-length chilies, sliced
2 cloves garlic, minced
2 tablespoons sugar
1 tablespoon fish sauce
1 tablespoon soy sauce
1 teaspoon salt
1 teaspoon ground coriander
1 tablespoon oil

1 Chill the beef in the freezer for 30 minutes, then slice it thinly across the grain.
2 Process the ginger or lemongrass, chilies, garlic and sugar to a smooth paste, adding a little of the fish sauce if needed to keep the blades turning. Transfer to a bowl and stir in the fish sauce, soy sauce, salt, coriander and oil, mixing well. Add the beef strips and massage with your hand for about 30 seconds to mix thoroughly. Cover the bowl with plastic wrap and refrigerate for 4 hours.
3 Spread the meat in a single layer on a bamboo tray or on a metal rack and dry in the sun, turning the meat after a few hours. Leave in the sun until the meat is completely dry; this will take around 8 hours of full sunshine. Alternatively, you can put the rack of meat slices in a large baking dish and cook in the lowest possible oven until the meat has completely dried out, about 4 hours. To serve, the dried beef can be cooked briefly over hot charcoal, about 2 minutes on both sides, or under a very hot grill. If you prefer, you could cook it on racks in a hot oven (425°F/220°C) until crisp, about 10 minutes.

# Balinese Seafood Satays    *Sate lilit*

I've made these sublime satay so many times that friends joke this is my signature dish. (The recipe is based on one created by Lother Arsana and Heinz von Holzen, with whom I worked on *The Food of Bali*.) Spicy fish, shrimp and coconut paste are molded around lemongrass skewers, which give the most incredible fragrance to the satay, although you could use alternatives if fresh lemongrass is not available.

**Serves 6–8**
**Makes about 20–24 sticks**
**Preparation time:** 1 hour
**Cooking time:** 10 mins

10 oz (300 g) boneless skinned white fish fillets
   (such as snapper, bream, or grouper), cubed
10 oz (300 g) fresh shrimp, peeled and deveined
2 cups (200 g) freshly grated coconut or
   1½ cups (120 g) desiccated coconut,
   moistened with ¾ cup (185 ml) milk
5 kaffir lime leaves, very finely shredded
1 teaspoon freshly ground black pepper
1 teaspoon salt
1 tablespoon shaved palm sugar
2–3 fresh red or green bird's-eye chilies, minced
   (optional)
20–24 stalks lemongrass, cut into 5–6 in
   (12.5–15 cm) lengths, or 16 trimmed pieces
   fresh or canned sugar cane, or bamboo
   skewers
¼ cup (60 ml) oil

**Seasoning Paste**
4 red finger-length chilies, deseeded and minced
6 shallots, minced
3 cloves garlic, minced
2 tablespoons grated ginger
5 candlenuts, finely chopped
½ teaspoon dried shrimp paste
¼ cup (60 ml) oil
2 teaspoons ground coriander
½ teaspoon ground turmeric
1 small tomato, peeled and minced
1 heaped tablespoon tamarind pulp, soaked in
   ¼ cup water, squeezed and strained to obtain
   the juice
1 *salam* leaf (optional)
1 stalk lemongrass, tender inner part of bottom
   third only, bruised and cut into 3 pieces

1 Prepare the Seasoning Paste by processing the chilies, shallots, garlic, ginger, candlenuts and dried shrimp paste to a smooth paste in a spice grinder; you may need to do this in two batches. Heat the oil in small pan, preferably nonstick. Add the ground paste and coriander, and stir-fry over low-moderate heat, 3 minutes. Add the turmeric, tomato, tamarind juice, *salam* leaf and lemongrass, and cook, stirring frequently, until the liquid has dried up and the oil starts to separate, about 10 to 12 minutes. Transfer to a bowl to cool, then remove the *salam* leaf and lemongrass. (The paste can be refrigerated in a covered container for up to a day before using, or even deep-frozen.)
2 Pulse the fish and shrimp in a food processor until they turn into a smooth paste. Put the coconut, Seasoning Paste, kaffir lime leaves, pepper, salt, palm sugar and chilies in a bowl and mix to combine well. Add the processed seafood mixture, and mix thoroughly, using your hand to make sure everything is evenly distributed.
3 Spread 2 tablespoons of the oil on a large plate. Make a shallow slit about 2 in (5 cm) long in the thick end of each lemongrass stem and bruise the stem lightly with pestle or back of a cleaver to help release the fragrance. Oil your hands lightly, then mold 2 to 3 heaped tablespoons of the seafood mixture around the thick end of each lemongrass stem, pressing firmly with your hands to make a cylinder about 4 in (10 cm) in length. Put each satay on the oiled plate, turning to cover with a little oil.
4 Grease the grill of a barbecue or broiler with oil. Cook the seafood skewers over moderate heat until golden brown, about 4 to 5 minutes, turning frequently and taking care they don't burn. Serve hot as an appetizer or as part of a main meal, with rice and other dishes.

**Balinese Seafood Satays**

# Chapter 2
# Soups and Salads

In Southeast Asia, soup is a liquid dish of broth or coconut milk containing vegetables, fruit, seafood, poultry, or meat, served together with rice and rarely eaten as a separate course. When you get used to eating soup the Asian way, spooning some of the solids on to your rice and either sipping the broth from the soup bowl or pouring a little directly over the rice, the logic of soup becomes apparent. Steamed rice on its own is dry. Add the liquid from your soup and it is just so much easier to eat. As many of the locals say, soup "helps the rice down." You can cook just about anything in a soup. Your main protein for the meal might come in Southern Thai Beefball Soup (page 52), or Thai Fragrant Coconut Chicken Soup (page 55). Put some of your vegetables into Creamy Coconut Pumpkin Soup (page 56), or make Javanese Tamarind Vegetable Soup (page 50), or healthy Clear Soup with Spinach and Corn (page 53). And don't stop at vegetables. You can enjoy fruit in the Cambodian Sweet and Sour Fish Soup (page 57). Noodle soups are included in this chapter. These substantial noodle soups, ranging from Vietnamese Beef Noodle Soup (page 62) to the incredible Singapore-style Laksa Noodle Soup (page 60) are enough to get you going for the day, to buck you up at lunch time, or to have as a late-night snack, just to make sure you're not going to be awake hungry during the night.

Salads are among some of the most exciting and creative food of Southeast Asia. Salads are by no means confined to vegetables: sour fruits, poultry, meat, fish, rice, noodles, cashew nuts—just about anything that will excite your palate while doing great things for your health ends up in a salad. Dressings are often piquant with lime juice, fish sauce, garlic and chilies, or sometimes come in the form of a creamy peanut sauce. Most salads are served at the same time as rice and other main meal dishes, their fresh flavor, crisp texture and bright green color adding a pleasing balance to the meal. For a genuine Southeast Asian meal, try to include a salad as part of every main, even if it's just a platter of raw vegetables (lettuce, cabbage, young long beans, for example) and an array of fresh herbs.

# Javanese Tamarind Vegetable Soup

*Sayur asam*

When I first tried this popular West Javanese soup, I was intrigued by the spray of red-skinned oval nuts and leaves floating in it. As I've subsequently learned, *melinjo* nuts and leaves are hard to find outside of Indonesia, but even without these, this mixture of vegetables and peanuts in sour broth tastes really great. Do try, however, to find fresh or dried *salam* leaves, which really make a difference to the flavor.

**Serves 4**
**Preparation time:** 10 mins
**Cooking time:** 20 mins

1/4 cup (40 g) raw peanuts
1/2 teaspoon dried shrimp paste, toasted (page 22)
6 shallots, thinly sliced
1 clove garlic, thinly sliced
1 red finger-length chili, deseeded and sliced
4 thick slices fresh galangal, bruised
2 fresh or dried *salam* leaves
4 cups (1 liter) light chicken or beef stock
2 cups (200 g) finely chopped cabbage
1 small zucchini or chayote (choko), peeled and diced
3 1/2 oz (100 g) green beans, cut into short lengths
2–3 tablespoons tamarind pulp, soaked in 1/2 cup (125 ml) warm water, squeezed and strained to obtain the juice
Shaved palm sugar, to taste
Salt, to taste

**1** Put the peanuts in a small saucepan with enough water to cover. Bring to a boil, reduce the heat and simmer for 10 minutes. Drain and set aside.
**2** Put the dried shrimp paste into a saucepan with the shallots, garlic, chili, galangal, *salam* leaves and stock. Bring to a boil, cover, reduce the heat and simmer for 5 minutes. Add the peanuts and vegetables and return to a boil. Lower the heat, cover and simmer until the vegetables are cooked, 10 to 15 minutes.
**3** Add the tamarind juice and simmer for about 1 minute. Add the sugar and salt to taste; if you prefer a really sour soup, omit the sugar. Remove the galangal and *salam* leaves. Transfer to a serving bowl and serve with steamed rice; this is particularly good with grilled fish or poultry.

# Spicy Thai Beef Soup  *Tom yam neua*

A Thai girlfriend taught me how to make this soup back in the early days when I was just beginning to learn about Thai food and thought that soups began and ended with the ubiquitous Tom Yam Kung, the hot sour soup made with shrimp. I think this beef soup—which has similar seasonings—is just as good and in areas where shrimp are expensive or hard to find, an excellent alternative. Saw-tooth coriander looks like a wide blade of grass with serrated edges; if you can't find it, regular fresh coriander leaves (cilantro) is fine.

**Serves 4–6**
**Preparation time:** 10 mins
**Cooking time:** 8 mins

4 cups (1 liter) water
2 stalks lemongrass, tender inner part of
   bottom third only, bruised and cut into
   4–5 pieces
1¼-in (3-cm) fresh galangal, thinly sliced
4–5 kaffir lime leaves, torn
4–6 bird's-eye chilies, lightly bruised
2–3 tablespoons Roasted Thai Chili Paste
   (page 31)
1½ tablespoons fish sauce
1 medium ripe but firm tomato, cut into
   8 wedges
2 tablespoons lime or lemon juice
7 oz (200 g) fillet or striploin beef, chilled in
   the freezer for 30 minutes, very thinly sliced
   across the grain
Salt, to taste
Several saw-tooth coriander leaves, torn, or
   fresh coriander leaves (cilantro), to garnish

1 Put the water, lemongrass, galangal, kaffir lime leaves and chilies into a saucepan. Bring to a boil, lower the heat and simmer, uncovered, for 5 minutes.
2 Stir in the chili paste, fish sauce, tomato and lime juice. Simmer for 1 minute, then add the beef and cook just until the beef is done.
3 Taste and add salt, if desired, and a little more lime juice if it is not sour enough. Sprinkle with coriander leaves and serve hot with rice and other dishes.

# Southern Thai Beefball Soup   *Sup bo vien*

The region's most famous beefball soup is found in the southern Thai town of Haadyai (though I'm not too reassured by the fact that Haadyai is also famous for bull fights). I prefer the fragrant beefball soup of Vietnam, where the beef is marinated then ground to a smooth paste with a touch of bicarbonate of soda to help give a characteristic springy texture. This soup is usually served as part of a main meal with rice, but you could transform it into a noodle soup (see Note). Beefballs are also added to beef stock with a mixture of other cuts (tripe, intestines, brisket, slivers of tender beef) to make what is sometimes irreverently called "spare parts soup."

**Serves 4–6**
**Preparation time:** 30 mins + 4 hours (or overnight) marinating
**Cooking time:** 25 mins

10 oz (300 g) lean topside beef, thinly sliced
2 teaspoons sesame oil
2 tablespoons minced fresh coriander leaves (cilantro)
Liberal sprinkling of freshly ground black pepper

**Marinade**
1 tablespoon fish sauce
1 tablespoon iced water
2 teaspoons lime juice
1 teaspoon tapioca flour or cornstarch
1/2 teaspoon bicarbonate of soda (baking soda)
1/4 teaspoon freshly ground black pepper
1/4 teaspoon sugar

**Stock**
6 cups (1.5 liters) beef stock, preferably home-made
1 tablespoon fish sauce
1 medium onion, minced
1 clove garlic, smashed and minced
1 stalk lemongrass, tender inner part of bottom third only, sliced
1 whole star anise
1/2 teaspoon black peppercorns
Salt, to taste

1 Put the sliced beef in a bowl and add the Marinade ingredients, massaging well with your hands until the liquid is completely absorbed. Cover the meat and refrigerate for at least 4 hours, or overnight if preferred.

2 Make the Stock by putting all the ingredients, except the salt, in a pan and bring to a boil. Cover the pan, lower the heat and simmer for 20 minutes. Strain, discarding the solids, then return the Stock to the pan. Taste and add salt, if desired.

3 Transfer the marinated beef to a food processor and process to a very smooth paste. Put the sesame oil in a small dish and use it to moisten your hands. You can use both hands to shape the mixture into very small balls about 3/4 in (2 cm) in diameter. Alternatively, you can try doing it the Vietnamese way, taking a handful of the beef mixture in one oiled hand and making a circle between your thumb and forefinger. Squeeze out some of the meat, scraping off the small ball that emerges with a teaspoon held in your other (non-oiled) hand. Repeat until you have used up the beef mixture. Set the balls aside on a plate. (You should have around 30 beefballs.)

4 Reheat the Stock, add the beefballs and bring to a boil. When the beefballs have risen to the surface of the Stock, lower the heat and simmer with the pan partially covered for 3 minutes. Transfer to individual soup bowls, sprinkle with coriander leaves and black pepper and serve immediately as an accompaniment to rice.

**NOTE:** If you'd like to convert this into a noodle soup, increase the amount of stock to 7 cups (1.75 liters) and add 7 oz (200 g) cooked rice vermicelli or wheat noodles before serving. You could add a handful of bean sprouts too, if you have them handy.

# Clear Soup with Spinach and Corn

## Sayur bayam

When I lived in Central Java in the mid-1970s, our cook, 'Bu Hardi, often prepared this delicious soup. I think it's nicest with English spinach, but I sometimes use amaranth (also called Chinese spinach); you could even substitute silver beet (Swiss chard) or Chinese flowering cabbage. Indonesians always use large chunks of sweet corn on the cob, but it's easier to eat if you add fresh or frozen corn kernels. Do try to find *salam* leaf for that distinctive Javanese flavor.

**Serves 4**
**Preparation time:** 10 mins
**Cooking time:** 15 mins

3 cups (750 g) chicken stock
3 shallots, thinly sliced
1/2-in (1-cm) sliced fresh galangal, lightly bruised
2 cloves garlic, minced
1/4 teaspoon ground turmeric
1 fresh or dried *salam* leaf
1 teaspoon shaved palm sugar
1 cup (125 g) fresh or defrosted sweet corn kernels
10 oz (300 g) English spinach, washed and coarsely chopped
Salt, to taste

1 Put the stock, shallots, galangal, garlic, turmeric, *salam* leaf and sugar in a saucepan and bring to a boil. Cover and simmer for 5 minutes.
2 Add the sweet corn and simmer with the pan partially covered until the corn is tender, 7 to 8 minutes. Add the spinach and simmer until it is tender.
3 Taste and add salt, if desired, and serve hot with rice and other dishes.

**Southern Thai Beefball Soup**

# Classic Shrimp Tom Yam Soup

*Tom yam kung*

This is one of the all-time favorite Thai dishes in restaurants around the world (and yes, even in Thailand too). With the fragrance of kaffir lime leaves, galangal and lemongrass, the saltiness of fish sauce, the sour bite of lime juice and the heat of chilies, this dish epitomizes the best of Southeast Asian food. All that and luscious shrimp too.

**Serves 4–6**
**Preparation time:** 15 mins
**Cooking time:** 20 mins

1 tablespoon oil
1 lb (500 g) medium-large fresh shrimp, peeled and deveined, heads and shells reserved
5 cups (1.25 liters) light chicken stock, preferably home-made
3 stalks lemongrass, tender inner part of bottom third only, bruised and cut into 4–5 pieces
2-in (5-cm) fresh galangal, thinly sliced
2 shallots, minced
2 tablespoons Roasted Thai Chili Paste (page 31)
4–6 kaffir lime leaves, torn
4–8 bird's-eye chilies, lightly bruised
1 medium tomato, cut into 8–10 wedges
2 tablespoons fish sauce
2–3 tablespoons lime juice

1 Heat the oil in a saucepan, then add the shrimp heads and shells and stir-fry until they turn pink. Add the stock, lemongrass, galangal and shallots. Bring to a boil, cover, lower the heat and simmer for 15 minutes. Pour through a sieve, pressing down firmly with a spoon to extract as much liquid as possible.
2 Put the chili paste in the saucepan and slowly stir in the strained stock. Add the kaffir lime leaves, chilies and tomato, and bring slowly to a boil, stirring all the time. Put in the shrimp and simmer for just 2 to 3 minutes, taking care not to over-cook. Stir in the fish sauce and lime juice to taste. Serve hot with rice and other dishes.

# Fragrant Coconut Chicken Soup

*Gaeng tom kha gai*

In Thailand, this wonderfully creamy soup is often served in an unglazed terracotta pot with a curved bottom, placed on a charcoal brazier to keep it warm throughout the meal. The galangal, lemongrass and kaffir lime leaves give a heavenly fragrance and as there are only a few bruised chilies, the flavor is fairly mild. Serve with rice and Simple Thai Fish Sauce and Chili Dip, which lets you intensify the heat as much as you like.

**Serves 4**
**Preparation time:** 10 mins
**Cooking time:** 20 mins

5 cups (1.25 liters) thin coconut milk
2-in (5-cm) fresh galangal, bruised and thickly
  sliced
4 stalks lemongrass, tender inner part of
  bottom third only, bruised and cut into 4–5
  pieces
1¹/2 lbs (700 g) chicken pieces, cut through the
  bone into bite-sized pieces, or 1 lb (500 g)
  boneless breast or thigh fillet
¹/2 cup (125 ml) thick coconut milk
¹/4 cup (60 ml) lime juice
¹/4 cup (60 ml) fish sauce
4–5 kaffir lime leaves, torn
4–6 bird's-eye chilies, bruised
Sprigs of fresh coriander leaves (cilantro)
Simple Thai Fish Sauce and Chili Dip (page 27)

1 Put the thin coconut milk, galangal and lemongrass into a saucepan and bring slowly to a boil, stirring frequently. Simmer gently with the pan uncovered for 5 minutes, then add the chicken and simmer gently, uncovered, until the chicken is tender.
2 Add the thick coconut milk, lime juice, fish sauce, kaffir lime leaves and chilies, and bring almost to a boil, stirring. Transfer to a large bowl and garnish with the coriander sprigs. Serve with the Simple Thai Fish Sauce and Chili Dip in separate bowls and allow everyone to add according to taste.

# Creamy Coconut Pumpkin Soup

## *Gaeng lian fak thong*

This easy and delicious soup is a Thai recipe, but I've enjoyed similar soups in both Laos and Cambodia. I'm not sure of the reason, but this soup is recommended "for nursing mothers and children." However, I've found that everyone loves it. Do try to find Asian basil leaves, which has a marvelous aniseed flavor lacking in sweet European basil.

**Serves 4**
**Preparation time:** 10 mins
**Cooking time:** 15 mins

2 tablespoons dried shrimp, soaked in water to soften
1/2 teaspoon dried shrimp paste, toasted (page 22)
3 shallots, minced
1–2 red or green finger-length chilies, sliced (some seeds removed if desired)
3 cups (750 ml) thin coconut milk
10 oz (300 g) butternut, kabocha, or other brightly colored pumpkin, peeled and diced
1/4 cup (60 ml) coconut cream
1 tablespoon fish sauce
1/2 cup (20 g) Asian basil leaves

**1** Process the dried shrimp to a powder in a spice grinder, then add the dried shrimp paste, shallots and chilies. Process to a smooth paste, adding a little of the coconut milk, if needed, to keep the blades turning. Transfer to a saucepan and stir in the coconut milk.
**2** Bring to a boil over medium heat and stir constantly. Add the pumpkin pieces and simmer with the pan uncovered until they are soft. Add the coconut cream and fish sauce, stirring gently for about 1 minute. Add the basil leaves and serve immediately.

**Cambodian Sweet and Sour Fish Soup**

# Cambodian Sweet and Sour Fish Soup

*Samlor machou khmer*

As the Cambodian name for this dish (*samlor*) indicates, this is a soupy stew eaten with rice. What the name doesn't tell you is how absolutely delicious it is. The delicate seasoning of galangal, lemongrass, other herbs and fish sauce is joined by the full-on flavor of crisp-fried garlic. The unusual addition of a beaten egg gives a lovely smooth texture to the soup, which has fresh pineapple and tomato for a touch of acidity. All in all, this has to be one of my favorite fish recipes.

**Serves 4**
**Preparation time:** 15 mins
**Cooking time:** 25 mins

4 cups (1 liter) chicken stock
1 heaped tablespoon tamarind pulp
1 tablespoon finely minced galangal
2 stalk lemongrass, tender inner part of bottom third only, bruised and cut into 4 pieces
1 thick slice of fresh pineapple (about ¼ lb/ 125 g), peeled, cored and cut into very small wedges
1 large ripe tomato, cut into 12 wedges
3 tablespoons fish sauce
1 tablespoon sugar, or more to taste
13 oz (375 g) boneless fish fillets (catfish if possible), cut into bite-sized pieces
2–3 tablespoons Crisp-fried Garlic (page 22)
1¼ cups (60 g) bean sprouts, tails removed
½ cup (20 g) Asian basil leaves, coarsely chopped
¼ cup (12 g) coarsely chopped rice paddy herb or fresh coriander leaves (cilantro)
1 egg, lightly beaten (optional)
Freshly ground black pepper, to taste
1 tablespoon sliced bird's-eye chilies

> **NOTE:** Chicken stock made with stock cubes (bouillon) or powder could be used, although home-made stock is preferable.

1 Put the chicken stock, tamarind pulp, galangal and lemongrass into a saucepan and bring to a boil. Lower the heat, cover and simmer for 10 minutes. Pour through a sieve, discarding the solids and return the stock to the pan.
2 Add the pineapple, tomato, fish sauce and 1 tablespoon of sugar. Bring to a boil, cover and simmer for 5 minutes. Add the fish and continue simmering, uncovered, until the fish is cooked, about 5 to 8 minutes depending on the thickness and type of fish. Add the Crisp-fried Garlic to taste, bean sprouts, Asian basil leaves and rice paddy herb (if using coriander leaves, do not add yet). Stir for a few seconds, until the sprouts start to wilt slightly. Taste and add a little more sugar if desired; this will depend on the sweetness of the pineapple.
3 Pour in the egg in a slow steady stream, stirring slowly until it sets. Add the coriander leaves, if using, then transfer the soup to a large bowl and serve hot with rice, accompanied by the chilies in a separate bowl for adding to taste. If you like, the soup can be transferred to individual bowls and spooned over the rice as required while eating.

# Penang Nonya Laksa Noodle Soup

## Asam laksa penang

Sour, fishy, fragrant, sweet, salty and hot, this Penang favorite is very different from the coconut-milk laksa found in the rest of Malaysia and Singapore. Some of the Penang Nonyas are descended from Chinese who migrated to this lovely island off the northwest Malay peninsula from southern Thailand in the 19th and early 20th centuries—and as this dish demonstrates, their food certainly shows it.

**Serves 4**
**Preparation time:** 45 mins
**Cooking time:** 30 mins

1¼ lbs (600 g) small whole mackerel, cleaned
6 cups (1.5 liters) water
2 tablespoons tamarind pulp, soaked in ½ cup (125 ml) warm water, squeezed and strained to obtain the juice
1 teaspoon sugar, or more to taste
1 teaspoon salt, or more to taste
1 ginger bud, halved lengthwise, thinly sliced across (optional)
4 large stalks Vietnamese mint (laksa leaf) or regular mint leaves
1¼ lbs (600 g) fresh round rice flour (laksa) noodles (see Note), or 10 oz (300 g) dried rice vermicelli

**Seasoning Paste**
4 shallots, minced
2 stalks lemongrass, tender inner part of bottom third only, finely sliced
¾-in (2-cm) fresh turmeric, minced, or ½ teaspoon ground turmeric
6–8 dried red finger-length chilies, cut into short pieces, soaked in hot water to soften
3 red finger-length chilies, sliced
1 teaspoon dried shrimp paste, toasted (page 22)

> **NOTE:** If fresh laksa noodles are not available, use 10 oz (300 g) dried laksa noodles or dried rice vermicelli, prepared according to directions on pack.

**Garnish**
½ small cucumber, halved lengthwise, pulp discarded, flesh cut into matchstick strips
5½ oz (150 g) pineapple, peeled and cored, cut into very small wedges
1 medium onion, halved lengthwise, very thinly sliced across
1 red finger-length chili, deseeded and sliced (optional)
4 large mint sprigs, leaves coarsely torn
2 tablespoons thick black shrimp paste
1 tablespoon warm water

1 Put the fish in a large saucepan and add the water. Bring to a boil, lower the heat and simmer, uncovered, until the fish is soft, about 5 minutes. Remove the fish and when cool enough, flake the flesh and keep aside, making sure you get rid of any tiny bones (local cooks use their fingers to be sure). Strain the stock back into the pan and add the tamarind juice, sugar, salt, ginger bud (if using), and Vietnamese mint.
2 Prepare the Seasoning Paste by processing all the ingredients in a spice grinder, adding a little water, if necessary, to keep the blades turning. Add to the fish stock, bring to a boil, lower the heat and simmer, uncovered, for 15 minutes. Taste and add more sugar or salt if desired. Return the flaked fish to the stock.
3 Heat a large saucepan of boiling water. Blanch the noodles for 30 seconds, drain and divide between four large noodle bowls. Add the fish soup to each bowl and garnish with cucumber, pineapple, onion, chili and mint.
4 Combine the thick black shrimp paste with water and serve in separate bowl for adding according to taste.

**Penang Nonya Laksa Noodle Soup**

# Thai Rice Soup with Pork or Chicken

*Khao tom*

I really love this easy, home-style dish, which many housewives in Thailand (as well as neighboring countries) whip up for a quick breakfast using rice left over from the night before. Ground pork—or chicken if you prefer—is simmered in chicken stock, then cooked rice and fish sauce are added, plus an egg if you like. The garnishes and dip are an important part of the overall flavor.

**Serves 4**
**Preparation time:** 10 mins
**Cooking time:** 12 mins

5 cups (1.25 liters) chicken stock
7 oz (200 g) ground lean pork or
   chicken
3 cups (400 g) cooked rice
1 tablespoon fish sauce
4 teaspoons sugar
4 teaspoons rice vinegar or white
   vinegar
4 eggs (optional)
2 tablespoons Crisp-fried Shallots or
   Garlic (page 22)
Sprigs of fresh coriander leaves
   (cilantro)
Crushed dried chili flakes, to taste
Simple Thai Fish Sauce and Chili Dip
   (page 27)

1 Put the chicken stock in a large saucepan and bring to a boil. Add the ground pork or chicken (break up the lumps with a fork) and simmer, uncovered, for 3 minutes. Add the rice and simmer for another 2 minutes, then add the fish sauce.

2 Put 1 teaspoon of sugar and 1 teaspoon of vinegar into each of four large bowls, stirring to dissolve the sugar. Break an egg into each bowl, then ladle the piping hot rice soup over the egg. Garnish with Crisp-fried Shallots or Garlic and sprigs of coriander leaves. Let the soup stand for a minute or two for the egg to start to set, then stir before eating. Serve hot accompanied by crushed dried chili flakes and Thai Fish Sauce and Chili Dip for adding to taste.

# Singapore-style Laksa Noodle Soup

*Laksa Singapura*

Extravagant. Time consuming. Absolutely delicious. Of all the versions of the famous Laksa noodle soup prepared in Malaysia and Singapore, this is my favorite. The fragrant coconut milk gravy is laced with chilies and dried shrimp, with the accompaniments giving even more flavor and texture. Serve this for a special lunch or dinner, followed by a delectable dessert and believe me, you won't regret it.

**Serves 4**
**Preparation time:** 40 mins
**Cooking time:** 30 mins

1¹/₂ lbs (700 g) fresh round rice flour (laksa) noodles, blanched in boiling water for 30 seconds, drained (see Note)
2 cups (100 g) bean sprouts, straggly tails removed
13 oz (375 g) cooked shrimp, peeled and deveined, tails intact
12 canned or fresh quail eggs, hard-boiled and peeled if fresh, or 2 hard-boiled eggs, quartered (see Note)
4 cakes dried deep-fried tofu, blanched in boiling water for 1 minute, sliced (see Note)
Sprigs of laksa leaves, to garnish

**Laksa Gravy**
10–12 dried red finger-length chilies, cut into short lengths, soaked in hot water to soften
2–3 red finger-length chilies, sliced
16 shallots, minced
2-in (5-cm) fresh galangal, minced
6 cloves garlic, minced
1-in (2.5-cm) ginger, minced
3 stalks lemongrass, tender inner part of bottom third only, sliced

³/₄-in (2-cm) fresh turmeric, or 1 teaspoon ground turmeric
1¹/₂ teaspoons dried shrimp paste, toasted (page 22)
¹/₃ cup (85 ml) oil
2 teaspoons coriander seeds, lightly toasted and ground to a powder
¹/₂ cup (60 g) dried shrimp, soaked in water to soften, ground to a powder
3 cups (750 ml) water
4 tablespoons finely minced laksa leaves
1¹/₂ teaspoons salt, or more to taste
1¹/₂ teaspoons sugar, or more to taste
12–16 small fish balls, or 1–2 fish cakes, thinly sliced
3 cups (750 ml) coconut milk

**Accompaniments**
4 tablespoons pounded red finger-length chili or Malaysian Chili and Dried Shrimp Paste Dip (page 28)
4 small round green limes (*limau kesturi*), stalk end sliced off, or 1 regular lime, quartered

1 Make the Laksa Gravy by processing both lots of chilies, shallots, galangal, garlic, ginger, lemongrass, turmeric and dried shrimp paste to a smooth paste, adding a little oil if needed to keep the blades turning.
2 Heat the oil in a large saucepan, add the chili paste and stir-fry over low-moderate heat until fragrant and the oil starts to separate, about 10 minutes. Add the ground coriander and stir-fry for 1 minute. Add the dried shrimp powder and stir-fry for 1 minute. Stir in the water, laksa leaves, salt and sugar.
3 Bring to a boil, lower the heat and simmer, uncovered, for 5 minutes. Add the fish balls and simmer for another 5 minutes. Add the coconut milk and bring almost to a boil, then remove from the heat. Taste and add more salt and sugar, if needed.
4 To serve, divide the noodles and bean sprouts between four large bowls. Fill each bowl with the hot Laksa Gravy, then top with the shrimp, fish balls, quail eggs (or 2 egg quarters) and tofu slices. Garnish with sprigs of laksa leaf and serve immediately with dipping bowls of Malaysian Chili and Dried Shrimp Paste Dip and a lime.

> **NOTE:** If boiling fresh quail eggs, add 1 tablespoon of salt to the water and boil for just 3 minutes; the salt makes it easier to peel off the shell. If fresh laksa noodles are not available, use 10 oz (300 g) dried laksa noodles, prepared according to directions on pack, or 13 oz (375 g) dried rice vermicelli, soaked to soften, then simmered for about 1 minute until cooked. Deep-fried tofu is also known as "taupok;" if you can't find this, use 1 square pressed tofu, deep-fried and thinly sliced.

# Vietnamese Beef Noodle Soup *Pho bo*

Variations of this classic noodle soup are found throughout Vietnam. It sounds simple: beef stock, slices of beef, noodles, bean sprouts and herbs. But what a fabulously rich beef stock, bathing silky rice flour noodles and crunchy sprouts, with morsels of rare beef, all perfumed with herbs and lime. This is a seriously satisfying soup. Eat it on its own for breakfast, lunch, or supper (or all three).

**Serves 4**
**Preparation time:** 30 mins
**Cooking time:** 3–4 hours

10 oz (300 g) beef brisket or gravy beef,
   in one piece
2 lbs (1 kg) beef shin bones
10 cups (2.5 liters) water
2-in (5-cm) ginger, unpeeled
1 medium onion, unpeeled
2 whole star anise
3-in (7.5-cm) cinnamon
1 teaspoon salt
13 oz (375 g) fresh wide rice noodles, or
   7 oz (200 g) dried rice-stick noodles,
   soaked in hot water to soften, drained
1/2 lb (250 g) sirloin or fillet steak, chilled
   in the freezer for 30 minutes, cut into
   paper-thin slices
1 medium onion, cut into paper-thin slices
2 green onions (scallions), thinly sliced

**Accompaniments**
1 1/4 cups (60 g) bean sprouts
Large handful of mint sprigs
Large handful of Asian basil leaves
1–2 red finger-length chilies, sliced
1 lime, quartered
Small bowls of fish sauce

1 Put the brisket beef and beef bones in a very large pan and add enough water to cover the meat and bones. Bring to a boil, then simmer, uncovered, for 10 minutes. Pour off the water and then add the 10 cups of fresh water.

2 While the beef is blanching, spear the ginger and the onion on a skewer and hold in a gas flame or place under a very hot grill. Cook, turning, until the ginger and onion are blackened. Do not remove the skin but add the whole piece of ginger and onion, skin and all, to the pan. Add the star anise, cinnamon and salt, and simmer over very low heat, with the pan uncovered, for 3 hours. By this time, the meat will be almost falling apart. Remove the piece of brisket and set aside to cool. Discard the beef bones and pour the stock through a sieve into a clean pan. If desired, the stock can be made one to two days in advance and refrigerated.

3 Cut the brisket beef into thin slices. Reheat the strained stock and keep warm. If using fresh noodles, plunge them in a large pan of boiling water for 10 seconds, then drain in a colander.

4 To serve, put some of the noodles into the bottom of four large soup bowls. Top with the sliced brisket beef and the raw sirloin slices. Fill each bowl with the hot stock and scatter with a little thinly sliced raw onions and green onions. Place the Accompaniments in the center of the table for each person to add to the noodle soup as desired.

# Madurese Chicken Noodle Soup

*Soto ayam*

Soto Ayam is one of the most popular soups in Indonesia, sold by mobile vendors and in basic restaurants throughout the archipelago. This recipe is from Madura—a rugged island northeast of Java. The addition of hard-boiled egg, bean sprouts and potatoes to the chicken, rice vermicelli and spiced chicken stock makes this a satisfying dish. Versions made at home often include potato croquettes or *pergedel* instead of sliced boiled potato.

**Serves 4**
**Preparation time:** 30 mins
**Cooking time:** 35 mins

1¹/₄ lbs (600 g) chicken pieces with the bone still in (preferably thigh)
4 cups (1 liter) water
1 teaspoon salt
3 tablespoons oil
1 cup (250 ml) coconut milk
2 kaffir lime leaves, edges torn
¹/₂–1 teaspoon chicken stock powder (optional)
2 small waxy potatoes, boiled, peeled and thickly sliced
2 hard boiled eggs, peeled and halved lengthwise
1¹/₂ cups (75 g) bean sprouts

7 oz (200 g) fine dried rice vermicelli, soaked in hot water to soften
3 tablespoons Crisp-fried Shallots (page 22)
2 tablespoons finely minced fresh coriander leaves (cilantro)
1 large lime, quartered

Seasoning Paste
1 teaspoon black peppercorns
1 teaspoon coriander seeds, lightly toasted
4 candlenuts, minced
6 shallots, minced
2 cloves garlic, minced
1 thin slice ginger, minced
¹/₂-in (1-cm) fresh turmeric, minced, or ¹/₄ teaspoon ground turmeric

**1** Put the chicken, water and salt in a saucepan. Bring to a boil, cover, lower the heat and simmer gently until the chicken is soft. When the chicken is cool enough to handle, discard the skin and remove the flesh from the bones, shredding it finely by hand. Set aside. Reserve the chicken stock.

**2** Prepare the Seasoning Paste by processing the peppercorns and coriander seeds to a powder in a spice grinder. Add the remaining ingredients and process to a smooth paste, adding a little of the oil, if needed, to keep the blades turning.

**3** Heat the oil in a saucepan with a heavy base, then add the Seasoning Paste and stir-fry over low-medium heat until fragrant, about 4 minutes. Add the reserved chicken stock and bring to a boil. Lower the heat, cover the pan and simmer for 5 minutes. Add the coconut milk and kaffir lime leaves, then bring gently to a boil, stirring. Taste and add a little chicken stock powder if desired. Simmer with the pan uncovered for 5 minutes.

**4** To serve, divide the noodles, potato, egg, bean sprouts and chicken between four large noodle bowls. Ladle the hot stock into each bowl, then garnish with the Crisp-fried Shallots and coriander leaves. Serve with a lime wedge and, if preferred, a chili sambal.

Madurese Chicken Noodle Soup

# Thai Lemongrass Soup with Mushrooms

*Tom yum hed*

Straw mushrooms, which have a firm yet slippery texture, are grown on a large scale in Thailand and have a wonderful woodsy perfume. They're excellent in this hot sour soup, which uses freshly made vegetable stock, although you could substitute this with chicken stock (preferably home-made) if you prefer. If you can't get fresh straw mushrooms, try the canned variety or use fresh button mushrooms.

**Serves 4**
**Preparation time:** 10 mins
**Cooking time:** 40 mins

**1–2 tablespoons Roasted Thai Chili Paste (page 31)**
**1 stalk lemongrass, tender inner part of bottom third only, bruised and cut into 4–5 pieces**
**3 kaffir lime leaves, torn**
**3 tablespoons lime or lemon juice**
**4 teaspoons fish sauce**
**1 teaspoon sugar**
**3¹/₂ oz (100 g) fresh straw mushrooms, halved if large**
**1 medium ripe tomato, quartered**
**2–3 bird's-eye chilies, lightly bruised**
**Sprigs of fresh coriander leaves (cilantro), to garnish**

**Vegetable Stock**
**5 cups (1.25 liters) water**
**1 medium onion, minced**
**1 large carrot, minced**
**1 stalk celery, sliced**
**1 whole coriander plant including roots, minced**
**1 teaspoon black peppercorns**

**1** Make the Vegetable Stock by combining the water, onion, carrot, celery, coriander and peppercorns in a large saucepan. Bring to a boil, cover, lower the heat and simmer until the liquid has reduced to 3¹/₂ cups (875 ml), about 30 minutes.

**2** Strain the Vegetable Stock into a medium saucepan. Stir in the chili paste, lemongrass and kaffir lime leaves. Bring to a boil, lower the heat and simmer, uncovered, for 3 minutes, stirring occasionally. Add the lime juice, fish sauce, sugar, mushrooms, tomato and chilies. Bring to a boil, reduce the heat and simmer, uncovered, until the mushrooms are cooked, 3 to 4 minutes. If using canned mushrooms, simmer for 3 minutes.

**3** Transfer to a serving bowl and garnish with coriander sprigs. Serve hot with steamed rice and other dishes.

# Sweet and Spicy Green Papaya Salad

*Som tum*

Versions of this hot, sour, salty green papaya salad are made for you on the spot at food stalls in Thailand, Vietnam, Cambodia and Laos. I was once asked in Central Thailand if I wanted it local style, with a pickled crab (shell and all) added. My policy is always to try something at least once, so I did, but I still wish they'd shelled the crab first. The traditional way to make this salad is using a mortar and pestle to bruise the ingredients—for once, a food processor just won't do.

**Serves 4–6**
**Preparation time:** 25 mins

3–4 cloves garlic
4–6 red or green bird's-eye chilies
2 tablespoons dried shrimp, soaked in
    water to soften
2 teaspoons sugar
2 green beans, cut into short lengths
1 small tomato, diced
1 unripe green papaya (about 10 oz/300 g),
    peeled and shredded
2 tablespoons fish sauce
2 tablespoons lime juice
2–3 tablespoons coarsely crushed dry-
    roasted peanuts
4–6 cabbage leaves, washed and torn into
    several pieces (optional)

**1** Divide the garlic, chilies and dried shrimp into two batches. Put half into a mortar, add 1 teaspoon of sugar into the mortar and pound until well broken up. Add half of the green beans and pound a little to bruise, then add half of the diced tomato and pound a few times just until they are broken up. Add half the papaya to the mortar, a little at a time, pounding until lightly bruised. Transfer the mixture to a bowl and repeat with the remaining garlic, chilies, dried shrimp, sugar, green beans, tomato and papaya.
**2** Add the fish sauce, lime juice and peanuts to the bowl of papaya mixture, tossing to mix well. Taste and add a little more lime juice, fish sauce, or sugar if you like and serve immediately. The salad is often eaten with cabbage leaves (served separately on a plate, with ice cubes to keep them cool and crisp). Each person uses a piece of the cabbage to scoop up the papaya salad.

# Thai Green Mango Salad with Cashews

## *Yam mamuang*

This salad is so superb that even though green mangoes are usually a fairly esoteric item outside of Southeast Asia, they're well worth tracking down just to make this recipe. The sourness of the mango is offset by a touch of sugar, a heady aroma provided by kaffir lime leaves and other herbs, with a splash of fish sauce for salty fragrance and chilies to give a bit of a bite. The cashew nuts add crunchy sweetness to the salad, which is great with just about anything, especially grilled or fried food. This recipe is a specialty of southern Thailand and northern Malaysia, where cashew nut trees are cultivated.

**Serves 4–6**
**Preparation time:** 10 mins

4–5 unripe green mangoes (about 1¹/₄ lbs/ 600 g), peeled
2–3 teaspoons caster sugar, or more to taste
2 kaffir lime leaves, finely shredded
2 tablespoons minced fresh coriander leaves (cilantro)
1 green onion (scallion), thinly sliced
2–3 red or green bird's-eye chilies, thinly sliced
3 shallots, thinly sliced
2 tablespoons fish sauce
¹/₃ cup (50 g) raw cashew nuts, dry roasted until golden and crisp

1 Hold a peeled mango over a shredder and grate to make matchstick shreds. Alternatively, hold the mango in the palm of one hand and with a sharp knife in your other hand, make vertical cuts down to the stone, keeping the cuts close together. Hold the knife horizontally and slice across to make shreds. Repeat on the other side of the mango.
2 Put the mango shreds in a bowl and sprinkle with the sugar. Massage with your fingers for about 30 seconds, then add the rest of the ingredients except the cashew nuts, tossing to mix well. Taste and if the mangoes seem too sour, add more sugar.
3 Add the cashew nuts, toss and serve immediately. This salad can also be used as a topping for Grilled Fish with Sweet Soy Dip (page 133).

# Tropical Fruit Salad with Palm Sugar Dressing

## *Rujak*

When hunger pangs suddenly strike during the day in Bali or Java, you can stop at roadside stall and indulge in this marvelous healthy snack of under-ripe fruit and vegetables mixed with a pungent dressing (a blend of dried shrimp paste, chilies, sweet palm sugar and sour tamarind). Toss your choice of under-ripe fruit, cucumber and jicama (*bangkwang*) with the dressing and enjoy the quintessential flavors of Southeast Asia.

**Serves 4–6**
**Preparation time:** 20 mins
**Cooking time:** 15 mins

Prepare about 4–6 cups of the following
 ingredients, peeled, cut into bite-sized
 pieces:
 Under-ripe pineapple
 Under-ripe mango or sour green apple
 Pomelo or grapefruit, membranes removed
  from each segment
 Under-ripe papaya
 Cucumber
 Jicama (*bangkwang*)

**Dressing**
1 teaspoon dried shrimp paste, toasted
 (page 22)
1/2 cup (90 g) shaved palm sugar
1–2 red finger-length chilies, minced,
 or 2–3 bird's-eye chilies, bruised
1/2 teaspoon salt
2–3 tablespoons tamarind pulp
1 cup (250 ml) water

1 Make the Dressing by combining all the ingredients in a small pan. Bring to a boil, stirring to dissolve the sugar. Lower the heat and simmer, uncovered, until the Dressing has thickened, about 12 to 15 minutes. Pour through a sieve, pressing to extract as much liquid as possible and leave to cool completely. (The prepared Dressing can be refrigerated for several days.)
2 Just before serving, put the prepared fruits and vegetables in a bowl. Pour over the Dressing, toss to mix well and serve immediately. *Rujak* is normally eaten as a snack, but you could serve it with rice and chicken or fish for a main meal.

# Crunchy Burmese Cabbage Salad

*Gawbi lethoke*

The Burmese have perfected the art of making salads, first choosing the vegetables, then adding extra ingredients for saltiness, texture, fragrance and acidity. In this simple yet really tasty recipe, shredded cabbage is mixed with onion, dried shrimp and lime juice, together with crisp-fried shallots or, even better, Burmese Crispy Dried Shrimp Sprinkle.

**Serves 4–6**
**Preparation time:** 20 mins + 1 hour soaking
**Cooking time:** 5 mins

5 cups (375 g) round cabbage or Chinese (Napa) cabbage, finely shredded
1 medium onion, halved lengthwise, thinly sliced across
1 teaspoon salt
3 tablespoons dried shrimp, dry roasted over low heat for 4–5 minutes, blended to a fine powder, or 3 tablespoons Burmese Crispy Dried Shrimp Sprinkle (page 30)
2–3 tablespoons lime juice
1 tablespoon oil, preferably shallot or garlic-flavored oil (page 22)
1 green finger-length chili, thinly sliced, or 1 teaspoon crushed dried chili flakes
1–2 tablespoons Crisp-fried Shallots (omit if using Burmese Crispy Dried Shrimp Sprinkle)

**1** Put the cabbage in a bowl, cover with cold water and refrigerate for 1 hour. Combine the onion with the salt, mixing well. Stand for 30 minutes, then rinse briefly and squeeze out the moisture. Set the onion aside.
**2** Drain the soaked cabbage thoroughly, then put into a bowl. Add the onion, dried shrimp powder, if using, 2 tablespoons lime juice, oil and chili. Mix thoroughly by hand, squeezing the cabbage slightly to bruise it. Taste and add more salt and lime juice if desired.
**3** Put the cabbage in a serving bowl and scatter with the Crisp-fried Shallots or Burmese Crispy Dried Shrimp Sprinkle. Serve immediately with rice and other dishes.

# Barbecued Pork Salad with Thai Herbs

*Yam chu yuk kan*

Seasoned and slightly sweetened pork, beaten into wafer-thin slices and grilled over charcoal, can be found in most Chinatowns around the world. In this creative Thai recipe, the pork (known in Chinese as *chu yuk kan*) is combined with cashew nuts and lashings of herbs to make a remarkable salad. The flavors are perfectly offset by plain rice; you can also serve a couple of other dishes for a complete meal.

**Serves 4**
**Preparation time:** 15 mins

5 1/2 oz (150 g) barbecued pork slices, cut into narrow strips
1 cup (150 g) raw cashew nuts, toasted in a wok over low heat until golden brown and crisp
2–3 shallots, thinly sliced
1 stalk lemongrass, tender inner part of bottom third only, very thinly sliced
1–2 stalks of Chinese celery, stems cut into short lengths to yield 1/3 cup (do not use the leaves)
1/3 cup (15 g) loosely packed fresh coriander leaves (cilantro), coarsely chopped
1/3 cup (15 g) loosely packed mint leaves, coarsely chopped
1 green onion (scallion), thinly sliced
1 tablespoon lime juice
1 tablespoon fish sauce
1/2–1 teaspoon crushed dried chili flakes

1  Put all the ingredients in a bowl and toss to mix thoroughly. Serve immediately.
2  This salad would be ideal partnered with Fragrant Coconut Chicken Soup (page 55), steamed rice and a simple cooked green vegetable dish.

# 'Big Salad' with Chicken, Pork and Shrimp

## *Yam yai*

This substantial northern Thai salad , known as 'Big Salad', is also found in Laos, although some of the traditional ingredients there (such as boiled pig's heart) don't appeal as much as this Thai version. Most of the preparation can be done in advance and all you need to do is just toss in the ingredients together with the dressing at the last minute. This salad is great for buffets (you may want to double the amounts) and as an accompaniment to barbecued poultry or fish.

**Serves 4–6**
**Preparation time:** 30 mins
**Cooking time:** 20 mins

1/2 cup (75 g) shredded daikon radish
1 teaspoon salt
1 1/4 cups (60 g) bean sprouts, straggly tails removed
1 small cucumber, skin left on, seeds removed, flesh thinly sliced
1 oz (30 g) transparent (bean thread) noodles, soaked in hot water to soften, cut into 2-in (5-cm) lengths
3 pieces dried wood ear fungus, soaked in hot water to soften, hard portions discarded, cut into bite-sized pieces
7 oz (200 g) boneless cooked chicken breast, shredded
7 oz (200 g) cooked lean pork, thinly sliced
7 oz (200 g) cooked small shrimp, peeled and deveined
2 hard-boiled eggs, peeled and sliced
1/2 cup (20 g) loosely packed mint leaves, washed and drained

**Dressing**
1/4 cup (60 ml) fish sauce
1 1/2 tablespoons lime or lemon juice
2 teaspoons sugar
1 teaspoon finely minced or crushed garlic
1–2 teaspoons crushed dried chili flakes

1 Put the shredded radish in a small bowl, sprinkle with the salt and mix well with your fingers. Stand for 15 minutes, rinse, drain and squeeze dry.
2 Scatter the bean sprouts in a wide serving bowl and spread the radish on top. Add the cucumber, noodles, wood ear fungus, chicken, pork and shrimp, scattering evenly. Arrange the egg slices on top and scatter with the mint leaves. (If preparing in advance, cover with plastic wrap and refrigerate.)
3 Make the Dressing by combining the rest of the ingredients in a small bowl, stirring to dissolve the sugar. Just before serving, pour over the prepared salad and toss.

**NOTE:** You could also add 3 to 4 sliced water chestnuts or 1/2 cup (75 g) grated jicama (*bangkwang*) to the salad. For a more decorative appearance, try using eight to twelve hard-boiled quail eggs, left whole, instead of chicken eggs.

'Big Salad' with Chicken, Pork and Shrimp

# Smoked Fish and Green Mango Salad

## *Yoam makah trey ang*

This is one of the first local dishes I ate in Cambodia, sitting under a shady tree in an open-air restaurant along the banks of the Mekong just north of Phnom Penh. It shows just how flavorful a dish can be with only a few seasonings—shallots, chilies, mint leaves, fish sauce and lime juice—but when you're starting with sour green mango and combining it with deep-fried smoked fish, it's hard to go wrong.

**Serves 4**
**Preparation time:** 7 mins
**Cooking time:** 5 mins

1 long-leaf Asian or butter lettuce leaves
  separated, washed and dried
Oil, for deep-frying
7 oz (200 g) boneless smoked fish, cut into
  bite-sized pieces (smoked mackerel or trout
  can be used)
3–4 unripe green mangoes (about 1 lb/500 g),
  peeled
1 tablespoon sugar
1 tablespoon fish sauce, or more to taste
3 shallots, thinly sliced
2–3 red or green bird's-eye chilies, thinly
  sliced
Lime juice, to taste
2 tablespoons minced mint or fresh coriander
  leaves (cilantro)

1 Place the lettuce leaves on a serving plate and set aside.
2 Heat the oil in a wok and when very hot, add the smoked fish and deep-fry until it becomes crisp and brown. Drain on paper towels and leave to cool.
3 Hold each peeled mango over a shredder and grate to make matchstick shreds. Alternatively, hold the mango in the palm of one hand and with a sharp knife in the other hand, make vertical cuts down to the stone, keeping the cuts close together. Hold the knife horizontally and slice across to make shreds. Repeat on the other side of the mango.
4 Put the mango shreds in a bowl. Sprinkle with the sugar, rub with your fingers to soften the mango slightly, then add the fish sauce, shallots, chilies and the cooled fish. Toss and taste, adding more fish sauce (you may not need this if the smoked fish is very salty) and a little lime juice only if the mangoes are not sufficiently sour. Toss in the mint or coriander leaves and serve in a bowl, together with the lettuce leaves. Each person puts some of the salad into a lettuce leaf and rolls it up to eat.

# Vietnamese Chicken Salad   *Ga xe phay*

I don't know anyone who doesn't love the fresh flavors and herbal aroma of this excellent salad (a dish that my friends insist I always bring along on picnics and boat trips). It's worth trying to track down Vietnamese mint (laksa leaf) or regular mint for the unique flavor it adds. The Vietnamese normally use long white Chinese or Napa cabbage, but I find regular round white cabbage is also very good. Some cooks add up to 50 percent more chicken, but I prefer the balance in this recipe.

> **NOTE:** If you're preparing the salad in advance, put the mixed cabbage, chicken and herbs in a sealed container, with the Sauce in a separate container. Combine immediately before serving.

**Serves 4–6**
**Preparation time:** 20 mins
**Cooking time:** 10 mins

13 oz (375 g) chicken thighs, or 7 oz
   (200 g) boneless thigh fillets, skin
   and fat removed
2 teaspoons salt
1 very large or 2 small to medium onions,
   halved lengthwise, very thinly sliced across
13 oz (375 g) Chinese (Napa) cabbage or round
   white cabbage, cored and finely shredded
1/4 cup (12 g) firmly packed fresh coriander
   leaves (cilantro), coarsely chopped
1/4 cup (12 g) firmly packed mint leaves,
   coarsely chopped
1/4 cup (12 g) firmly packed Vietnamese mint
   (laksa leaf) or regular mint leaves
Liberal amount of freshly ground black pepper

Dressing
4 tablespoons lime juice
3 tablespoons fish sauce
3 tablespoons caster sugar
1 tablespoon rice vinegar
1 red finger-length chili, minced

**1** Put the chicken thighs in a saucepan with 1 teaspoon of the salt and add just enough water to cover. Bring to a boil, cover and simmer until the chicken is cooked. Cool in the stock if you have time, then remove the meat from the bones and shred the flesh into fine, lengthwise strips with your fingers. Keep the stock for some other purpose.
**2** While the chicken is cooking, sprinkle the remaining teaspoon of salt over the onion, rub with your fingers and set aside for 30 minutes.
**3** Prepare the Dressing by combining all the ingredients in a small bowl, stirring to dissolve the sugar. Set aside for the flavors to blend.
**4** Just before serving, put the cabbage and all the herbs in a large bowl. Rinse the salted onion under running water, then squeeze dry and add to the cabbage. Add the chicken and Dressing, tossing to combine well. Grind over a liberal amount of black pepper, toss again and serve with other dishes.

## Chapter 3

# Noodles, Rice and Breads

Southeast Asians adore noodles, especially those made from rice flour, but you'll also find wheat noodles and transparent noodles made from mung beans. Noodles come in different shapes and sizes and are truly versatile; they can be served stir-fried (as in the classic Classic Pad Thai Rice Noodles, page 78), or swimming in huge bowls of noodle soup. (Noodle soups are featured in the Soups and Salads chapter.)

Rice—the symbol of fertility and the embodiment of the life force—is so much more than the grain which nourishes millions throughout Southeast Asia. The Rice Goddess, who hovers over paddy fields and dry hillside rice plantations, is honored in countless festivals related to the rice cycle. Rice is cooked with the respect it deserves: steamed to a soft, fragrant and fluffy mound; stir-fried; enriched with coconut milk; turned into a salad; or made into a type of soup.

# Burmese Noodles in Coconut Broth

When I first tried these excellent noodles—basically, a very liquid chicken curry served in a bowl with noodles—in northern Thailand, I didn't realize that the recipe actually originated in Burma. I must admit I prefer the seasonings of this aromatic Thai version, which makes an excellent lunch or light meal, or could be served with a side salad and followed by dessert for a dinner.

**Serves 4**
**Preparation time:** 25 mins
**Cooking time:** 30 mins

1/4 cup (60 ml) oil
2 cups (500 ml) chicken stock
1 stalk lemongrass, tender inner part of bottom third only, bruised, cut into short lengths
13 oz (375 g) boneless chicken breast or thigh fillets, cut into 1/4-in (0.5-cm) strips about 2 in (5 cm) in length
2 cups (500 ml) coconut milk
Salt, to taste
7 oz (200 g) dried round or flat egg noodles
1 red finger-length chili, deseeded and sliced
1 green onion (scallion), finely sliced
2 tablespoons Crisp-fried Shallots (page 22)
1 large lime, quartered lengthwise

**Curry Paste**
2 teaspoons coriander seeds, lightly toasted
1 teaspoon cumin seeds, lightly toasted
1 teaspoon finely minced coriander root
2 tablespoons minced galangal
2 cloves garlic, minced
2 teaspoons dried shrimp paste
2 1/2 tablespoons curry powder
1/2 teaspoon ground red pepper (cayenne)
3 tablespoons water

**1** Make the Curry Paste by processing the coriander and cumin seeds to a powder in a spice grinder. Add the coriander root, galangal, garlic and dried shrimp paste and process until fine, adding a little of the water if needed to keep the blades turning. Transfer to a small bowl and mix in the curry powder, ground red pepper and water.

**2** Heat the oil in a medium saucepan and stir-fry the Curry Paste over low-medium heat until fragrant and cooked, 4 to 5 minutes. Add the chicken stock and lemongrass and bring to a boil. Simmer, uncovered, for 5 minutes, then add the chicken and cook until tender, 10 to 15 minutes. Add the coconut milk and heat, stirring frequently, until it almost comes to a boil. Season with the salt and keep warm.

**3** Bring a saucepan of water to a boil, then add the noodles and boil until cooked, 3 to 4 minutes depending on the thickness of the noodles. Rinse, drain and divide between four large bowls. Ladle the chicken curry broth over the top of each portion of noodles. Garnish each bowl of noodles with the sliced chili, green onion and Crisp-fried Shallots. Serve the lime wedges on a separate plate for adding the lime juice to taste.

Burmese Noodles in Coconut Broth

# Nonya Rice Noodles with Toasted Coconut

One of my friends in Singapore, whose grandmother was a Nonya, gave me her basic recipe for this salad, which is a fabulous mixture of rice vermicelli, toasted coconut, bean sprouts, shallots, herbs, lime juice, fish sauce and the favorite local condiment, Malaysian Chili and Dried Shrimp Paste Dip (Sambal Belacan). Julia also adds dried shrimp and salted fish and sometimes throws in chopped bird's-eye chilies for those who like it hot. As she says, "It's up to you, lah!"

**Serves 4–6**
**Preparation time:** 20 mins
**Cooking time:** 8 mins

7 oz (200 g) dried rice vermicelli
1 cup (100 g) freshly grated coconut, or
    1 cup (80 g) desiccated coconut
¹/₃ cup (40 g) dried shrimp, lightly
    toasted until fragrant, processed to a
    powder
¹/₂ cup (40 g) thinly sliced salted fish,
    fried until crisp and golden, coarsely
    crumbled
2 cups (100 g) bean sprouts, straggly
    tails discarded
8 shallots, thinly sliced
2 stalks lemongrass, tender inner part of
    bottom third only, thinly sliced
4–5 kaffir lime leaves, finely shredded
2 green onions (scallions), finely minced
¹/₄ cup (12 g) minced fresh coriander
    leaves (cilantro)
1 ginger bud, thinly sliced (optional)
¹/₄ cup (60 ml) lime juice
2–3 tablespoons Malaysian Chili and
    Dried Shrimp Paste Dip (page 28)
2 tablespoons fish sauce
1¹/₂ tablespoons sugar
1 teaspoon sesame oil
Salt, to taste
Freshly ground black pepper, to taste

1 Do not pre-soak the dried rice vermicelli but put it dry into a saucepan of boiling water and simmer until it is just cooked but still firm, about 3 to 4 minutes, separating the noodles as they start to soften. Drain, rinse under cold running water, then drain thoroughly and set aside.
2 Put the coconut in a dry wok and cook over very low heat, stirring constantly, until it turns golden brown. Transfer to a plate and leave to cool.
3 To finalize the salad, cut the rice vermicelli into short lengths, then put in a large bowl and add the coconut, dried shrimp, salted fish, bean sprouts, shallots, lemongrass, kaffir lime leaves, green onions, coriander and ginger bud, if using. Toss gently.
4 Combine the lime juice, Malaysian Chili and Dried Shrimp Paste Dip, fish sauce, sugar and sesame oil in a small bowl, stirring to mix well, then pour over the rice vermicelli, tossing gently to mix. Taste and add salt and pepper if you like and a little more lime juice or sugar depending on the degree of acidity you enjoy. Toss again and serve immediately.

# Classic Pad Thai Rice Noodles

This Thai classic combines rice-stick noodles with pork or chicken, shrimp and eggs, plus a little tofu if you like. The fried noodles have a faint sweet-sour tang, thanks to the lime juice and sugar, as well as a lovely contrast in textures, with soft noodles snuggling up to crunchy bean sprouts and peanuts. You can vary the protein, using either pork or chicken, or adding tofu. Served with Simple Thai Fish Sauce and Chili Dip, these noodles make a great lunch.

**Serves 4**
**Preparation time:** 20 mins
**Cooking time:** 7 mins

1/4 cup (60 ml) oil
6 cloves garlic, minced
3–4 shallots, minced
1 teaspoon crushed dried chili flakes
7 oz (200 g) lean pork or chicken, shredded
1/2 lb (250 g) small or medium shrimp, peeled and deveined
4 tablespoons fish sauce
2 eggs
13 oz (375 g) dried rice-stick noodles, soaked in warm water to soften, drained
1 tablespoon lime juice
1 tablespoon sugar
1 1/4 cups (60 g) bean sprouts, straggly tails removed

**Garnish**
4 tablespoons coarsely crushed unsalted roasted peanuts
1 tablespoon dried shrimp, toasted over low heat 4–5 minutes, processed to a powder
1 green onion (scallion), finely sliced
2 tablespoons coarsely chopped fresh coriander leaves (cilantro)
1 lime, quartered
1 1/4 cups (60 g) bean sprouts, straggly tails removed

**Accompaniments**
**Crushed dried chili flakes**
**Simple Thai Fish Sauce and Chili Dip (page 27)**

> **NOTE:** You could reduce the amount of pork or chicken to 4 oz (125 g) and add 1 cake pressed tofu. Cut the tofu in 1/2-in (1- cm) dice and add as soon as the shrimp have started to turn pink.

**1** Heat the oil in a wok, add the garlic, shallots and chili flakes, and stir-fry for a few seconds. Add the pork or chicken and stir-fry over high heat for 2 minutes. Add the shrimp and stir-fry until they are just cooked, 2 to 3 minutes. Splash over the fish sauce, stir, then add the eggs, stirring briefly to break up the yolks. Leave for a few seconds until the egg starts to set, then mix it with the pork and shrimp.

**2** Push the cooked ingredients up the sides of the wok and put in the drained noodles in the center. Leave them for a few seconds, then toss to mix well. Add the lime juice and sugar and give a quick stir. Put in the bean sprouts and stir-fry for just 30 seconds, mixing well.

**3** Transfer immediately to a large serving dish or four individual dishes. Garnished with crushed peanuts, dried shrimp powder, green onion and coriander leaves. Arrange the bean sprouts and lime wedges around the edge of the noodles and serve together with chili flakes and Simple Thai Fish Sauce and Chili Dip.

# 'Birthday Noodles' with Pork and Shrimp

Want to take out a little life insurance next time you celebrate your birthday? Then try this recipe, a mixture of typical Chinese ingredients with Malay garnishes. The Chinese custom of serving noodles (which symbolize a long life) at birthday dinners is continued by the Nonyas of both Malaysia and Singapore. But you don't have to wait for your birthday to try this tasty noodle dish. Whatever you do, don't cut the noodles before eating them—this is considered very bad luck as it implies cutting your life short.

**Serves 4–6**
**Preparation time:** 25 mins
**Cooking time:** 12 mins

7 oz (200 g) belly pork, in one piece
2–3 cups (500–750 ml) water
2 tablespoons oil
3 shallots, finely sliced
1 clove garlic, crushed and finely minced
2 tablespoons salted soybeans
1/2 lb (250 g) small fresh shrimp, peeled and deveined
1/2 teaspoon salt
1/2 teaspoon sugar
3 1/2 oz (100 g) Chinese flowering cabbage, cut into 2-in (5-cm) lengths
1 1/4 cups (60 g) bean sprouts, straggly tails removed
13 oz (375 g) fresh wheat noodles, rinsed and drained (see Note)
Malaysian Chili and Dried Shrimp Paste Dip (page 28)

**Garnish**
1 egg, cooked to make a thin omelet, cut into thin strips
5-in (12.5-cm) piece cucumber, deseeded, flesh cut into matchstick shreds
1 red finger-length chili, sliced
1 tablespoon Crisp-fried Shallots (page 22)
Sprigs of fresh coriander leaves (cilantro)
4 lime wedges

> **NOTE:** If you prefer, you could use 6 oz (175 g) dried wheat or egg noodles, preferably thin and round; cook them in boiling water just until tender; rinse and drain thoroughly.

1 Put the pork and enough water to cover it in a small saucepan. Bring to a boil, cover the pan, lower the heat and simmer until the meat is tender. Cool and cut the pork into thin slices, reserving the stock. Measure the stock and add water if needed to make up 1 cup (250 ml). Set aside.
2 Heat the oil in a wok and add the shallots and garlic. Stir-fry until transparent, then add the salted soybeans and stir-fry for 1 minute. Add the shrimp and stir-fry just until they change color, then sprinkle with the salt and sugar. Add the vegetable and stir-fry until it starts to soften, about 1 minute. Add the bean sprouts and stir-fry for a few seconds, then add the noodles and pork.
3 Stir-fry to mix well. Add the reserved stock and cook over high heat, stirring frequently, until the stock has been absorbed and the noodles are cooked, about 3 minutes. Transfer the noodles to a large serving dish and decorate with the Garnish ingredients. Sprinkle with lime juice to taste and serve with Malaysian Chili and Dried Shrimp Paste Dip.

# Malay Rice Noodles in Sweet Tamarind Gravy

*Mee siam*

The hot, sour, spicy flavor of many Malay dishes makes them remarkably similar to some Thai food, a good example being this fragrant noodle soup. Although this Malay version of Thai noodles (hence the name "Siam") takes a while to prepare, the spice paste, gravy and garnishes can be done well ahead of serving. Then it's just a matter of a short time in the kitchen when you're ready to eat.

**Serves 4**
**Preparation time:** 30 mins
**Cooking time:** 20 mins

2 cups (100 g) bean sprouts, straggly tails removed
1/2 cup (20 g) garlic chives, cut into short lengths
10 oz (300 g) cooked shrimp, peeled, heads removed, halved lengthwise
10 oz (300 g) dried rice vermicelli, soaked in hot water to soften, drained, cut into 2 1/2-in (6-cm) lengths
1 cake pressed tofu, deep-fried until golden, halved crosswise and thinly sliced
2 hard-boiled eggs, peeled and quartered
2 limes, quartered, or 4 small round green limes (*limau kesturi*), top portion sliced off

**Spice Paste**
8–10 dried red finger-length chilies, soaked to soften, some seeds discarded if preferred, to reduce the heat
8 shallots, minced
6 candlenuts, minced
1/4 cup (60 ml) oil
4 tablespoons salted soybeans, lightly crushed with the back of a spoon
3–4 teaspoons sugar

**Gravy**
4 cups (1 liter) water
3 tablespoons dried shrimp, soaked in water to soften, blended to a powder
2 heaped tablespoons tamarind pulp, soaked in 1/2 cup (125 ml) warm water, mashed and strained to obtain the juice
Sugar, to taste

1 Prepare the Spice Paste by grinding the chilies, shallots and candlenuts in a spice grinder, adding a little oil if needed to keep the blades turning. Heat the oil in a wok for 30 seconds, then add the Spice Paste and stir-fry over low-medium heat, stirring frequently, for 4 minutes. Add the salted soybeans and stir-fry for 30 seconds, then sprinkle in the sugar and cook for another 30 seconds.

2 Prepare the Gravy by putting half the Spice Paste in a large saucepan, reserving the other half in the wok for frying the noodles. Add the water and dried shrimp powder to the saucepan, bring to a boil, then add the tamarind juice. Taste and add a little sugar if desired. Simmer for 3 minutes. Remove from the heat but keep the gravy in the saucepan.

3 Heat the reserved Spice Paste in the wok, then add the bean sprouts and stir-fry over high heat for 30 seconds. Add half the chives and half the shrimp and stir-fry for 30 seconds. Add the rice vermicelli, a little at a time, stirring vigorously to mix it thoroughly with the other ingredients. Stir-fry for 2 minutes, then transfer to a large serving dish.

4 Arrange the remaining chives and shrimp decoratively on top of the noodles and garnish with the pressed tofu, eggs and lime. Reheat the gravy and transfer to a deep bowl or jug. Serve hot. (Alternatively, you can divide the noodles, chives, shrimp, tofu and eggs between four large noodle bowls, topping each up with Gravy and adding two pieces of lime to each portion.)

# Singapore Hokkien Noodles   *Hokkien mee*

The majority of Singapore's Chinese population is Hokkien in origin, their ancestors coming from Fujian province in southern China. You won't be surprised to learn, then, that the nation's favorite noodle dish is this Hokkien mixture of fresh yellow noodles and dried rice vermicelli in a rich pork and seafood stock. It's always served with something you won't find in China: a side-dish of the very local Malaysian Chili and Dried Shrimp Paste Dip or Sambal Belacan.

**Serves 4**
**Preparation time:** 25 mins
**Cooking time:** 15 mins

1 lb (500 g) fresh thick yellow noodles
5¹/2 oz (150 g) dried rice vermicelli, soaked in hot water to soften, cut into 3-in (7.5-cm) lengths
¹/2 lb (250 g) belly pork, covered with water and boiled until cooked, stock reserved, meat thinly sliced
3 tablespoons oil
10 oz (300 g) small fresh shrimp, peeled and deveined, heads and shells reserved
5 cups (250 g) bean sprouts, washed and drained, straggly tails discarded
8–10 cloves garlic, crushed
2 eggs, lightly beaten
1 teaspoon salt
¹/4 teaspoon white pepper
¹/4 cup (10 g) minced garlic chives or green onions (scallions)
Malaysian Chili and Dried Shrimp Paste Dip (page 28)
4 small round green limes (*limau kesturi*), top portion sliced off, or 1 regular lime, quartered

> **NOTE:** Some cooks like to add fresh squid to the noodles; substitute 5¹/2 oz (150 g) of the shrimp with squid; slice the squid and simmer together with the shrimp.

1 Put the fresh yellow noodles in a bowl and pour in enough boiling water to cover the noodles. Stand for 1 minute, then drain in a colander and put on a plate with the soaked and drained rice vermicelli.

2 Measure the reserved pork stock and add more water, if necessary, to make up 1 cup (250 ml). Set aside.

3 Heat 1 tablespoon of the oil in a saucepan and stir-fry the shrimp heads and shells until they turn pink. Add the reserved pork stock, bring to a boil, cover and simmer for 5 minutes. Strain, pressing down on the shrimp shells to extract as much liquid as possible. Discard the solids. Return the stock to the pan, add the shrimp and simmer until just cooked, about 3 minutes. Strain and reserve the stock and shrimp separately. (The recipe can be prepared in advance to this stage and all ingredients refrigerated for several hours.)

4 Heat the remaining oil in a wok and stir-fry the garlic until it turns golden brown and flavors the oil. Discard the garlic and increase the heat. When the oil is very hot, pour in the beaten eggs and stir for 1 minute. Add the noodles, bean sprouts and ¹/2 cup (125 ml) of the stock. Stir-fry over high heat for 1 minute, then add the pork, shrimp, salt and pepper. Stir-fry for 2 to 3 minutes until everything is heated through and well mixed, adding a little more stock if the noodles threaten to stick.

5 Add the Chinese chives, stir for a few seconds, then transfer to a large serving dish. Serve with Malaysian Chili and Dried Shrimp Paste Dip, and limes, or, if preferred, small bowls of dark soy sauce with sliced red chili.

Singapore Hokkien Noodles

# Vegetarian Noodles with Chinese Mushrooms

Although most Southeast Asian noodle dishes have a little meat, poultry, or seafood in them, here's an easy vegetarian version from Cambodia with tofu, broccoli, mushrooms, carrot and bean sprouts. There's just enough seasoning to give a delightful flavor to the combination and you can adjust the amount of chili to suit your taste. This would be good for a quick and healthy lunch, especially if followed by fresh fruit.

**Serves 4**
**Preparation time:** 10 mins
**Cooking time:** 3 mins

13 oz (375 g) dried egg noodles
1/2 cup (125 ml) oil
2 cakes pressed tofu
1 tablespoon minced garlic
1–2 red finger-length chilies, finely minced
4 dried black Chinese mushrooms, soaked to soften, stems discarded, caps shredded
5 1/2 oz (150 g) broccoli, broken into very small florets
1 medium carrot (about 3 1/2 oz/100 g), cut into matchstick pieces
4 tablespoons soy sauce
4 tablespoons dark soy sauce
1 1/2 teaspoons sugar
1 1/4 cups (60 g) bean sprouts
1/2 teaspoon salt
Sprigs of fresh coriander leaves (cilantro), to garnish or 1 green onion (scallion), thinly sliced

1 Bring a large pot of water to a boil and add the dried noodles. Boil rapidly, stirring from time to time to separate the noodles, until they are just soft. Transfer the noodles to a colander and rinse well under cold running water. Drain and set aside.
2 Heat the oil in a wok for 30 seconds and when very hot, add the tofu and fry until golden brown all over, about 2 minutes on each side. Remove and drain on paper towels. When cool enough to handle, cut each tofu in half across, then slice thinly.
3 Remove all but 3 tablespoons of oil from the wok. Heat, then add the garlic and stir-fry for 5 seconds. Add the chili and mushrooms and stir-fry for 30 seconds, then put in the broccoli and carrot and stir-fry for 1 minute. Add the drained noodles and stir-fry, mixing well, for 1 minute.
4 Sprinkle both lots of soy sauce and sugar over the noodles, then add the bean sprouts, tofu slices and salt. Stir-fry for 1 minute, mixing thoroughly to incorporate the noodles and vegetables. Serve immediately garnished with the coriander leaves.

# Thai River Noodles with Beef and Broccoli

## Guey teow pad sei ew

Fresh wide rice flour noodles are the basis of this Thai dish, particularly popular in Bangkok (you could use dried noodles if the fresh ones aren't available). The silky noodles are mixed with beef and broccoli, both of which have strong flavors that seem to have been made for each other. Although this is similar to many Chinese stir-fried noodle dishes, the addition of fish sauce, chili and crushed peanuts gives this recipe a true Thai accent.

**Serves 4**
**Preparation time:** 25 mins + 10 mins marinating
**Cooking time:** 8 mins

10 oz (300 g) boneless sirloin or rump steak, thinly sliced across the grain, cut into bite-sized pieces
3 tablespoons oil
3 cloves garlic, minced
10 oz (300 g) broccoli, cut into small florets
1/4 cup (60 ml) water
2 tablespoons fish sauce
1 tablespoon dark soy sauce
1 3/4 lbs (800 g) fresh wide rice flour noodles, blanched briefly in boiling water and drained (see Note)
3 tablespoons coarsely crushed dry-roasted peanuts
2 tablespoons dried chili flakes

**Marinade**
1 tablespoon cornstarch
1 egg, lightly beaten
1 clove garlic, minced
1 tablespoon Chinese rice wine (preferably Shaoxing)
1 tablespoon fish sauce
1 tablespoon oyster sauce
1 tablespoon sugar
1 teaspoon sesame oil
1/2 teaspoon white pepper

**1** Put the beef in a bowl and marinate by sprinkle it with the cornstarch and toss to coat, then add the remaining Marinade ingredients, mixing well. Marinate for 10 minutes.
**2** Heat the oil in a wok and stir-fry the garlic for 5 seconds. Add the beef and its Marinade and stir-fry over very high heat until the meat starts to change color, about 1 minute. Add the broccoli and stir-fry for 1 minute, then put in the water and continue stir-frying until the broccoli is just cooked, about 2 minutes. (The broccoli must be cut into very small pieces so it will cook quickly.)
**3** Splash in the fish sauce and soy sauce, then add the noodles, stir-frying for about 1 minute to mix well and heat through. Transfer to a serving dish and sprinkle with peanuts. Serve hot with dried crushed chili flakes served separately for adding to taste.

**NOTE:** If fresh noodles are not available, use 13 oz (375 g) dried wide rice flour noodles or regular rice-stick noodles, soaked in hot water to soften, then simmered until cooked.

# Singapore Fried Kway Teow

*Char kway teow*

There used to be a Chinese cook in a coffee shop opposite Singapore's Newton Circus where the version of fried rice flour noodles was so fantastic that you could queue for as long as 30 minutes if you went during the lunch-hour rush. The cook and the coffee shop have long gone, but the basic way of cooking the noodles still remains. The addition of crisp-fried pork fat is a real no-no in these health-conscious days, but it gives a unique and authentic flavor to the noodles. (You could, however, omit this if you prefer.)

**Serves 4**
**Preparation time:** 20 mins
**Cooking time:** 18 mins

3 1/2 oz (100 g) hard pork fat (cut from the back), cut into 1/2-in (1-cm) dice (see Note)
2 tablespoons water
4 cloves garlic, minced
2 red finger-length chilies, crushed to a paste, or 2 teaspoons crushed chili
7 oz (200 g) lean pork, shredded
13 oz (375 g) fresh shrimp, peeled and deveined
7 oz (200 g) squid, cleaned, peeled and sliced
1 tablespoon soy sauce
1 tablespoon dark soy sauce
2 teaspoons oyster sauce
1/2 teaspoon salt
Liberal sprinkling of white pepper
5 cups (250 g) bean sprouts, straggly tails removed
2 lbs (1 kg) fresh wide rice flour noodles, scalded in boiling water, rinsed and drained
1 red finger-length chili, sliced
Sprigs of fresh coriander leaves (cilantro)

**1** Put the pork fat and water in a wok and cook over medium heat, stirring from time to time, until the water has dried up and the oil run out. Keep cooking until the pieces of fat turned crisp and golden brown, then remove and drain on paper towels. Leave 3 tablespoons of the pork oil in the wok and discard the remainder.
**2** Heat the pork oil and stir-fry the garlic and chili over low-medium heat for about 30 seconds. Increase the heat, add the pork and stir-fry for 2 minutes. Add the shrimp and squid and stir-fry for 2 minutes. Season with both lots of soy sauce, oyster sauce, salt and pepper.
**3** Add the bean sprouts and stir-fry for 2 minutes, then put in the noodles and stir-fry until well mixed and heated through. Stir in the crisp pork fat and transfer to a serving dish. Garnish with sliced chili and sprigs of coriander leaves.

> **NOTE:** If you prefer, the pork crisps can be omitted and 3 tablespoons oil used instead of the pork oil for frying.

# Thai Rice Salad with Toasted Coconut  *Khao yam pak thai*

Want something refreshingly light, healthy, and herbal for lunch or a warm evening? This lovely Thai rice salad has a refreshing mixture of tastes and textures. Start off with cooked rice, then add toasted coconut, bean sprouts, cucumber, and long beans for a lovely crunch. Shredded omelet, dried shrimp, and sweet-sour pomelo join the party, with plenty of sour, fragrant notes in the lime juice and herbs. The salad looks really pretty if you arrange each portion of rice and accompaniments separately on individual serving plates.

**Servess 4**
**Preparation time:** 30 mins
**Cooking time:** 15 mins

1 teaspoon oil
4 cups (520 g) room-temperature cooked rice
1 cup (100 g) freshly grated or desiccated coconut, toasted in wok until golden brown, cooled
1 cup (125 g) shredded pomelo or grapefruit segments (juice drained off if using grapefruit)
1¼ cups (60 g) bean sprouts, straggly tails removed
2 eggs, lightly beaten and cooked to make 2 thin omelets, shredded
⅓ cup (40 g) dried shrimp, soaked in water to soften, drained and minced
1 cup (100 g) thinly sliced young long beans or green beans
1 cup (100 g) finely diced cucumber
4 stalks lemongrass, tender inner part of bottom third only, very thinly sliced
1 tablespoon minced red or green bird's-eye chilies
½ cup (20 g) loosely packed coriander leaves (cilantro)
1 large lime, quartered
2 kaffir lime leaves, cut in hair-like shreds

**Sauce**
2 tablespoons preserved fish or 3 tablespoons chopped canned anchovies
2 tablespoons shaved palm sugar
2 tablespoons minced galangal
4 shallots, finely minced
1 stalk lemongrass, tender inner part of bottom third only, thinly sliced
2 kaffir lime leaves, torn
2 teaspoons dark soy sauce
1 cup (250 ml) water

**1** To prepare the Sauce, put all the ingredients in a small saucepan, and bring to a boil, stirring. Lower the heat and simmer very gently, with the pan uncovered, until the liquid is reduced by half, 10 to 15 minutes. Pour through a sieve into a small bowl, pressing with the back of a spoon to extract as much liquid as possible. Leave the liquid to cool, discarding the solids.

**2** You can either arrange the rice in the center of a large serving plate, putting all the other ingredients around it, or you can prepare individual servings. To do the latter, lightly grease a small bowl with oil. Add 1 cup rice, pressing down to make the grains adhere, then invert the bowl over a plate. Repeat, putting each portion of rice on a separate plate. Put small piles of coconut, pomelo or grapefruit, bean sprouts, omelet, dried shrimp, green beans, cucumber, lemongrass, bird's-eye chilies and coriander leaves around each rice mound. Add 1 lime quarter to each plate, and top the rice with the kaffir lime shreds.

**3** Divide the Sauce between four small sauce dishes and serve with the salad for everyone to drizzle over according to taste. The garnish ingredients are normally mixed through the rice just before eating.

# Classic Indonesian Fried Rice *Nasi goreng*

Fried rice is a common breakfast throughout Indonesia. It is often very simple—cooked rice tossed with a seasoning paste of chili and a dash of sweet soy sauce—or can be more substantial, like this recipe, which adds beef instead of the pork often used in non-Muslim parts of Southeast Asia. You could also add some shrimp and top each serving with a fried egg (which the Indonesians call a "bull's-eye egg"). This is a quickly made lunch or supper dish.

**Serves 4**
**Preparation time:** 10 mins
**Cooking time:** 10 mins

⅓ cup (85 ml) oil
7 oz (200 g) sirloin or rump steak, thinly sliced across the grain, shredded
7 oz (200 g) small fresh shrimp, peeled and deveined, or add another 7 oz (200 g) beef
6 cups (800 g) cold cooked rice, stirred with a fork to separate the grains
2 tablespoons sweet soy sauce
1 teaspoon salt
4 eggs
2 tablespoons Crisp-fried Shallots (page 22)
1 green onion (scallion), minced
1 large ripe tomato, sliced

**Seasoning Paste**
6 shallots, minced
2 cloves garlic, minced
2–3 red finger-length chilies, sliced
½ teaspoon dried shrimp paste, toasted (page 22)

**1** Prepare the Seasoning Paste by processing all the ingredients together to a coarse paste.
**2** Heat ¼ cup (60 ml) of the oil in a wok and add the Seasoning Paste. Stir-fry over medium heat until softened and fragrant, about 4 minutes. Increase the heat, add the beef and shrimp, if using, and stir-fry until cooked, about 3 minutes. Add the rice and stir-fry over high heat for 1 minute. Sprinkle with the sweet soy sauce and salt and stir-fry for another minute.
**3** Transfer the rice to a large bowl and keep warm. Use the remaining oil to fry the eggs, one at a time, in the wok, or cook them all at one time in a skillet. Transfer the rice to four plates. Top each serving with a fried egg and garnish with the Crisp-fried Shallots and green onion. Add a few tomato slices and serve with a chili sambal.

**NOTE:** As with all fried rice dishes, it is preferable to use rice that was cooked the previous day, so that it has completely dried out.

# Cambodian Rice Noodle Soup   *K'tieu*

If you're prepared to brave the exhaust fumes from the endless flow of motorcycles weaving along Phnom Penh's busy streets, you can grab a bowl of this noodle soup at just about any food stall. K'tieu is to the Cambodians what Beef Noodle Soup is to the Vietnamese, the national dish, slurped with pleasure at any time of day. Both pork fillet and ground pork are simmered in rich chicken or pork stock, which is poured over noodles and bean sprouts. Uniquely Cambodian touches come in the form of shredded salted cabbage and dried shrimp powder, with chilies, fresh herbs and crisp-fried garlic and shallots all adding their magic.

**Cambodian Rice Noodle Soup**

**Serves 4**
**Preparation time:** 10 mins
**Cooking time:** 30 mins

10 oz (300 g) pork fillet or loin, in one piece
6 cups (1.5 liters) chicken or pork stock
7 oz (200 g) ground lean pork
1–2 teaspoons sugar
1/2 teaspoon freshly ground black pepper
2 oz (60 g) finely shredded salted cabbage
1/2 lb (250 g) dried rice-stick noodles, soaked in hot water to soften, drained
2 cups (100 g) bean sprouts, straggly tails removed
12 cooked medium shrimp, peeled and deveined
2 tablespoons Crisp-fried Shallots (page 22)
1–2 tablespoons Crisp-fried Garlic (page 22)
1 green onion (scallion), finely minced
3 tablespoons minced fresh coriander leaves (cilantro) or mint leaves
3 tablespoons dried shrimp, soaked in water to soften, processed to a powder
2–3 green or red bird's-eye chilies, minced

**1** Put the pork fillet or loin into a saucepan with the stock. Bring to a boil, cover, lower the heat and simmer until tender, about 15 minutes for fillet, 30 to 40 minutes for loin. Remove the pork, slice thinly and set aside, leaving the stock in the pan.
**2** Add the ground pork to the stock and simmer until cooked, 4 to 5 minutes. Return the sliced pork to the stock and add the sugar, pepper and salted cabbage. Bring to a boil, cover and remove from the heat.
**3** Bring a large saucepan of water to a boil. Add the noodles and cook until done, 1 to 2 minutes. Drain, rinse under running water, drain again, then divide between four large bowls.
**4** Divide the bean sprouts evenly into each bowl. Top each serving with 3 of the cooked shrimp. Add the meat and stock, and garnish each serving with the shallots, garlic, green onion, coriander leaves, dried shrimp powder and chili. Serve immediately.

# Vietnamese Mixed Coconut Rice

## Com hua mimosa

The Vietnamese name this beautifully presented rice dish after the yellow mimosa flower, which the garnish of egg yolk is supposed to resemble. The rice is cooked in coconut milk for a rich creamy taste, then mixed with seasoned diced chicken, pork, dried Chinese sausage, peas and carrots. This recipe makes enough for a light meal with a simple salad, or you could serve it with a soup, salad, or another dish for a more substantial dinner.

**Serves 4–6**
**Preparation time:** 40 mins
**Cooking time:** 1 hour

2 1/4 cups (560 ml) coconut milk
1/2 teaspoon salt
2 cups (400 g) uncooked rice, washed and drained
4 oz (125 g) chicken breast fillet, diced
4 oz (125 g) pork fillet or loin, diced
2 teaspoons fish sauce
1/4 teaspoon sugar
Sprinkling of freshly ground black pepper
2 dried Chinese sausages (*lap cheong*)
1 tablespoon oil
1 clove garlic, crushed and finely minced
2 green onions (scallions), minced
1/2 cup (75 g) green peas, boiled 30 seconds, drained
1 small carrot, diced, simmered in boiling water for 2 minutes and drained
2 hard-boiled eggs, separated, yolks sieved and whites finely minced
Sprigs of fresh coriander leaves (cilantro), to garnish

**1** Put the coconut milk and salt in a saucepan with a heavy base. Bring to a boil over low-medium heat, stirring constantly. Add the rice, stir, then partially cover the pan. Cook over low heat until the coconut milk is completely absorbed, about 5 minutes.
**2** Cover the pan firmly and remove from the heat. Stand for 5 minutes. Wipe the inside of the lid with a towel and cover again. Put over the lowest possible heat and cook for 20 to 30 minutes until tender. Remove from the heat, fluff up the rice with a fork, cover and let it stand while preparing the rest of the ingredients.
**3** Put the chicken and pork in a bowl and sprinkle with the fish sauce, sugar and pepper. Toss, then set aside. Put the Chinese sausages in boiling water in a saucepan and simmer gently until softened, about 3 to 4 minutes. Remove and cut into 1/2-in (1-cm) slices.
**4** Heat the oil in a wok, then stir-fry the garlic and green onions for 10 seconds. Add the chicken and pork and stir-fry over medium heat for 5 minutes. Add the peas, carrots and Chinese sausage and stir-fry until cooked, 3 to 4 minutes.
**5** Add the rice, stirring to mix well. Transfer to a well-oiled ring mold, pressing down lightly. Turn out onto a serving dish. Place the egg white in the center, then sprinkle the top of the egg white with half of the yolk. Scatter the remaining yolk over the rice and garnish with coriander leaves.

**Vietnamese Mixed Coconut Rice**

# Malaysian Coconut Rice

## *Nasi lemak*

Nasi lemak is the Malay name for rice cooked in coconut milk, and also for the popular breakfast combination of coconut rice, cucumber, egg, crunchy deep-fried anchovies and peanuts, plus a chili sambal. You could serve the coconut rice as part of a main meal (for a balance of flavors, make sure that the other dishes do not contain coconut milk), or go the whole way and serve the rice with the traditional accompaniments for breakfast or lunch.

**Serves 4**
**Preparation time:** 20 mins
**Cooking time:** 40 mins

2¹/₂ cups (625 ml) coconut milk
1 teaspoon salt
2 pandanus leaves, tied into a knot, or 1 *salam* leaf
2 cups (400 g) uncooked rice, washed and drained

**Crisp-fried Anchovies**
¹/₃ cup (85 ml) oil
2 cups (50 g) cleaned dried anchovies
¹/₂ cup (80 g) raw peanuts
6 shallots, processed until coarsely ground
2 teaspoons sugar
¹/₂–1 teaspoon ground red pepper (cayenne)
¹/₄ teaspoon ground turmeric
1–2 small round green limes (*limau kesturi*), halved, or wedges of lime or lemon, optional

**Additional Accompaniments**
2 eggs, lightly beaten, cooked to make a thin omelet, shredded, or 4 fried eggs
¹/₂ small cucumber, skin raked with a fork, sliced
Malaysian Chili and Dried Shrimp Paste Dip (page 28)

1 Bring the coconut milk, salt, pandanus or *salam* leaves to a boil in a saucepan with a heavy base, stirring constantly. Pour in the rice, stir, then partially cover the pan. Cook over low heat until the coconut milk is completely absorbed, about 5 minutes. Cover the pan firmly and remove from the heat. Stand for 5 minutes. Wipe the inside of the lid with a towel and cover again. Put over the lowest possible heat and cook for 15 minutes.
2 Remove from the heat, fluff up the rice with a fork, cover and let it stand until required, up to 20 minutes. Discard the pandanus leaves before serving.
3 To prepare the Crisp-fried Anchovies, heat all but 2 tablespoons of the oil in a wok. Add the anchovies and stir-fry over moderate heat until crisp and golden brown.

Remove from the wok and drain on paper towels. Discard the oil and wipe the wok clean. Reheat the wok, add the peanuts and stir-fry over low-medium heat until the peanuts are cooked, about 8 minutes. Remove from the wok.
4 Heat the remaining oil in the wok and stir-fry the shallots over low heat for 2 minutes. Add the sugar, ground red pepper and turmeric, and fry for another minute or two, until fragrant. Return the anchovies and peanuts to the wok and stir-fry for about 1 minute to mix thoroughly. Allow to cool before serving.
5 Serve the rice as an accompaniment to other dishes, or if serving Additional Accompaniments, put one-quarter of the rice on each of the four plates. Add some of the omelet, Crisp-fried Anchovies, cucumber, and Malaysian Chili and Dried Shrimp Paste Dip to each portion and serve hot.

# Thai Fried Rice with Shrimp and Pork

*Khao phad*

Thai fried rice dishes are usually quite mild, but are always pepped up by the accompanying Simple Thai Fish Sauce and Chili Dip or lots of dried crushed chili. There is no hard and fast recipe—cooks use whatever is on hand, taking their pick from pork, chicken, shrimp, crabmeat or tofu. This recipe is a basic guideline and makes enough to serve four for lunch or a light supper. It could also be served instead of steamed rice as part of a main meal for six to eight persons.

**Serves 4**
**Preparation time:** 10 mins
**Cooking time:** 7 mins

4 tablespoons oil
1 onion, halved lengthwise, thinly sliced
6–8 cloves garlic, crushed and finely minced
1/2 lb (250 g) lean pork or chicken, cut into thin strips
10–13 oz (300–375 g) fresh shrimp, peeled and deveined, halved lengthwise if large
2 eggs, lightly beaten
3 tablespoons fish sauce
6 cups (800 g) cold cooked rice
1 tablespoon lime juice
3/4 cup (100 g) cooked crabmeat (optional)
3 tablespoons coarsely chopped coriander leaves (cilantro)
1 green onion (scallion), minced
Freshly ground black pepper, to taste
1 large ripe tomato, halved, then sliced across
12 slices cucumber
Simple Thai Fish Sauce and Chili Dip (page 27)

**1** Heat the oil in a wok and stir-fry the onion and garlic over moderate heat until softened, 1 to 2 minutes. Add the pork or chicken. Stir-fry until it changes color, then add the shrimp and stir-fry over high heat until cooked, about 3 minutes. Slowly pour in the eggs around the upper edges of the wok, stirring as they set.
**2** Add the fish sauce, then the rice and stir-fry for 2 to 3 minutes. Season with the lime juice, add the crabmeat, if using, and cook, stirring, until it is heated through. Sprinkle on the coriander leaves, green onion and black pepper, stir, then immediately transfer the rice to a large serving dish. Arrange the tomato and cucumber slices around the plate and serve hot with the Simple Thai Fish Sauce and Chili Dip.

# Lacy Malay Pancakes

*Roti jala*

In the old days, Malay cooks used to make these lacy pancakes by putting their hand in the batter and then swirling it over the skillet, letting the batter dribble down their fingers. Then sophistication struck and the *roti jala* cup was born, a cup-like funnel with four spouts. You could use a regular kitchen funnel, or a Japanese soy sauce dispenser to get the appropriate lacy look to these pancakes, which are fabulous for mopping up curry gravy.

**Serves 4**
**Preparation time:** 7 mins
**Cooking time:** 40 mins

1¹⁄₂ cups (185 g) plain flour
¹⁄₂ teaspoon salt
2 eggs, lightly beaten
2¹⁄₂ cups (625 ml) coconut milk or fresh milk
Oil, for greasing the pan
*Roti jala* cup or kitchen funnel

**1** Sift the flour into a bowl and stir in the salt and eggs. Add the coconut or fresh milk gradually, stirring to make a smooth batter.
**2** Lightly grease a skillet, preferably nonstick, with a little oil. Hold a *roti jala* cup, a Japanese soy sauce dispenser with a narrow hole, or a regular kitchen funnel with the end partly closed with one finger to let through a thin stream of batter, over the skillet. Use the other hand to pour in about ¹⁄₄ cup (60 ml) of the batter, swirling the cup or funnel rapidly in circles over the pan to make a lacy pattern as the batter goes in.
**3** Allow the pancake to set on top, then turn over and cook for another 30 seconds. Use a spatula to fold the pancake in half, then half again, and transfer to a plate. Continue, greasing the pan after each pancake, until all the batter has been used up. If the batter thickens towards the end, add a little more milk. Serve with any curry.

Chapter 4

# Poultry and Meat

All of these poultry or meat dishes can be ready within 30 minutes and this includes measuring, slicing, chopping, seasoning and cooking. Several of the following recipes are for stir-fried combinations of meat or poultry with vegetables and seasonings; basically, a meal in a wok, to be served with rice. These include Chicken with Green Curry Paste and Basil (page 99), Lemongrass Beef with Peanuts (page 109) and Cambodian Garlic Pork (page 108). One of my favorites, however, just has to be the Vietnamese recipe for Chicken with Mango and Cashews (page 106)—this is a real winner on any occasion.

There's a particularly elegant modern recipe for Roast Duck on a Bed of Crispy Noodles (page 105); even though it's quick and easy to prepare, it could star at any dinner party. Eggs come quickly in the form of the simple but really good Simple Thai Pork Omelet (page 113) and one of our family stand-bys, Vietnamese Scrambled Eggs with Chinese Sausages (page 116).

There's no denying that some Southeast Asian dishes take time, although the recipes which appear in this chapter are not necessarily complex. Some are actually very easily and quickly prepared, but need time to cook slowly to perfection: Burmese Green Mango Pork (page 117), Thai Red Beef Curry (page 115), Sweet Soy Balinese Pork (page 114), Laotian Beef Stew with Asian Herbs (page 118) and a Nonya favorite, Nonya Soy Braised Pork (page 112), all fall into this category.

Others recipes—such as Thai Barbecued Chicken (page 100) and Vietnamese Honey-glazed Chicken (page 96)—don't really require that much preparation time, but need to be left aside for the fragrant marinade to penetrate.

# Vietnamese Honey-glazed Chicken

*Ga quay mat on*

To make this sophisticated Vietnamese recipe, chicken—first marinated with black pepper, sugar, salt and sesame oil—is brushed during cooking with a piquant glaze. This is a good recipe if you're entertaining, not just because it's sure to be enthusiastically received, but because the chicken can be marinated and the Honey Glaze prepared several hours in advance. Then all you need to do is start roasting the chicken about an hour before you want to eat.

**Serves 4**
**Preparation time:** 20 mins + 1 hour marinating
**Cooking time:** 1 hour

2 teaspoons salt
2 teaspoons freshly ground black pepper
2 tablespoons sugar
2 teaspoons sesame oil
1 whole fresh chicken (about 2¹/₂–3 lbs/ 1.25–1.5 kg), fatty deposits and excess skin removed, pat dry with paper towels
2 stalks lemongrass, tender inner part of bottom third only, bruised and cut into 4 pieces

**Honey Glaze**
1 tablespoon oil
2 teaspoons annatto seeds or a little red food coloring (optional)
¹/₄ cup (60 ml) honey
2 tablespoons sweet soy sauce, or 2 tablespoons dark soy sauce mixed with 2 teaspoons soft brown sugar
4 teaspoons lime or lemon juice
1 teaspoon sesame oil

> **NOTE:** It is important to baste the chicken every 15 minutes so that the skin becomes crisp and turns a rich golden brown. Stir the glaze each time before basting to amalgamate the honey.

1  Mix the salt, pepper, sugar and sesame oil in a small bowl. Rub half the mixture inside the chicken and the remainder over the outside. Leave the chicken to marinate at room temperature for 1 hour, or cover and refrigerate for several hours if preferred.

2  Prepare the Honey Glaze by heating the oil in a small saucepan. Add the annatto seeds and cook over medium heat until the oil turns light orange, 2 to 3 minutes. Strain the oil into a large bowl, discarding the seeds. Add the honey, soy sauce, lime juice and sesame oil, mixing well. If using red food coloring, just mix all the Honey Glaze ingredients together, including the oil. (The glaze can now be kept aside for several hours if you are preparing the recipe in advance.)

3  To finalize the dish, put the lemongrass inside the chicken and place it in a baking dish. Use a pastry brush to paint the Honey Glaze over the outside of the chicken, reserving the remaining glaze. Roast the chicken at 425°F (220°C), breast side up, for 15 minutes.

4  Stir the glaze thoroughly, baste the chicken again and return it to the oven. Reduce the heat to 350°F (180°C) and roast for 15 minutes. Brush the chicken with the glaze and oil which has run into the baking dish, then with the reserved glaze. Turn the chicken breast side down and cook for another 15 minutes. Brush again and roast for a final 15 minutes. Cut the chicken with a cleaver into 14 to 16 serving pieces, put on a serving dish and serve hot with the glaze from the baking dish poured over.

**Vietnamese Honey-glazed Chicken**

# Fragrant Cambodian Chicken

## *Larb muan*

This mild yet fragrant Cambodian chicken dish is similar to the spicy beef popular in Laos and northeastern Thailand. Ground chicken is stir-fried with a fragrant spice paste, seasoned with fish sauce and accentuated with aromatic roasted rice powder and herbs. Plenty of black pepper (rather than the crushed dried chili flakes of Thailand) and lime juice give a very Cambodia accent. You can serve this either straight from the wok or at room temperature, together with rice and other dishes.

**Serves 4**
**Preparation time:** 15 mins
**Cooking time:** 10–12 mins

3 cloves garlic, minced
2 tablespoons finely minced galangal
2 red finger-length chilies, minced
2 teaspoons dried shrimp paste
3 tablespoons oil
1¼ lbs (600 g) ground chicken
2 green onions (scallions), thinly sliced
3 tablespoons fish sauce
½ cup (125 ml) water
3 tablespoons Roasted Rice Powder (page 22)
3 tablespoons minced Vietnamese mint (laksa leaf) or regular mint leaves
2 tablespoons minced Asian basil leaves
3 tablespoons lime juice, or more to taste
Salt, to taste
½ teaspoon freshly ground black pepper

**1** Process the garlic, galangal, chilies and dried shrimp paste to a smooth paste in a spice grinder, adding a little of the oil, if necessary, to keep the blades turning.
**2** Heat the oil in a wok, then add the processed mixture and stir-fry over low heat until fragrant, 2 to 3 minutes. Increase the heat and add the ground chicken and green onions. Stir-fry until the chicken has changed color all over, about 2 minutes, then splash with the fish sauce and stir-fry for about 30 seconds. Add the water and cook, stirring occasionally, until the liquid has dried up and the chicken is done, about 3 to 4 minutes.
**3** Remove from the heat and stir in the Roasted Rice Powder, Vietnamese mint, basil leaves and lime juice. Taste and add salt if you like and more lime juice if you think it needs it. Sprinkle with the black pepper and transfer to a serving bowl. Serve hot or at room temperature.

# Thai Basil Chicken

*Gai pad bai horapa*

The flavor of this dish is so good no one will believe how ridiculously quick and easy it is to make (once you've located the bird's-eye chilies and fragrant Asian basil leaves). The bruised chilies add pungency and flavor to the chicken, but be sure to warn anyone who is not a chili addict to put them to one side rather than eating them whole, as the Thais do.

**Serves 4**
**Preparation time:** 7 mins
**Cooking time:** 7 mins

3 tablespoons oil
1¹/4 lbs (600 g) boneless chicken thigh fillet or
    breast, cut into ¹/2-in (1-cm) dice
1–2 tablespoons whole bird's-eye chilies,
    lightly bruised
1 cup (50 g) firmly packed Asian basil leaves,
    coarsely torn
2 tablespoons fish sauce

1  Heat the oil in a wok, then add the chicken and stir-fry over high heat for 3 to 4 minutes. Add the chilies and ¹/2 cup (25 g) of the basil and stir-fry for another minute.
2  Splash on the fish sauce, stirring to mix thoroughly. Transfer to a serving dish and scatter the rest of the basil on top.
3  Serve immediately with plain rice and a salad; a simple chicken stock with some diced tofu would be good to help moisten the rice when eating, as this chicken dish is dry.

# Chicken with Green Curry Paste and Basil

*Pad bai horapa keow wan gai*

If you've got some Thai Green Curry Paste ready (preferably home-made) this is one of the easiest chicken recipes around and wonderfully fragrant too. All you need do is stir-fry the curry paste for a moment, add some chicken breast and flavor it with kaffir lime leaves, Asian basil leaves and a splash of fish sauce. Yes, that's really all there is to it.

**Serves 4–6**
**Preparation time:** 7 mins
**Cooking time:** 7 mins

3 tablespoons oil
3 tablespoons Thai Green Curry Paste
  (page 101)
1 lb (500 g) chicken breast, cut into 1$^1$/$_2$-in
  (4-cm) pieces
2 kaffir lime leaves, edges torn (optional)
$^1$/$_2$ cup (20 g) loosely packed Asian basil
  leaves
2 tablespoons fish sauce

1  Heat the oil in a wok for 30 seconds, then add the Thai Green Curry Paste and stir-fry over medium heat for 1 minute.
2  Increase the heat and add the chicken, then stir-fry until it has changed color and is almost done, about 3 minutes.
3  Add the kaffir lime leaves and half the basil leaves. Stir-fry over high heat for 1 minute. Add the fish sauce to taste and stir to mix well.
4  Transfer to a serving dish and scatter with the remaining basil leaves. Serve hot with white rice.

# Thai Barbecued Chicken   *Gai yang*

Years ago, my young son made it his mission to try barbecued chicken in as many places as possible every time we visited Thailand. After a few years of research, he finally declared that the best version was the chicken served on the bridge linking Thailand with Burma at Mae Sai. I must confess that we never get tired of eating this chicken, which is marinated in the Thai trinity of garlic, black pepper and coriander root. Cook it over charcoal for that authentic Thai flavor and serve it with sweet Thai chili sauce.

**Serves 4–6**
**Preparation time:** 10 mins + 4 hours marinating
**Cooking time:** 15–20 mins

2¹/2 lbs (1.25 kg) chicken pieces (thighs, drumsticks and breasts)
1 tablespoon black peppercorns
6 large cloves garlic, minced
1¹/2 tablespoons coarsely minced coriander root
1¹/2 tablespoons coarsely minced coriander stems and leaves (cilantro)
1¹/2 teaspoons salt
1 tablespoon Thai Mekong whisky or Chinese rice wine (preferably Shaoxing), (optional)
Oil, for brushing
Sweet Thai chili sauce, to serve

**1** Remove any excess skin and fatty deposits from the chicken and prick the skin all over with a fork to allow the marinade to penetrate.
**2** Pound or process the peppercorns to a coarse powder in a mortar or spice grinder, then add the garlic, coriander root, stems and leaves, and the salt. Process to a smooth paste, adding the whisky or rice wine a little at a time.
**3** Rub the chicken pieces all over with the mixture, then leave to marinate for at least 4 hours, or refrigerate in a covered container up to 24 hours if preferred. Brush liberally with the oil and cook over hot charcoal, turning several times, until golden brown and cooked through, about 15 minutes. Alternatively, grill or broil until cooked. Serve with sweet Thai chili sauce.

**Green Curry Chicken**

# Green Curry Chicken    *Gaeng kiew wan gai*

Intensely aromatic Thai Green Curry Paste—which gets its color from green chilies and coriander—goes particularly well with chicken and duck and is sometimes also cooked with beef. You can either add bamboo shoots or straw mushrooms to the pot—or both if you like. This recipe uses home-made curry paste, which has a really fresh taste; if you decide to use the commercial variety, you may need to adjust the amount as the intensity varies from brand to brand.

**Serves 4–6**
**Preparation time:** 40 mins
**Cooking time:** 35 mins

1/2 cup (125 ml) thick coconut milk
3–4 tablespoons Thai Green Curry Paste (see below)
1 fresh chicken (about 2 1/2 lbs/1.25 kg), cut into 12–14 pieces, or 1 small duck, cut into bite-sized pieces
3 cups (750 ml) thin coconut milk
4 kaffir lime leaves
2 tablespoons fish sauce
3 1/2 oz (100 g) sliced bamboo shoots (optional)
3 1/2 oz (100 g) fresh or canned straw mushrooms (optional)
4–6 green bird's-eye chilies, bruised
1/2 cup (20 g) loosely packed Asian basil leaves

**Thai Green Curry Paste**
2 green finger-length chilies, minced
8–12 bird's-eye chilies, green if possible, minced
3 shallots, minced
4 cloves garlic, minced
1 tablespoon minced galangal
2 teaspoons minced coriander root
2 teaspoons minced coriander stem
2 teaspoons dried shrimp paste
1 teaspoon ground coriander
1 teaspoon salt
2 kaffir lime leaves, central rib discarded, minced
2 stalks lemongrass, tender inner part of bottom third only, thinly sliced
1 teaspoon grated kaffir lime rind or lemon rind
1 tablespoon oil

1  Make the Green Curry Paste by putting all the ingredients, except the oil, in a spice grinder (you will probably need to do this in two batches) and process to a smooth paste, adding a little of the oil, if needed, to keep the blades turning. If using the paste for some other recipe, transfer to an airtight container and refrigerate for up to 1 week. Alternatively, store in small ziplock bags in the freezer in two-tablespoon quantities for future use.

2  Pour the thick coconut milk into a saucepan and stir in the Thai Green Curry Paste. Cook uncovered, stirring frequently, over low-medium heat until the oil separates and the mixture starts to fry and smells fragrant, about 8 to 10 minutes.

3  Add the chicken pieces and stir-fry over medium heat for 10 minutes. Add the thin coconut milk, kaffir lime leaves and fish sauce and bring to a boil, stirring constantly. Lower the heat and simmer very gently, uncovered, for 15 minutes. If you are using bamboo shoots and mushrooms, add these now and keep simmering until the chicken is tender. Stir in the chilies and basil leaves just before serving.

# Laotian Chicken with Onions and Tomatoes

## Kai pad som mak kheua khua dong

In this simple Laotian recipe, chicken pieces are seasoned with garlic, pepper and salt before being gently braised with shallots, onion and green onions. This combination of types of onion ensures a really good flavor and fragrance, while the sliced tomatoes, chicken stock and fish sauce cook down to make a delicious sauce.

**Serves 4**
**Preparation time:** 20 mins
**Cooking time:** 25 mins

2$^{1}$/$_{2}$–3 lbs (1.25–1.5 kg) chicken, cut into
    serving pieces, or 2 lbs (1 kg) chicken pieces
1 tablespoon minced garlic
$^{1}$/$_{2}$ teaspoon salt
$^{1}$/$_{2}$ teaspoon freshly ground black pepper
2 tablespoons oil
6 shallots, finely minced
2 tablespoons fish sauce
1 large onion, sliced lengthwise
6 green onions (scallions), white part finely
    minced, green part cut into 1$^{1}$/$_{4}$-in (3-cm)
    lengths to make $^{1}$/$_{2}$ cup (50 g)
3 medium ripe tomatoes, sliced
$^{1}$/$_{2}$ cup (125 ml) chicken stock, preferably
    home-made
Salt, to taste
1 heaped tablespoon minced fresh coriander
    leaves (cilantro)

**1** Put the chicken pieces in a bowl and rub in the garlic, salt and pepper. Set aside for 10 minutes.
**2** Heat the oil in a wok, then add the shallots and stir-fry over low-medium heat for 1 minute. Add the chicken pieces and cook gently, turning so that they change color all over. Sprinkle with the fish sauce, then add the sliced onions and cook until the onions soften, 4 to 5 minutes.
**3** Add the white part of the green onions, the $^{1}$/$_{4}$ cup of green onion greens and the tomatoes. Cook, stirring several times, until the tomatoes start to soften, 2 to 3 minutes.
**4** Add the chicken stock, bring to a boil, cover the wok and simmer, stirring from time to time, until the chicken is tender, 15 to 20 minutes. You may need to add a little more stock if the sauce threatens to dry out before the chicken is cooked. Taste and add a little salt if desired, then sprinkle with a few extra grindings of black pepper. Transfer to a serving dish and garnish with the coriander leaves.

# Mild Javanese Chicken Bathed in Coconut Milk

*Opor ayam*

If you're not in the mood for chili-hot food, try this Indonesian chicken, fragrant with coriander, cumin and fennel and simmered in coconut milk. There is plenty of sauce, which is aromatic with lemongrass, *salam* leaves and kaffir lime leaves. Even if you are unable to obtain all of these herbs, you can be sure of a beautiful mild chicken curry.

**Serves 4**
**Preparation time:** 25 mins
**Cooking time:** 35 mins

3 cups (750 ml) coconut milk
1 stalk lemongrass, tender inner part of
    bottom third only, bruised
1 thin slice fresh galangal, bruised
2 *salam* leaves (optional)
2 kaffir lime leaves, torn
1 teaspoon shaved palm sugar
3/4–1 teaspoon salt
1 fresh chicken (about 3 lbs/1.5 kg), cut into
    14 pieces
1–2 teaspoons lime or lemon juice
1 tablespoon Crisp-fried Shallots (page 22)

**Spice Paste**
1 tablespoon coriander seeds
3/4 teaspoon cumin seeds
1/4 teaspoon fennel seeds
4 candlenuts, minced
6 shallots, minced
2 cloves garlic, minced
1 tablespoon minced ginger
1/2 teaspoon white pepper

1 Prepare the Spice Paste by toasting the coriander, cumin and fennel seeds in a dry saucepan over low heat, shaking the pan frequently, until fragrant, 1 to 2 minutes. Process to a fine powder in a spice grinder, then transfer to a small bowl. Add the candlenuts, shallots, garlic and ginger to the spice grinder. Process to a smooth paste, adding a little of the coconut milk, if necessary, to keep the blades turning. Combine with the ground spices, add the white pepper and stir.
2 Transfer the Spice Paste to a large saucepan. Place over low-medium heat and stir in the coconut milk, a little at a time. When well mixed, add the lemongrass, galangal, *salam* and kaffir lime leaves, sugar and salt. Bring to a boil, stirring frequently, then simmer, uncovered, for 2 minutes. Add the chicken and cook uncovered, stirring from time to time, until the chicken is tender, about 30 minutes. Just before serving, add the lime or lemon juice to taste. Transfer to a serving dish and garnish with Crisp-fried Shallots.

# Indonesian Grilled Chicken

## *Ayam panggang menado*

If you're concerned about your fat consumption, here's a chicken recipe from northern Sulawesi, Indonesia, that doesn't contain coconut milk. Chicken pieces are simmered in a tangy mixture of fresh seasonings and chili, together with herbs, sweet soy sauce and tomatoes, then barbecued for even more succulence and flavor. This is great for entertaining or taking on a barbecue picnic as most of the work can be done in advance.

**Serves 4**
**Preparation time:** 25 mins
**Cooking time:** 35 mins

4 chicken quarters (leg or breast portions), about 2 lbs (1 kg)
1 tablespoon lime or lemon juice
1 teaspoon salt
1/4 cup (60 ml) oil
1 stalk lemongrass, tender inner part of bottom third only, slit and bruised
1/2 cup (20 g) loosely packed lemon basil or Asian basil sprigs
2 pandanus leaves, raked with a fork and tied into a knot
3 tablespoons sweet soy sauce, or 3 tablespoons dark soy sauce with 2 teaspoons soft brown sugar
4 medium-sized ripe tomatoes, minced
1 cup (250 ml) water

**Seasoning Paste**
6–8 red finger-length chilies, sliced
10–12 shallots, minced
2 tablespoons minced ginger
2 cloves garlic, minced

**1** Rub the chicken pieces with the lime juice and salt. Set aside.
**2** Process all the Seasoning Paste ingredients to a smooth paste in a spice grinder, adding a little of the oil, if necessary, to keep the blades turning.
**3** Heat 3 tablespoons of the oil in a wok. Add the Seasoning Paste and stir-fry until fragrant, about 4 minutes. Add the lemongrass, basil, pandanus leaves, soy sauce and tomatoes. Cook, stirring frequently, until the tomatoes are reduced to a pulp, about 5 minutes. Add the water and chicken, cover the wok and simmer, turning the chicken several times, until the sauce has dried up and the chicken is tender, about 25 minutes. Take care that the sauce does not burn, because of the sugar content of the sweet soy sauce; if it threatens to dry up before the chicken is cooked, add a little more water to the wok. When the chicken is tender, remove from the wok, picking off any pieces of herb or tomato skin and leave to cool.
**4** Shortly before the chicken is required, brush each piece with the remaining oil and cook over charcoal or under a hot grill until golden brown on both sides, taking care that it does not burn. Chop into smaller pieces before serving.

**Indonesian Grilled Chicken**

# Roast Duck on a Bed of Crispy Noodles

This is one of my favorite dinner party dishes, a modern Singapore recipe combining elements of both Chinese and Western cuisines. Chinese-style roast duck (found in just about any Chinatown in the world) is tossed with shredded raw vegetables and a tangy dressing, then laid on a bed of crisp deep-fried rice vermicelli. Gravy is normally provided together with the roast duck, so if you can lay your hands on some of this, be sure to include it in the sauce.

**Serves 4**
**Preparation time:** 15 mins
**Cooking time:** 3 mins

Oil, for deep-frying
1³/4 oz (50 g) dried rice vermicelli, broken into
   short lengths
¹/2 small green bell pepper, very finely sliced
2¹/2-in (6-cm) carrot, very finely sliced
2¹/2-in (6-cm) daikon radish, very finely sliced
1 cup (75 g) finely shredded red cabbage
¹/2 roast duck, preferably Chinese-style, skin
   discarded, meat cut into ¹/2-in (1-cm) slices

Sauce
¹/2 teaspoon very finely minced garlic
¹/4 teaspoon salt
¹/2 teaspoon French Dijon mustard
Liberal sprinkling of white pepper
3 tablespoons rice or white vinegar
3 tablespoons oil
¹/2 teaspoon sesame oil
1 tablespoon roast duck gravy (see Note)

1 Prepare the Sauce by crushing the garlic, salt and mustard in a small bowl with the back of a spoon, then stir in the pepper, vinegar, oil, sesame oil and gravy, mixing well. Set aside.
2 Heat the oil in a wok for 30 seconds. When smoking hot, add a small handful of vermicelli and deep-fry until puffed and crisp, about 3 to 4 seconds. Remove with a wire basket or slotted spatula and drain on paper towels. Repeat until all the noodles are cooked. Arrange the fried noodles on a large serving plate.
3 Combine the bell pepper, carrot, radish, cabbage and duck meat in a bowl. Add the Sauce, tossing to mix well. Lay the salad over the center of the noodles and serve immediately.
4 This dish is best eaten as a separate course; you could begin the meal with a non-fried appetizer, follow by a soup, and then serve the duck.

> **NOTE:** If you can't get the roast duck gravy, use 1 tablespoon chicken stock mixed with 1 teaspoon oyster sauce and a large pinch of five spice powder.

# Chicken with Mango and Cashews

*Ga xao hot dieu*

Chicken stir-fried with cashew nuts is a Chinese restaurant cliché in the West, but this Vietnamese combination has a more complex (and in my opinion, infinitely superior) flavor. The Vietnamese add juicy sweet mango, tomato and snow peas, flavoring it all with a touch of fish sauce, lime juice, pepper and sugar. Not only does this dish look beautiful, it has a perfect balance of salty, sweet and sour flavors.

**Serves 4**
**Preparation time:** 15 mins
**Cooking time:** 7 mins

1 large ripe but firm mango (about 7 oz/200 g
   flesh after slicing)
3 tablespoons fish sauce
1 teaspoon lime juice
1 teaspoon sugar
1/2 teaspoon salt
1/4 teaspoon freshly ground black pepper
1 cup (250 ml) oil
1 lb (500 g) boneless chicken breast, cut into
   bite-sized pieces, dried with paper towels
2 teaspoons very finely minced garlic
1 teaspoon very finely minced red finger-
   length chili
7 oz (200 g) sugar snap or snow peas, tips,
   tails and strings removed (halved diagonally
   if large)
1 medium ripe tomato, peeled and cut into
   1/2-in (1-cm) dice
1/2 cup (75 g) dry-roasted cashew nuts

**1** Using a sharp-pointed knife, cut the mango lengthwise, following the stone to remove the two "cheeks" of flesh. Cut diagonal slashes across each mango cheek, 1/2-in (1-cm) apart, taking care not to cut right through the skin. Use a spoon to ease out the mango slices.
**2** Combine the fish sauce, lime juice, sugar, salt and pepper in a small bowl, stirring to dissolve the sugar and salt.
**3** Heat the oil in a wok until very hot, then add the chicken and deep-fry in two separate batches, stirring frequently, until just cooked, 2 minutes. Remove with a slotted spatula and drain on paper towels.
**4** Pour out all but 3 tablespoons of oil from the wok. Reheat the oil and stir-fry the garlic and chili over medium heat for a few seconds. Increase the heat, add the snow peas and stir-fry for 1 minute. Return the chicken and fish sauce mixture to the wok, stirring to mix well, then add the mango slices, tomato and cashew nuts. Stir for about 30 seconds until heated through, taking care not to smash the mango. Transfer to a dish and serve with steamed white rice.

# Spicy Tamarind Chicken with Lemongrass

*Ga xao sa ot me*

To make this simple dish, chicken thighs are briefly marinated in a mixture of fish sauce, crushed chili, garlic, lemongrass and sugar. The sugar helps give the chicken a rich brown color when it is stir-fried, but the sweetness is offset by the sour fruitiness of tamarind juice, another example of the clever balance of flavors typical of Vietnamese cuisine.

**Serves 4**
**Preparation time:** 20–25 mins
**Cooking time:** 5 mins

1 lb (500 g) chicken thigh fillets, cut into
    1³/4-in (4.5-cm) pieces
1 tablespoon fish sauce
1¹/2 tablespoons sugar
1–3 red finger-length chilies, ground to a paste
¹/4 teaspoon freshly ground black pepper
1 stalk lemongrass, tender inner part of
    bottom third only, very thinly sliced
3 cloves garlic, very finely minced
1 tablespoon oil
¹/2 cup (125 ml) chicken stock
1 heaped tablespoon tamarind pulp, soaked in
    ¹/4 cup (60 ml) warm water, squeezed and
    strained to obtain the juice
Salt, to taste
Sprigs of fresh coriander leaves (cilantro), to
    garnish

**1** Put the chicken in a bowl and add the fish sauce, sugar, chili, pepper, lemongrass and half of the garlic, stirring to mix well. Cover and marinate for 15 minutes.
**2** Heat the oil in a wok for 30 seconds, then add the remaining garlic and stir-fry for 5 seconds.
**3** Add the marinated chicken and stir-fry over high heat until it has turned brown, about 2 minutes.
**4** Reduce the heat and add the chicken stock and tamarind juice. Simmer until tender, stirring frequently, about 3 minutes. Taste, adding salt if desired. Transfer to a serving dish and garnish with the fresh coriander leaves.

# Cambodian Garlic Pork *Loc lac chrouk*

This uncomplicated recipe uses just a few basic ingredients, but it has a delightfully fresh flavor thanks to the unique Cambodian Salt, Lime and Black Pepper Dip (page 27). Serve this stir-fried pork and salad with rice as part of a main meal; you might like to add a soup (Creamy Coconut Pumpkin Soup, page 56, or Cambodian Sweet and Sour Fish Soup, page 57); if time is short, just toss together some Vietnamese Bean Sprout Pickles (page 29) before starting this recipe.

**Serves** 4
**Preparation time:** 15 mins
**Cooking time:** 3 mins

1–1¹/₄ lbs (500–600 g) pork fillet or
    loin, thinly sliced, shredded
1 tablespoon finely minced garlic
2 teaspoons fish sauce
1 teaspoon sugar
¹/₄ teaspoon freshly ground black
    pepper
Lettuce leaves, to line a serving
    plate
1 small onion, thinly sliced, rings
    separated
2 medium ripe tomatoes, each cut
    into 8 wedges
2 tablespoons oil
Cambodian Salt, Lime and Black
    Pepper Dip (page 27)

1 Put the pork in a bowl and add the garlic, fish sauce, sugar and pepper. Massage to mix well and set aside to marinate while preparing the salad.
2 Line a serving plate with the lettuce leaves. Scatter with the onion rings and surround with the tomato wedges. Set aside.
3 Heat the oil in a wok, add the pork and stir-fry over high heat until cooked, about 3 minutes.
4 Arrange the cooked pork in the center of the lettuce and serve, accompanied by the dip and steamed white rice. Each person squeezes lime or lemon juice to taste into the dipping sauce. A little of the pork can be rolled up with a tomato wedge in a lettuce leaf and seasoned with the dip before eating.

Lemongrass Beef with Peanuts

# Lemongrass Beef with Peanuts

## Sach ko cha kroeung

In this Cambodian recipe, beef is mixed with a seasoning paste of fragrant lemongrass, kaffir lime leaves, fresh coriander leaves (cilantro), chilies and garlic. There's no waiting around for it to marinate—just toss it in the wok with onion, bell pepper and green onions, splash in some fish sauce, add a bit of sugar, salt and crushed peanuts and there you have it: a really tasty meal to serve with rice.

**Serves 4**
**Preparation time:** 20 mins
**Cooking time:** 5 mins

1–1¹/4 lbs (500–600 g) sirloin or fillet steak, thinly sliced
3 tablespoons oil
3 tablespoons fish sauce
1 tablespoon sugar
¹/2 teaspoon salt
1 large onion, ¹/2 in (1 cm) cut off root end and discarded, cut into wedges
1 large red bell pepper, thinly sliced
¹/3 cup (50 g) coarsely crushed dry-roasted peanuts
4 green onions (scallions), white part halved lengthwise, white and green parts cut into 1³/4-in (4.5-cm) lengths
Sprigs of fresh coriander leaves (cilantro), to garnish

**Seasoning Paste**
3 shallots, minced
4 cloves garlic, minced
2–3 dried red finger-length chilies, cut into short lengths, soaked in hot water to soften, or ¹/2–1 teaspoon ground red pepper (cayenne)
1 tablespoon finely minced fresh coriander stem and leaves (cilantro)
5 kaffir lime leaves, central ribs discarded, torn
2 stalks lemongrass, tender inner part of bottom third only, thinly sliced
1 tablespoon finely minced galangal
¹/2 teaspoon ground turmeric
¹/2 cup (125 ml) water

1 Make the Seasoning Paste by processing the shallots, garlic, chilies, coriander stem and leaves, kaffir lime leaves, lemongrass and galangal in a spice grinder until smooth, adding a little water, if needed, to keep the blades turning. Transfer to a bowl and stir in the remaining water.
2 Add the beef, stirring to coat thoroughly.
3 Heat the oil in a wok. Add the beef, fish sauce, sugar and salt, and stir-fry over high heat for 2 minutes. Add the onion and stir-fry until it starts to soften, about 1 minute.
4 Add the bell pepper and stir-fry over high heat, 1 minute. Reserve 1 tablespoon each of the peanuts and the green onions. Add the remaining peanuts and green onions to the wok, stir-fry for 1 minute, then transfer to a serving dish.
5 Garnish with the remaining peanuts and green onions and the coriander sprigs. Serve hot with rice. You could also serve Vietnamese Bean Sprout Pickles (page 29) or Vinegared Cucumber Salad (page 25) and perhaps a simple soup for an even more sumptuous meal which will, of course, take a little longer.

# Thai Grilled Beef Salad  *Yam neua*

If you happen to have any left-over grilled steak or roast beef, this recipe is really quick to prepare and it takes only a little longer if you need to grill the steak just before you want to serve the salad. The room-temperature beef is sliced and mixed with a fragrant bouquet of lemongrass, coriander leaves (cilantro), mint and kaffir lime leaves, then tossed with a spicy dressing of fish sauce, lime juice, garlic and chilies. Arrange the meat on a bed of lettuce and serve it as part of a meal with rice.

**Serves 4**
**Preparation time:** 20 mins
**Cooking time:** 5 mins

1 lb (500 g) roast, grilled or barbecued beef, preferably medium-rare, cut into thin slices 2 in (5 cm) in length
1 stalk lemongrass, tender inner part of bottom third only, very thinly sliced
4 shallots, thinly sliced
1 tablespoon minced fresh coriander leaves (cilantro)
2 tablespoons mint leaves, coarsely torn
4 kaffir lime leaves, very finely shredded
6–8 lettuce leaves, washed and dried
1 firm ripe tomato, sliced
Cucumber slices
4 sprigs of mint

**Sauce**
2 cloves garlic, minced
2 red finger-length chilies, sliced
1 tablespoon sugar
1/4 cup (60 ml) lime juice
2 tablespoons fish sauce

1  Put the beef in a bowl. Add the lemongrass, shallots, coriander leaves, mint and kaffir lime leaves. Toss to mix well.
2  Prepare the Sauce by blending the garlic, chilies and sugar in a spice grinder, adding a little of the lime juice if needed to keep the blades turning. Transfer to a bowl and stir in the lime juice and fish sauce.
3  Pour the Sauce over the beef and herbs, mix well. Cover with plastic wrap and leave to marinate for 10 minutes.
4  Line a serving plate with the lettuce leaves. put the beef (at room temperature, not chilled) on top and surround with the tomato and cucumber slices. Garnish with the mint sprigs and serve.

# Malaysian Lamb Curry

A genuine Malaysian curry that uses commercial curry powder? Yes, local cooks do sometimes use blended spice mixtures (see curry powder, page 15), but also add whole spices, fresh seasonings and lemongrass for a more complex blending of flavors. The seasoning is softened with a little coconut milk and given a touch of sourness with tamarind juice. Add a few potato cubes and you have a fragrant, mouth-watering dish. You can make this curry a day before you intend to serve it, as the flavors actually improve with keeping.

**Serves 4**
**Preparation time:** 30 mins
**Cooking time:** 1 hour

3 tablespoons curry powder for meat
1/2 teaspoon ground fennel
3 tablespoons water
3 tablespoons oil
1 1/4 lbs (600 g) lean lamb leg, in 1/2-in (1-cm) thick slices, cut into 1 3/4-in (4.5-cm) squares
2 cups (500 ml) water
1 stalk lemongrass, tender inner part of bottom third only, bruised
1 teaspoon salt, or more to taste
2 potatoes, peeled and cubed
1/2 cup (125 ml) coconut milk
1 heaped tablespoon tamarind pulp, soaked in 1/4 cup (60 ml) warm water, squeezed and strained to obtain the juice
1 teaspoon sugar

**Seasoning Paste**
6 shallots, minced
3 cloves garlic, minced
1 1/2 tablespoons minced ginger
4 dried red finger-length chilies, cut into short lengths, soaked in hot water to soften, seeds discarded

**Whole Spices**
1 1/2-in (4-cm) cinnamon
2 petals of star anise
2 cardamom pods, slit and bruised
2 cloves

1 Prepare the Seasoning Paste by processing the shallots, garlic, ginger and chilies in a spice grinder to make a smooth paste, adding a little of the oil, if necessary, to keep the blades turning. (You may need to process the shallots first to reduce them and make enough space in your grinder jar before adding the remaining ingredients.)

2 Combine the curry powder, fennel and water in a small bowl, stirring to make a smooth paste. Set aside.

3 Heat the oil in a wok, then add the Whole Spices and stir-fry over low-medium heat until fragrant, about 1 minute. Add the Seasoning Paste and stir-fry for 2 minutes, then add the curry powder paste and stir-fry for another 2 minutes.

4 Add the lamb and stir-fry until it changes color and is coated with the spices, 3 to 4 minutes.

5 Add the water, lemongrass and salt, and bring to a boil, stirring to remove any spice paste stuck to the bottom of the wok. Cover and simmer until the meat is just tender.

6 Add the potato cubes and a little more water if needed and simmer until both the potatoes and meat are tender. Add the coconut milk, tamarind juice and sugar and simmer gently, uncovered, until the gravy has thickened, about 5 minutes. Serve hot with white rice or Lacy Malay Pancakes (page 93).

**Malaysian Lamb Curry**

# Nonya Soy Braised Pork   *Tau yu bak*

The Nonyas of Malaysia and Singapore take a classic Chinese braised pork dish, add a cinnamon stick, substitute sweet little purple shallots for onions and potatoes for bamboo shoots, then add a touch of sugar. You'll be surprised how these touches improve an already delicious dish, which embodies the best of home-style cooking—simple but oh, so good. A very close Chinese friend from Kuching, in Malaysian Borneo, paid me the ultimate compliment by saying this recipe is even better than the one prepared by his mother.

**Serves 4**
**Preparation time:** 20 mins + 30 mins marinating
**Cooking time:** 1 hour 10 mins

1¼ lbs (600 g) belly or shoulder pork, skin left on
3 tablespoons dark soy sauce
3 tablespoons soy sauce
2 teaspoons sugar
¼ teaspoon white pepper
10 shallots, minced
4 cloves garlic, minced
2–3 tablespoons oil
2-in (5-cm) cinnamon
1 tablespoon salted soybeans
8 dried black Chinese mushrooms, soaked to soften, stems discarded, soaking water reserved
3–4 cups (750 ml–1 liter) water, (including water reserved from soaking mushrooms)
2–3 medium potatoes (about 10 oz/300 g), peeled and quartered

1 Cut the pork in ¾-in (2 cm) thick slices, then cut into pieces about 1¼ x 2½ in (3 x 6 cm). Sprinkle with both lots of soy sauce, sugar and pepper. Mix well and leave to marinate for 30 minutes.
2 Process the shallots and garlic in a spice grinder until finely ground.
3 Heat the oil in a wok or large saucepan, then add the processed mixture and stir-fry over low-medium heat for 2 minutes. Add the cinnamon and stir-fry for a few seconds, then add the salted soybeans and stir-fry for 30 seconds.
4 Put in the mushrooms and stir-fry for 1 minute. Drain the meat in a sieve, saving the marinade. Increase the heat, add the meat and stir-fry until it changes color, 3 to 4 minutes. Add enough water to just cover the meat and bring to a boil. Reduce the heat, cover and simmer until the meat is just tender, about 45 minutes.
5 Add the potatoes and a little more water if needed, cover and simmer, stirring occasionally, until the potatoes are cooked and the meat is very soft, about 15 to 20 minutes. Serve hot with steamed white rice. You can make this well in advance and reheat it if you like, or even refrigerate it for 24 hours.

# Simple Thai Pork Omelet  *Gai tod gup moo*

I particularly enjoy this omelet with a salad for lunch, but you could just as well serve it as part of a main meal with rice (adding a soup and a salad or vegetable dish). Omelets with a filling of ground seasoned pork are common in Thailand, but in this easy recipe, the meat is mixed with the egg before cooking. The omelets are not chili-hot, so are good for those who prefer mild food. For the genuine Thai taste, however, spoon over liberal amounts of the chili-spiked Simple Thai Fish Sauce and Chili Dip when eating.

**Serves 4**
**Preparation time:** 7 mins
**Cooking time:** 7 mins

8 eggs
1/2 tablespoon fish sauce
1/2 lb (250 g) finely ground lean pork, separated with a fork
3–4 shallots, finely minced
2 cloves garlic, minced
3 tablespoons finely minced fresh coriander leaves (cilantro)
1 tablespoon oil
1/4 teaspoon freshly ground black pepper
Sprigs of fresh coriander leaves (cilantro), to garnish (optional)
Simple Thai Fish Sauce and Chili Dip (page 27)

**1** Whisk the eggs with the fish sauce, then stir in the ground pork, shallots, garlic and minced coriander leaves, mixing well.
**2** You can either cook 1 large omelet and cut it in quarters to serve (the quicker option), or use a small skillet to make individual omelets. Assuming you're taking the latter option, put about 1/2 teaspoon of oil in a small skillet (about 6 in /15 cm in diameter) and heat, swirling the pan to grease the sides as well as the bottom. When moderately hot, pour in 1/4 of the egg mixture and cook until the edges are starting to set, about 1 minute.
**3** Lift the edges of the omelet with a spatula and let the liquid portion of egg run underneath. Cook until the bottom of the omelet is golden brown and the top almost set, 1 to 2 minutes. Slide the omelet out onto a plate, then flip it over into the pan and continue cooking until the other side is golden brown, about another 2 minutes.
**4** Put the omelet on a plate and continue cooking, adding a little oil to grease the pan each time, to make four omelets. Arrange the omelets on a serving plate and garnish each with a sprig of coriander leaves if desired. Serve at room temperature accompanied by the dip.

# Sweet Soy Balinese Pork   *Babi masak kecap*

Like many Indonesian dishes, this excellent recipe doesn't contain any dried spices but what it does have is plenty of chilies, shallots, garlic, ginger and dried shrimp paste, with sweet soy sauce offset by a touch of lime juice. This dish is one of my personal favorites and makes me very glad that the Balinese are Hindu and therefore not forbidden to eat pork like Indonesia's Muslims.

**Serves 4**
**Preparation time:** 12 mins
**Cooking time:** 1 hour

4–6 red finger-length chilies, sliced
8 shallots, minced
4 cloves garlic, minced
2-in (5-cm) ginger, minced
1 teaspoon dried shrimp paste, toasted (page 22)
3 tablespoons oil
1¹/4 lbs (600 g) pork shoulder, into bite-sized slices, cut into 1¹/4-in (3-cm) squares
3 tablespoons sweet soy sauce, or 3 tablespoons dark soy sauce with 2 teaspoons soft brown sugar
1 tablespoon lime juice
1¹/2 cups (375 ml) water
Salt, to taste

1 Process the chilies, shallots, garlic, ginger and dried shrimp paste to a smooth paste in a spice grinder, adding a little of the oil, if necessary, to keep the blades turning.
2 Heat the oil in a wok or saucepan with a heavy base, then add the chili paste and stir-fry over low-medium heat, 4 minutes. Add the pork and stir-fry over medium heat until it changes color, about 5 minutes.
3 Add the sweet soy sauce, lime juice and water. Bring to a boil, cover and simmer over low heat, stirring occasionally, until the pork is tender and the sauce has thickened, about 1 hour. Taste and add salt if desired. Transfer to a serving dish and serve hot with steamed white rice and vegetables.

Thai Red Beef Curry

# Thai Red Beef Curry

*Gaeng ped neua normai*

This Thai classic is a really gutsy dish, with the no-nonsense flavor of beef emphasized by the robust and fragrant Thai Red Curry Paste. You can make your own following the recipe below; if you use commercial curry paste, you may need to adjust the amount slightly as the intensity seems to vary from one brand to another. Coconut milk helps soften the bite of the chilies and the rather neutral flavor of bamboo shoots (or eggplant, if you prefer) acts as foil to the spicy sauce.

**Serves 4**
**Preparation time:** 20 mins
**Cooking time:** 1 hour 30 mins

1/2 cup (125 ml) thick coconut milk
4 tablespoons Thai Red Curry Paste (see below)
3 cups (750 ml) thin coconut milk
1 1/4 lbs (600 g) topside beef, in 3/4-in (2-cm) slices, cut into 1 1/4-in (3-cm) squares
4 kaffir lime leaves, torn
1/2 lb (250 g) canned bamboo shoots, boiled in fresh water for 10 minutes, drained and sliced, or 1–2 slender Asian eggplant, cut into 1 1/4-in (3-cm) slices
1–2 tablespoons fish sauce
Salt, to taste

**Thai Red Curry Paste**
2 teaspoons coriander seeds
1 teaspoon cumin seeds
1 teaspoon black peppercorns
10–12 dried red finger-length chilies, cut into short lengths, soaked in hot water to soften
1/3 cup (50 g) minced shallots
1/4 cup (40 g) minced garlic
2 tablespoons finely minced galangal
2 tablespoons thinly sliced lemongrass, tender inner part of bottom third only
1 tablespoon ground coriander root
1 teaspoon dried shrimp paste, toasted
1/2 teaspoon grated kaffir lime rind, or 1–2 kaffir lime leaves, minced

1 Prepare the Thai Red Curry Paste if you are not using the commercial variety. Dry-roast the coriander, cumin and peppercorns in a small dry pan, shaking the pan, until fragrant, 1 to 2 minutes. Transfer to a spice grinder and grind to a fine powder, then keep aside in a small bowl.
2 Process the rest of the ingredients to a smooth paste in a spice grinder; you will probably need to do this in several small batches. You may need to add a teaspoon or two of water to keep the blades turning; the resulting paste must be absolutely smooth. Combine this paste with the dry ground spices, stirring to mix well. Refrigerate in an airtight jar for about three weeks, or deep-freeze in small portions if not using for this curry.
3 Make the beef curry by combining the thick coconut milk and the Thai Red Curry Paste in a saucepan. Cook uncovered, stirring frequently, over low-medium heat until the oil separates and the mixture starts to fry and turns aromatic, about 8 to 10 minutes. Add the thin coconut milk and bring to a boil, stirring constantly. Put in the beef and kaffir lime leaves and simmer, uncovered, until the beef is tender, 1 to 1 1/4 hours.
4 Add the bamboo shoots or eggplant and continue cooking until the vegetables are done and the meat is very tender; if the sauce seems to be drying out before the cooking is done, add a little water.
5 Just before serving, add the fish sauce and a little salt, if you desire. Transfer to a serving dish and serve with rice.

# Scrambled Eggs with Chinese Sausages

## *Trung ga xot xet*

This recipe (based on one by Vietnamese culinary authority, Nicole Routhier) is one of my stand-by dishes for days when I "haven't a thing in the fridge." I always keep dried Chinese sausages in my store cupboard (they seem to last forever) and these lift the usual scrambled eggs to the level of a gourmet treat. You can serve this dish with either rice or crusty French bread and a simple salad for a delicious light meal.

**Serves 4**
**Preparation time:** 10 mins
**Cooking time:** 3 mins

3 dried Chinese sausages (*lap cheong*), cut
    into ¹/₂-in (1-cm) slices
8 large eggs
2–3 green onions (scallions), thinly sliced
2 tablespoons fish sauce
1 tablespoon finely minced shallot
3–4 cloves garlic, minced
3 small-medium tomatoes, diced
2 tablespoons coarsely chopped fresh
    coriander leaves (cilantro)
Freshly ground black pepper, to taste

1  Put the sausages in a saucepan, preferably with a nonstick surface. Cook over moderate heat, stirring from time to time, until the sausages release their fat and just start to brown, about 2 to 3 minutes.

2  While the sausages are cooking, break the eggs into a bowl and whisk lightly. Stir in the green onions (use only two if they are large) and the fish sauce.

3  Add the shallot and garlic to the sausages and stir-fry for 30 seconds, then put in the tomatoes. Stir-fry until the tomatoes soften, about 2 to 3 minutes. Add the egg mixture to the pan and cook over low heat, stirring constantly with a wooden spoon, until the eggs are set but not too firm. Add the fresh coriander leaves and stir to mix well. Transfer the cooked eggs to a serving dish and grind plenty of black pepper over the top. Serve hot.

# Green Mango Pork

## *Wettha thayet thi chet*

It won't take you long to prepare this Burmese pork dish, which can be left to simmer gently for about an hour while you get on with other things. Although it has only a few seasonings—garlic, ginger, onion, chili and turmeric, plus the ubiquitous dried shrimp paste and a touch of sesame oil —what lifts it out of the ordinary is the sour green mango. If you can't find unripe mangoes, there are alternative suggestions for obtaining that irresistible sour tang.

Serves 4
**Preparation time:** 15 mins
**Cooking time:** 1 hour 10 mins

1 large onion, minced
2–3 cloves garlic, minced
1³/4-in (4.5-cm) ginger, minced
1 teaspoon dried shrimp paste
3 tablespoons oil
1 teaspoon sesame oil
2–3 teaspoons crushed dried chili flakes,
    or 1 teaspoon ground red pepper (cayenne)
¹/4 teaspoon ground turmeric
1¹/4 lbs (600 g) boneless pork shoulder,
    cut into bite-sized slices, about 1¹/2-in/
    4-cm) square
1¹/2 tablespoons fish sauce
1–2 unripe green mangoes (about ¹/2 lb/250 g),
    peeled and coarsely grated (see Note)
1¹/2–2 cups (375–500 ml) water
Sugar, to taste
Salt, to taste

**1** Process the onion, garlic, ginger and dried shrimp paste to a smooth paste.
**2** Heat both lots of oil in a saucepan and add the processed paste, chili flakes and turmeric. Stir-fry over low-medium heat until fragrant, about 4 to 5 minutes. Add the pork and stir-fry until it changes color and is well coated with the seasonings, about 5 minutes.
**3** Splash in the fish sauce, stir for about 1 minute, then add the green mango and stir-fry for 5 minutes. Add just enough water to cover the pork and bring to a boil. Cover the pan, lower the heat and simmer until the pork is tender and the sauce has reduced, about 1 hour. (I sometimes add a couple of cubed potatoes towards the end of the cooking time.) Taste and add sugar and salt, if needed, to balance the flavors. Serve hot with steamed rice.

> **NOTE:** If you can't find green mango, you could use 1 grated sour green apple to replace unripe green mango; add this with the pork for stir-frying, then add 1 tablespoon lime or lemon juice with the water after the pork has been stir-fried. Taste at the end of cooking and add more lime juice as needed for a sour tang.

# Laotian Beef Stew with Asian Herbs

*Or lam*

When I asked the women vegetable sellers at a street market in Luang Prabang what went into the popular local beef stew, I was shown bundles of woody sticks. I was skeptical when they insisted that these were cooked together with the meat, vegetables and herbs, but I later found out that this vine is related to the pepper family and gives a faintly bitter flavor. Even without this esoteric ingredient and using the easily available vegetables and herbs suggested here, you'll find this is still a very tasty dish.

**Serves 4**
**Preparation time:** 30 mins
**Cooking time:** 1 hour 30 mins

2 tablespoons preserved fish, or 3 tablespoons chopped canned anchovies
1¼ lbs (600 g) topside or chuck steak, cut into ¾-in (2-cm) slices, about 1¼-in (3-cm) square
1 stalk lemongrass, tender inner part of bottom third only, thinly sliced
6 shallots, thinly sliced
4–6 slender Asian eggplants (about 1½ lbs/700 g), left whole
4 red finger-length chilies, left whole
3–4 cups (750 ml–1 liter) water
6 green onions (scallions)
13 oz–1 lb (375–500 g) leafy greens (watercress, water spinach, English spinach, amaranth, silver beet, etc), coarsely chopped
½ teaspoon freshly ground black pepper
Salt, to taste
½ cup (20 g) loosely packed Asian basil leaves
Small bunch of dill or mint leaves, minced

> **NOTE:** You can use just one type of leafy green vegetable, or a combination of several.

1 If using preserved fish, put it in a small bowl and add enough warm water to cover. Stir, then leave to soak for a few minutes before pouring the contents into a sieve. Press down on the solids to extract the salty liquid.
2 Put the meat in a wide saucepan and add the preserved fish liquid (or chopped anchovies), lemongrass, shallots, chilies, eggplants and enough water to cover. Bring to a boil, then reduce the heat, cover and leave to simmer until the eggplants and chilies are very soft, 15 to 20 minutes. Lift out the eggplants and chilies and remove the stem end of each. Slice the eggplants in half and scoop out the flesh. Chop the chilies, then process the eggplants and chilies to a paste; alternatively, you can mash them finely with a fork. Return to the pan.
3 Cut the green onions in 1¾ in (4.5 cm) lengths, then mince enough of the green portion to make 2 tablespoons. Set aside the minced green onions and add the rest to the pan, together with the leafy greens. Bring to a boil, cover and continue cooking until the meat is very tender, about 1¼ hours. If there is still a lot of liquid in the pan, uncover and cook over moderately high heat to reduce it slightly.
4 Add the black pepper and salt to taste, then stir in the basil and the dill or mint leaves. Transfer to a serving bowl and scatter with the reserved minced green onions.

**Laotian Beef Stew with Asian Herbs**

# Spicy Laotian Ground Beef

## Larb neua

The first time I tried this Lao dish (which is also popular in northeast Thailand), I was presented with raw ground buffalo, moistened with a liberal splash of fresh blood and mixed with herbs and lashings of chili. To my surprise, it actually tasted great, but I'm not advocating that you strive for total authenticity. Use good ground beef, stir-fry it briefly and take a rain check on the blood. Add the seasonings, herbs and crunchy rice powder and you'll love the result.

**Serves 4**
**Preparation time:** 10 mins
**Cooking time:** 3 mins

1 lb (500 g) lean rump or sirloin beef, finely
   ground
1 teaspoon oil
1 tablespoon Roasted Rice Powder (page 22)
3 stalks lemongrass, tender inner part of
   bottom third only, thinly sliced
4–6 shallots, thinly sliced
1 teaspoon crushed dried chili flakes,
   or more to taste
1 red finger-length chili, thinly sliced
1/4 cup (60 ml) lime juice, or more to taste
2 tablespoons fish sauce
1/2 cup (20 g) loosely packed mint leaves,
   coarsely chopped
Cabbage or lettuce leaves (optional)

1 Break up the beef with a fork. Heat the oil in a wok and when very hot, add the beef and stir-fry just until it starts to change color, about 1 minute. Transfer to a large bowl and leave to cool.
2 Add the remaining ingredients to the beef, tossing to mix well and serve immediately. Traditionally, the *larb* is spooned into cabbage or lettuce leaves and eaten with steamed rice, although you could just serve it beside the rice and omit the leafy wrappers if you like.

# Chapter 5

# Seafood and Fish

Here are a few simple but wonderful seafood recipes. Try Delicate Squid with Thai Herbs (page 125), an easy room-temperature dish, or Thai Fried Fish with Ginger Sauce (page 129) and you'll see what I mean.

There are even a couple of fish recipes, Grilled Fish with Sweet Soy Dip (page 133) and Fish with Sweet Tamarind Sauce (page 130), that take only a little more than 30 minutes from start to finish.

But, it must be admitted, there are a number of recipes where you really do need to spend time peeling, chopping, squeezing, processing, or wrapping in banana leaf. These are the times when you might wish you were part of an extended Asian family, with plenty of willing hands to help, or that you were one of those cooks lucky enough to have household help. But when you try them, you're sure to agree that these more time-consuming recipes are well worth every moment.

Pick a day when you have plenty of time, or can persuade someone to join you in the kitchen to help peel the shallots and garlic, slice the lemongrass, process curry pastes or wilt squares of banana leaf so that you can enjoy such wonderful dishes as Fish Mousse with Basil and Red Curry (page 128) and Famous Singapore Chili Crab (page 127).

So put your rice on to cook, then get to work preparing one of these recipes and you'll be enjoying a marvelous meal within just 30 minutes.

# Crunchy Thai Stuffed Shrimp  *Kung tiparot*

You can find some amazing seafood at the coastal stalls in Thailand, but I was still surprised to find this sophisticated recipe in a simple shack on the beach near Songkla, on the southeast coast (perhaps the cook had learned it from someone in Bangkok). Jumbo shrimp were filled with seasoned ground pork, dipped in a light batter, deep-fried until golden brown and served with sweet Thai chili sauce. I find that home-made Vietnamese Fish Sauce Dip, while not traditional, also works very well.

**Serves 4–6**
**Preparation time:** 30 mins
**Cooking time:** 15 mins

12 fresh jumbo shrimp (about 5 in/12.5 cm)
1/4 teaspoon black peppercorns
1 teaspoon finely ground coriander root
2 1/2 oz (75 g) lean ground pork
2 teaspoons fish sauce
1/2 teaspoon sugar
Oil, for deep-frying
3 tablespoons rice flour
2 tablespoons plain flour
1/4 teaspoon salt
2 eggs, lightly beaten
Sweet Thai chili sauce or Vietnamese Fish
  Sauce Dip (page 27)

1 Remove the heads and shells from the shrimp, but leave on the final tail section. Cut down the back of each shrimp with a sharp knife. Remove the black vein and use the palm of your hand to press gently on each shrimp to open out the back, taking care not to squash it completely flat. Set aside.
2 Process the peppercorns to a powder in a spice grinder or mortar, then add the coriander root and process to a paste. Transfer to a bowl and stir in the pork, fish sauce and sugar, mixing well with your hand.
3 Spread some of the pork filling down the back of each shrimp, carefully pushing it in with your fingers and smoothing the top. When all the shrimp have been filled, heat the oil for deep-frying in a wok.
4 Combine both lots of flour and salt in a bowl and have the beaten eggs in a separate bowl nearby. Hold a shrimp by the tail over the flour mixture and spoon the flour over to coat the shrimp. Shake the shrimp gently to dislodge any excess flour, dip in the egg to coat all over, then lower into the hot oil. Repeat with another three to four shrimp and deep-fry until they are golden brown and cooked, about 3 to 4 minutes. Drain on paper towels and keep warm while cooking the remaining shrimp. Serve hot with a bottled sweet Thai chili sauce or Vietnamese Fish Sauce Dip.

# Marinated Shrimp Skewers   *Satay kung*

Satay—skewers of seasoned meat, poultry or seafood grilled to perfection over charcoal—is most commonly associated with Malaysia and Indonesia, but the Thais also prepare some amazingly good satay in the south. In this version, the natural sweetness of shrimp is accentuated by the marinade of coconut cream, galangal, lemongrass and spices. You could eat these with a peanut dipping sauce, but I think a squeeze of lime or lemon juice is all that's needed (and it's fat-free as well).

**Makes about 20 sticks**
**Preparation time:** 12 mins
**Cooking time:** 5 mins

4 teaspoons coriander seeds, lightly toasted
1 teaspoon cumin seeds, lightly toasted
2 teaspoons very finely minced galangal
2 stalks lemongrass, tender inner part of
   bottom third only, thinly sliced
4 teaspoons sugar
1 teaspoon salt
1/2 teaspoon white pepper
1/4 teaspoon ground turmeric
1/2 cup (125 ml) coconut cream
1/4 cup (60 ml) water
2 lbs (1 kg) large or medium fresh shrimp,
   peeled and deveined, head and tail intact
Bamboo skewers, soaked in cold water for
   30 minutes
1 tablespoon oil
1 large lime or lemon, quartered

**1** Process the coriander and cumin seeds in a spice grinder until fine. Add the galangal, lemongrass, sugar, salt, pepper, turmeric and 1 tablespoon of the coconut cream and process to a smooth paste.
**2** Transfer the paste to a bowl. Stir in the coconut cream and water to make a smooth marinade. Add the shrimp and stir to coat with the marinade. Cover with plastic wrap and marinate at room temperature for at least 30 minutes, or refrigerate for up to 4 hours.
**3** Grease the grill of a barbecue or broiler with oil. Heat until very hot. Thread a shrimp horizontally onto each skewer, then cook over high heat for 2 minutes. Turn and cook for another 2 minutes; check to see if the shrimp is cooked. Serve accompanied by lime wedges.

# Squid with Garlic and Black Pepper

## Pla mok phat

A Thai dish without chilies might seem strange, but before chilies were introduced to Southeast Asia, black peppercorns were relied on for heat. This recipe is quickly prepared, although if you want to impress everyone by scoring the squid decoratively, it'll take a little longer. Despite the use of only a few seasonings, the flavor is excellent. Be sure to use fresh, not frozen, squid.

**Serves 4**
**Preparation time:** 10 mins
**Cooking time:** 4 mins

1 1/4 lbs (600 g) small fresh squid or calamari with tentacles intact, or 1 lb (500 g) fresh squid hoods
2 teaspoons black peppercorns
6 cloves garlic, minced
1 teaspoon oyster sauce
1 teaspoon fish sauce
1 teaspoon soy sauce
1/2 teaspoon sugar
1/4 cup (60 ml) oil
2 green onions (scallions), cut into 1 3/4-in (4.5-cm) lengths

1  If you're dealing with whole squid, pull out the heads and cut the tentacles off just above the eyes. Squeeze to remove the hard portion in the center of the tentacles, then keep the tentacles aside. Remove the reddish-brown skin from the squid and clean out the central cavity. Cut the squid hoods in half lengthwise and pat dry on both sides with paper towels. For a decorative "pine cone" look to the squid, score the soft inside of the squid pieces with diagonal lines using a very sharp knife, taking care not to cut right through the flesh. Turn the piece of squid and score diagonally across the lines already made, resulting in a criss-cross pattern. Cut each squid half into bite-sized pieces. If you don't have time to score the squid, just cut it into bite-sized pieces. Dry the squid pieces and tentacles on paper towels and set aside.

2  Process the peppercorns in a spice grinder until very coarsely ground. Add the garlic and process another few seconds to get a coarse paste; you do not want a fine paste for this dish. If you have a mortar and pestle, you can do the job quickly and easily. Set aside. Put the oyster sauce, fish sauce, soy sauce and sugar in a small bowl, stirring to dissolve the sugar. Set aside.

3  Heat oil in a wok until smoking hot, then add the squid pieces and stir-fry over maximum heat for 1 minute. Add the pepper-garlic mixture and stir-fry for 2 minutes, then pour in the prepared sauce, mixing well. Add the green onions and stir-fry just until they are wilted, about 30 seconds. Serve hot with rice.

# Delicate Squid with Thai Herbs

*Yam pla muk*

Fresh squid or calamari has a delicate flavor and texture, provided you start with really fresh squid and cook it just until it turns white—over-cooking makes the flesh tough. In this Thai recipe, the squid is mixed with a tangy dressing of chili, garlic, lime juice and fish sauce. Add lemongrass, shallots and mint leaves, and you have a superb salad to serve with rice. If you prefer, you could substitute some of the squid with shrimp and fish.

**Serves 4**
**Preparation time:** 15 mins
**Cooking time:** 1 min

2 lbs (1 kg) whole squid (calamari),
    or 1³/4 lbs (800 g) squid hoods
2 cups (500 ml) water
2 red finger-length chilies, finely minced
4 shallots, thinly sliced
1 stalk lemongrass, tender inner part of
    bottom third only, very thinly sliced
2 teaspoons caster sugar
¹/4 cup (60 ml) lemon juice
¹/4 cup (60 ml) fish sauce
¹/4 cup (12 g) firmly packed mint leaves, torn

1 If you're using whole squid, pull out the heads and cut the tentacles off just above the eyes. Squeeze to remove the hard portion in the center of the tentacles, then keep the tentacles aside. Pull off the flaps from the squid bodies and put with the tentacles. Remove the reddish-brown skin from the squid and clean out the central cavity. Cut the squid bodies (hoods) in half lengthwise and pat dry on both sides with paper towels.
2 For a decorative "pine cone" look to the squid, score the soft inside of the squid pieces with diagonal lines using a very sharp knife, taking care not to cut right through the flesh. Turn the piece of squid and score diagonally across the lines already made, resulting in a fine criss-cross pattern. Cut each squid half into bite-sized pieces. If you don't have time to score the squid, just cut it into bite-sized pieces.
3 Bring the water to a boil in a saucepan, then add the squid and cook uncovered just until the squid turns white, about 1 minute. Tip into a colander, rinse under cold water, drain well and cool to room temperature.
4 Put the squid in a serving bowl. Add the chilies, shallots, lemongrass, sugar, lemon juice, fish sauce and mint leaves, tossing to mix well. Serve at room temperature.

# Fragrant Steamed Mussels

*Hoy mangpoo ob mor din*

This is quite the most delicious way of preparing mussels you'll ever try. The fragrance of kaffir lime leaves, lemongrass and Asian basil leaves totally transforms the mussels, which are briefly simmered in the herb-seasoned stock and eaten with sweet Thai chili sauce. The mussels can be served with rice and also make a perfect first course for a Western meal, served with crusty French bread and a good Sauvignon Blanc.

**Serves 4**
**Preparation time:** 15 mins
**Cooking time:** 8 mins

3 cups (750 ml) water
6 kaffir lime leaves, torn
3 stalks lemongrass, tender inner part of bottom third only, bruised and cut into 4 pieces
1 teaspoon salt
2 lbs (1 kg) mussels, preferably green-lipped variety, scrubbed to remove grit, washed and drained
1–2 red finger-length chilies, sliced
1/2 cup (25 g) firmly packed Asian basil sprigs
Sweet Thai chili sauce

1 Put the water into a wok or large saucepan and add the kaffir lime leaves, lemongrass and salt. Bring to a boil, lower the heat and simmer, uncovered, for 5 minutes. Add the mussels and continue simmering, stirring frequently, removing each mussel immediately the shell opens and transferring it to a serving bowl. Discard any mussels which do not open.
2 Pour the stock through a cloth-lined sieve. Put 2 cups of the strained stock back into the wok and bring to a boil. Add the chilies and basil and simmer, uncovered, for 1 minute.
3 Pour the stock over the mussels and serve with sweet Thai chili sauce as a dipping sauce.

# Famous Singapore Chili Crab

Back in the late 1960s in Singapore, it was still possible to sit at a table with your feet in the sand and to inspect the live crabs kept in huge baskets under the coconut trees before ordering the famous Palm Beach chili crab. Singapore has changed enormously since those days, but its chili crab is still one of the great seafood dishes of the world. This recipe takes time, but believe me, it's worth every moment. The crab is traditionally eaten with chunks of crusty bread to mop up the sauce.

**Serves 4–6**
**Preparation time:** 40 mins
**Cooking time:** 20 mins

3–4 lbs (1.5–2 kg) live mud crabs
2 tablespoons oil
6 shallots, minced
6–8 large cloves garlic, minced
2–3 tablespoons minced ginger
3–4 red bird's-eye chilies, minced
3 1/2 cups (875 ml) chicken stock
4 tablespoons hot bean paste, or
   3 tablespoons salted soybean paste
   plus 2 extra bird's-eye chilies
1/4 cup (60 ml) bottled chili sauce
1/2 cup (125 ml) bottled tomato sauce
1 tablespoon sugar
2 tablespoons Chinese rice wine
   (preferably Shaoxing)
2 teaspoons salt
1 teaspoon white pepper
2 tablespoons cornstarch, mixed with
   3 tablespoons water
2 eggs, lightly beaten

**Chili-Ginger Sauce**
6 red finger-length chilies, minced
5–6 cloves garlic, minced
2 tablespoons finely minced ginger
2 teaspoons sugar
1/2 teaspoon salt
1 teaspoon rice vinegar
1 tablespoon water

1 Put the crabs in the freezer for 15 to 20 minutes to immobilize them. Cut in half lengthwise with a cleaver and remove the back and spongy grey matter. Remove the claws and crack in several places with a cleaver. Cut each body half into two to three pieces, leaving the legs attached.
2 Make the Chili-Ginger Sauce by blending all the ingredients in a spice grinder. Set aside.
3 Heat the oil in a wok and add the shallots, garlic, ginger and bird's-eye chilies. Stir-fry over low-medium heat until fragrant, about 3 minutes, then add the Chili-Ginger Sauce, chicken stock, hot bean paste, chili sauce, tomato sauce, sugar, rice wine, salt and pepper. Bring to a boil, then lower the heat and simmer for 2 minutes. Add the crab pieces and simmer, uncovered, turning several times, until the shells are bright red and the crabs are cooked, about 10 minutes.
4 Add the cornstarch mixture and stir until the sauce thickens and clears. Add the eggs and stir until set, then transfer the chili crab to a serving dish and serve with crusty French bread.
5 You could follow the crab with something simple, perhaps some steamed rice with stir-fried mixed vegetables and a soup.

**Famous Singapore Chili Crab**

# Fish Mousse with Basil and Red Curry

*Hor mok pla*

This Thai favorite is a recipe to prepare when you really want to impress. The decorative banana-leaf cups filled with fish mousse not only look exotic but smell divine. (You can, however, take the easier option and cook the fish in small ramekins or soufflé dishes). The fish is processed to a smooth paste and flavored with red curry paste, fish sauce and fresh herbs, giving it an incredible flavor. You can enjoy this either hot or at room temperature.

**Serves 4**
**Preparation time:** 20–40 mins
**Cooking time:** 20 mins

16 pieces banana leaves, 5-in (12.5-cm) square, softened in a gas flame or boiling water
1 lb (500 g) firm boneless white fish fillets, skinned and cubed
2 cups (500 ml) thick coconut milk
1 egg
2 tablespoons Thai Red Curry Paste (page 115)
1 tablespoon fish sauce
1/4 teaspoon salt
1 green onion (scallion), minced
1 cup (40 g) loosely packed Asian basil leaves
1 red finger-length chili, deseeded and sliced
2 kaffir lime leaves, cut into hair-like shreds

**1** If you are using banana leaf, fold in the sides of each square by about 1 in (2.5 cm), pressing to make a line. Lift up the marked edges to make a square container with sides 1 in (2.5 cm) high and fold over at each corner, stapling to hold the shape.

**2** Put the fish in a food processor and process at high speed until it forms a coarse paste. Add the thick coconut milk, egg, Thai Red Curry Paste, fish sauce, salt and green onion, and process until smooth.

**3** Put two basil leaves in the bottom of each banana leaf cup. Fill with the fish mixture, repeating until all the cups have been filled. Lay one basil leaf, a slice of chili and a few shreds of kaffir lime leaf across the top of each cup. If you are using four to six small bowls instead of banana leaf cups, divide the basil, chili and kaffir lime leaves between them.

**4** Transfer the banana leaf cups or bowls to a steaming basket, or set on a perforated metal disc and place in a wok over boiling water. Steam until the mousse is set, about 20 minutes (or up to 10 minutes longer if using bowls), adding more boiling water to the wok after 10 minutes to prevent it from drying out. Serve the fish cups either hot or at room temperature.

Serves 4    **Preparation time:** 5 mins
**Cooking time:** 15 mins

2–2¹/₂ lbs (1–1.25 kg) whole fish or fresh white
    fish (snapper bream or sea bass), or 1¹/₄ lbs
    (600 g) fish fillets
Oil, for deep-frying
2 tablespoons cornstarch
1 heaped tablespoon very finely shredded pickled
    ginger
Cucumber slices, to garnish
Sprigs of fresh coriander leaves (cilantro), to
    garnish

Sauce
2 cloves garlic, finely minced
¹/₂ cup (125 ml) water
¹/₄ cup (60 g) soft brown sugar
¹/₄ cup (60 ml) rice vinegar
4 teaspoons fish sauce
2 teaspoons cornstarch
3 tablespoons water
2¹/₂-in (6-cm) ginger, very finely sliced
1 red finger-length chili, deseeded and very finely
    sliced
3 green onions (scallions), cut into 1¹/₄-in (3-cm)
    lengths

**1** Wash the whole fish, dry thoroughly and cut two
deep diagonal slashes on each side.
**2** Heat the oil in a wok and when smoking hot,
sprinkle the cornstarch on both sides of the fish,
rubbing it in with your fingers. Shake the fish to
remove excess flour. If using fish fillets, coat them
with cornstarch in the similar way.
**3** Lower the fish carefully into the oil and fry, turning once, until the fish is golden brown and cooked
through, about 10 to 12 minutes, flicking the hot oil
up over the surface of the fish during cooking. If you
are using fish fillets, they will need around 4 minutes. Drain the fish on paper towels and keep warm
in a low oven.
**4** Make the Sauce by pouring out all but 1 tablespoon of oil from the wok. Reheat the oil and fry
the garlic until golden, then add the water, sugar,
vinegar and fish sauce. Bring to a boil. Mix the
cornstarch and water together and add to the wok,
stirring over moderate heat until the Sauce thickens
and clears, about 30 seconds. Add the ginger, chili
and green onions and simmer for 1 minute.
**5** Put the fish on a serving dish, pour over the hot
Sauce and scatter with the pickled ginger. Garnish
with the cucumber slices and fresh coriander leaves.

# Thai Fried Fish with Ginger Sauce

*Pla priu wan*

It's always impressive when you serve a whole fish and this Thai dish tastes even better
than it looks. The fish is bathed with a piquant sweet and sour sauce, enhanced by plenty of
fresh and pickled ginger, fish sauce and fresh coriander leaves (cilantro). Although it won't
look as impressive, you could use fish fillets as a quicker alternative.

# Fish with Sweet Tamarind Sauce

*Ca chien sot me chua*

I'm not usually a fan of fish fillets, preferring to buy whole fish (it's easier to check the freshness) and cook it whole so that I don't waste any of the flesh. However, when I can be sure of really fresh fillets (or if I have time to cut them off a whole fish), I love to prepare this Vietnamese recipe, a beautifully orchestrated blend of taste sensations—sweet, sour, salty, spicy and aromatic with fresh mint leaves. Use a nonstick pan so that you can minimize the amount of oil needed for frying.

**Serves 4–6**
**Preparation time:** 15 mins
**Cooking time:** 20 mins

1¹/₂–2 heaped tablespoons tamarind pulp, soaked in ³/₄ cup (185 ml) warm water, squeezed and strained to obtain the juice
4 tablespoons fish sauce
3 tablespoons sugar
1 teaspoon soy sauce
1¹/₄–1¹/₂ lbs (600–700 g) white fish fillets (snapper or bream), cut into 4 serving pieces, bones removed but skin left on
¹/₂ teaspoon freshly ground black pepper
¹/₃ cup (40 g) cornstarch
3 tablespoons oil
1 tablespoon minced garlic
1 tablespoon finely minced ginger
1 red finger-length chili, minced
2 tablespoons minced mint leaves
Additional mint sprigs, for garnish

1 Combine the tamarind juice, fish sauce, sugar and soy sauce in a bowl, stirring to dissolve the sugar. Set aside.
2 Dry the fish with paper towels, then sprinkle both sides with the black pepper. Dredge in the cornstarch to coat both sides. Shake to remove the excess.
3 Heat 2 tablespoons of the oil in a skillet (preferably nonstick) until smoking hot. Add the fish pieces, skin side down. Reduce the heat to medium and cook until the skin is crisp and golden brown, about 4 to 5 minutes. Turn the fish and fry until cooked through, about another 2 minutes. Transfer to a serving plate and keep warm.
4 Heat the remaining oil in the skillet and stir-fry the garlic, ginger and chili over medium heat for 30 seconds. Add the tamarind mixture and simmer for 1 minute, stirring constantly. Stir in the mint leaves and immediately pour the sauce over the fish. Garnish with additional mint sprigs and serve.

**Grilled Whole Sambal Fish**

# Grilled Whole Sambal Fish
## *Sambal ikan panggang*

It doesn't take long to make the fragrant spicy filling that lifts these Malay-style fish out of the ordinary. To be honest, Malays are more likely to fry fish now that the wood or coconut husk fire has virtually disappeared from modern kitchens, but I prefer to use a grill or broiler because it reduces the consumption of fat and the fish still tastes great. For best results, you need really fresh fish. Work quickly and you'll have the fish ready and waiting to be devoured in just 30 minutes.

**Serves 4**
**Preparation time:** 15 mins
**Cooking time:** 12 mins

4 small whole fish, about 1¹/₂–2 lbs (700 g–1 kg) preferably mackerel or herring, scaled and cleaned, heads left on
1 teaspoon salt
1 teaspoon ground turmeric
1–2 tablespoons oil

**Spicy Filling**
4 shallots, minced
1 clove garlic
2 teaspoons minced galangal
4 red finger-length chilies, sliced, some seeds removed if preferred
4 candlenuts, minced
1 stalk lemongrass, tender inner part of bottom third only, thinly sliced
¹/₂ teaspoon dried shrimp paste
2 tablespoons oil
¹/₂ teaspoon sugar
¹/₂ teaspoon salt

1 Pat the fish dry inside and out with paper towels. Make slits right along both sides of the back bone of each fish to create a pocket. Sprinkle the fish on both sides with the salt and turmeric and leave to marinate while you prepare the filling.
2 Make the Spicy Filling by processing the shallots, garlic, galangal, chilies, candlenuts, lemongrass and dried shrimp paste in a spice grinder until smooth, adding a little of the oil, if needed, to keep the blades turning. Heat the oil in a small pan. Add the smooth paste, sugar and salt and stir-fry over low heat until it starts to smell fragrant, 3 to 4 minutes.
3 Put your grill on to heat so that it will be hot immediately the fish are ready for cooking.
4 Use a teaspoon to push some of the Spicy Filling into both pockets of each fish. Brush the fish on both sides with oil, then grill or broil until golden brown on both sides and cooked through, about 4 minutes for each side. Serve with rice and a cooked vegetable and salad, such as Cucumber and Pineapple Salad (page 25).

# Fragrant Grilled Fish Cakes

## *Pepes ikan*

My friend Rani, with whom I lived in Ubud while working on a book on Balinese cuisine, was always making little banana-leaf packets of chopped fish, poultry, meat, or even eels caught in a nearby paddy field. This is her version of diced fish fillets mixed with a chili-coconut sauce, scented with lemon basil and lime juice. These packets can be prepared in advance and steamed or (even better) cooked over a grill just before they're needed. If you can't obtain banana leaf (which does wonderful things to the texture and flavor) you could steam the mixture in four to six small heat-proof bowls.

**Serves 4–6**
**Preparation time:** 35 mins
**Cooking time:** 10–20 mins

1¼ lbs (600 g) white fish fillets, skinned, boned and cut into ½-in (1-cm) dice
3 tablespoons minced lemon basil leaves (see Note)
1 teaspoon lime or lemon juice
12 pieces banana leaves, each about 8 in- (20-cm) square, softened in boiling water or in a gas flame

**Spice Paste**
4 shallots, minced
2 cloves garlic, minced
1 tablespoon finely minced galangal
1 stalk lemongrass, tender inner part of bottom third only, thinly sliced
2 red finger-length chilies, minced, deseeded if desired
4–6 bird's-eye chilies, minced
4 candlenuts, minced
1 teaspoon salt
½ teaspoon dried shrimp paste, toasted (page 22)
⅔ cup (170 ml) thick coconut milk

> **NOTE:** If lemon basil leaves are not available, add two finely shredded kaffir lime leaves or 1 teaspoon grated kaffir lime or lemon rind.

1 Prepare the Spice Paste by processing all the ingredients except the coconut milk in a spice grinder until very smooth, adding a little of the coconut milk, if necessary, to keep the blades turning. Put the paste in a small saucepan and stir in the coconut milk. Bring to a boil over medium heat, stirring. Lower the heat and simmer, uncovered, stirring frequently, for 3 minutes.

2 Transfer the Spice Paste to a bowl and add the fish, lemon basil leaves and lime juice, stirring to mix well.

3 Place a piece of banana leaf on a clean work bench. Put about 2 heaped table-spoons of the fish mixture in a rectangle across the center of the banana leaf. Fold over the end closest you to cover the fish, then tuck in both sides, turning the package over to make an envelope. Repeat until the fish is used up, stirring the mixture each time to distribute the coconut milk evenly.

4 Cook over moderately hot charcoal or under a broiler for about 5 minutes on each side. Alternatively, put the packets in a steamer and steam over a wok of rapidly boiling water for 15 minutes, adding more boiling water after 10 minutes and making sure the water does not touch the packets during the steaming. If using heat-proof bowls, steam for 20 to 25 minutes. Serve hot or at room temperature.

# Grilled Fish with Sweet Soy Dip

One of the easiest, healthiest and most delicious ways of cooking fish is to grill it over hot charcoal (or use a table-top griller or broiler). If green mangoes are available, try the grilled fish with piquant Thai Green Mango Salad with Cashews spooned over the top, or make the Indonesian dip of sweet soy sauce with lime or lemon juice, shallots, chili and lemon-scented or Asian basil leaves. Both options are really tasty—the choice is yours. (You could also grill one large fish rather than four small ones.)

**Serves 4**
**Preparation time:** 15 mins
**Cooking time:** 30 mins

4 small whole fish or 1 whole fresh fish, about 3 lbs (1.5 kg) (such as snapper, bream, trevally, grouper, or barramundi), cleaned and scaled
1–2 teaspoons salt
2–3 tablespoons oil
Half quantity of Thai Green Mango Salad with Cashews (page 67)
1/2 cup (125 ml) sweet soy sauce
1/4 cup (60 ml) lime or lemon juice, or more to taste
2 shallots, thinly sliced
1 red finger-length chili, deseeded if desired, thinly sliced
2 tablespoons coarsely chopped lemon basil or Asian basil leaves

1 Wash the fish, drain well, then wipe inside and out with paper towels. Cut two deep diagonal slashes on each side of each fish and sprinkle both sides with salt.
2 Grease the grill of a barbecue, table-top grill or broiler liberally with oil. Brush both sides of the fish with the oil and put it on the grill. Cook small fish for 3 to 5 minutes on each side, until golden brown and cooked through. A large fish will take 20 to 30 minutes to cook, depending on the thickness. Check to see if it is cooked through by inserting the tip of a knife to ensure that the flesh in the center is white. If not, put it back and cook a little longer.
3 While the fish is cooking, make the Thai Green Mango Salad with Cashews. To prepare the spicy soy sauce dip, combine the soy sauce, lime or lemon juice, shallots, chili and basil. Taste, adding more lime juice if desired, then divide between four small sauce bowls.
4 Transfer the cooked fish to a large platter. Spoon the Thai Green Mango Salad with Cashews over the top of the fish, and serve with the bowls of spicy soy sauce dip.

# Chapter 6

# Vegetables and Tofu

To start with, the variety of vegetables found in most local markets is astonishing and cultivated vegetables aren't the only option. Rural cooks have an impressive knowledge of wild edible plants and go on a daily forage to pluck young leaves from trees and shrubs, pick herbs growing beside a stream or a paddy field, or gather wild ferns and immature fruits. In most regions, cultivated and wild vegetables are often preferred raw in salads, or served with a spicy dip, rather than eaten cooked. (Salads are featured in the Soups and Salads Chapter.)

Cooked vegetable dishes are never dull. For example, this chapter includes Cabbage Braised in Creamy Coconut Milk (page 137), Stir-fried Pumpkin and Snowpeas (page 139), a classic recipe for Stir-fried Vegetables with Oyster Sauce (page 136), some interesting tofu dishes and even a recipe for Fragrant Spiced Pineapple (page 140).

# Stir-fried Vegetables with Oyster Sauce

*Kanaa namman hoi*

Many Thai cooks prepare leafy green vegetables and *gai larn*, a type of kale sometimes known as Chinese broccoli, using this basic method. It is very similar to the Chinese way of stir-frying vegetables, yet the use of fish sauce as well as oyster and soy sauce adds a definite Thai touch. You can use *gai larn*, regular broccoli, or any dark leafy Asian greens.

**Serves 4**
**Preparation time:** 5 mins
**Cooking time:** 5 mins

1¹/₄ lbs (600 g) *gai larn*, or 13 oz (375 g) broccoli, broken into florets, or a bunch of leafy Asian greens (Chinese flowering cabbage, Chinese white cabbage or *bok choy*)
1 tablespoon oil
2 cloves garlic, minced
Water or chicken stock, if needed
1 teaspoon oyster sauce
1 teaspoon fish sauce
1 teaspoon soy sauce
¹/₂ teaspoon sugar

**1** If using *gai larn*, cut the leaves away from the stems and discard (these are too tough to eat). Peel the stems if the skin seems thick, then cut the stems lengthwise into ¹/₄-in (0.5-cm) strips. Cut the strips across into 2-in (5-cm) lengths. Bring a large saucepan of water to a boil and blanch the *gai larn* or broccoli for 1 minute. Drain in a sieve, then cool in a bowl of cold water.
**2** If using Chinese greens, cut across into 2 in-(5-cm) lengths, discarding the hard bottom part of the stems if using Chinese flowering cabbage. Do not blanch, but set aside.
**3** Heat the oil in a wok for 30 seconds. Add the garlic and stir-fry for a few seconds until it starts to smell fragrant. Add the blanched *gai larn* or broccoli, or the raw leafy greens and stir-fry until they are just cooked, adding a tablespoon or two of water or chicken stock if the vegetables start to stick. Usually, the moisture from washing the vegetables (especially if you're using leafy greens) is enough to prevent this happening.
**4** Add the oyster sauce, fish sauce, soy sauce and sugar and stir-fry for a few seconds. Transfer to a serving dish and serve immediately.

# Cabbage Braised in Creamy Coconut Milk

*Kobis masak lemak*

It makes sense in areas where ripe coconuts literally drop from the trees (if not plucked with the help of a trained monkey) to use coconut milk in cooking, its creamy sweetness transforming everything from meat to poultry, seafood and vegetables. This Malay recipe for cabbage braised in lightly seasoned coconut milk can be adapted to many other vegetables and makes a perfect accompaniment to rice and other dishes, particularly fried or grilled food that is dry.

**Serves 4–6**
**Preparation time:** 10 mins
**Cooking time:** 20 mins

1 tablespoon oil
4 shallots, finely sliced
1 clove garlic, minced
1 red or green finger-length chili, sliced
3 cups (750 ml) coconut milk
1/2 small round cabbage (1 lb/500 g), halved lengthwise, cored and coarsely sliced across
2 tablespoons dried shrimp, soaked in water to soften
1/2 teaspoon salt, or more to taste

1 Heat the oil in a saucepan, then add the shallots, garlic and chili, and stir-fry over low-medium heat until soft, 3 minutes. Add the coconut milk, increase the heat slightly and bring almost to a boil, stirring constantly.
2 Put in the cabbage, dried shrimp and salt, stirring to mix well. Bring almost to a boil, then lower the heat.
3 Simmer gently with the pan uncovered until the cabbage is soft, about 15 minutes, stirring occasionally. Taste and add more salt if desired. Transfer to a serving bowl and serve hot or warm with plain white rice.

> **NOTE:** Try using two small sweet potatoes, cut into chunks, with a bunch of English spinach or amaranth instead of the cabbage; pumpkin and long beans are also very good cooked in this way.

# Spicy Sambal Eggplant

### *Sambal terong hay bee*

If you think eggplant is rather dull, this flavorful Nonya recipe is sure to change your mind. Most Nonya cooks deep-fry the eggplants first, but I prefer to keep the fat content low by cooking them whole in a tiny bit of oil in a covered pan. For maximum flavor, halve the eggplants before spreading them with sambal topping; this may be a bit tricky if using miniature eggplants, so try to find the regular slender Asian variety.

**Serves 4–6**
**Preparation time:** 15 mins
**Cooking time:** 15 mins

4 tablespoons oil
1 lb (500 g) slender Asian eggplants, skin left on, stems trimmed
1/3 cup (40 g) dried shrimp, dry-roasted for 3–4 minutes
1 medium onion, halved lengthwise, thinly sliced across
1 teaspoon sugar
1/2 teaspoon salt
Juice of 1 small round green lime (*limau kesturi*), or lime juice, to taste

**Seasoning Paste**
2 red finger-length chilies, sliced
6 shallots, minced
1 large clove garlic, minced
1 teaspoon dried shrimp paste, toasted (page 22)

1  Heat 1 tablespoon of the oil in a wide saucepan or covered skillet. Put in the whole eggplants. Cover the pan and cook the eggplants over low heat, turning until they are cooked through. Remove the eggplants, cut in half lengthwise, then cut across in two or three pieces, depending on their size. Keep warm.
2  Process the dried shrimp to a powder in a spice grinder. Remove and set aside.
3  Process all the Seasoning Paste ingredients to a smooth paste in a spice grinder, adding a little of the oil, if necessary, to keep the blades turning.
4  Heat the remaining 3 tablespoons of oil in a wok, then add the onion and stir-fry over low-medium heat until softened, about 2 to 3 minutes. Add the Seasoning Paste and dried shrimp powder and stir-fry over low heat, until cooked and fragrant, about 4 minutes. If the mixture starts to stick, add a little more oil or about a tablespoon of water. When the mixture is cooked, add the sugar and salt, stirring until dissolved.
5  Spread the cooked mixture over the top of each piece of eggplant. Squeeze the lime juice to taste and serve hot or at room temperature with rice and other dishes.

> **NOTE:** If slender Asian eggplants are not available, miniature eggplants could be used.

Spicy Sambal Eggplant

# Stir-fried Pumpkin and Snowpeas

*Cha bonle*

This Cambodian recipe is the essence of simplicity: pumpkin stir-fried with sugar snap or snow peas and green onion, flavored with garlic, fish sauce, a touch of sugar and black pepper. Apart from looking beautiful —the golden orange pumpkin contrasting with bright green peas—this versatile recipe can be served as part of any Southeast Asian meal.

**Serves 4–6**
**Preparation time:** 15 mins
**Cooking time:** 5 mins

3 tablespoons oil
2–3 cloves garlic, very finely minced
1¹/₂–2 tablespoons fish sauce
1 teaspoon sugar
1 lb (500 g) butternut or other bright yellow pumpkin, peeled, seeds and fibers discarded, flesh thinly sliced
7 oz (200 g) snow peas, tips and strings removed (if using large snow peas, cut into half diagonally)
2 green onions (scallions), cut into 2-in (5-cm) lengths
¹/₂ teaspoon freshly ground black pepper

1 Heat the oil in a wok, then add the garlic and stir-fry for a few seconds. Add the fish sauce and sugar, stirring, then put in the pumpkin and stir-fry over medium-high heat, 2 minutes.
2 Add the snow peas and stir-fry for 2 minutes. Add the green onions, stir-fry for 30 seconds. Sprinkle with the black pepper and transfer to a serving dish.

**NOTE:** In Cambodia, pork is often added to this dish; you could add 7 oz (200 g) shredded pork fillet after putting in the fish sauce and sugar and stir-fry for 1 minute before adding the pumpkin and snow peas.

# Fragrant Spiced Pineapple

## *Pacheri nanas*

Pineapples are often used as a vegetable when they're still a little under-ripe, as in this Malay/Indonesian recipe, which you'll often find at weddings. This is partly because of the pineapple's bright yellow color—yellow is the color of royalty and a bride and groom are regarded as "king and queen" on their marriage day—and also because this hot, sour, fragrantly spiced dish is irresistible. Be sure not to use ripe pineapple for the best result.

**Serves 4–6**
**Preparation time:** 15 mins
**Cooking time:** 15 mins

1 medium under-ripe fresh pineapple (about 3 lbs/1.5 kg), peeled, quartered lengthwise, core discarded, each quarter halved across
3–4 cups (750 ml–1 liter) water
1¹/₂ teaspoons ground turmeric
3 tablespoons oil
1 large onion, thinly sliced
1 whole star anise
6 cardamom pods, slit and bruised or ¹/₄ teaspoon cardamom seeds or ground cardamom
2-in (5-cm) cinnamon
8 cloves
4 cloves garlic, minced
2-in (5-cm) ginger, minced
1 teaspoon salt
2 tablespoons sugar, or more to taste
1–2 red finger-length chilies, halved length-wise, leaving stem attached

**1** Put the pineapple in a medium saucepan and add just enough water to cover. Add the turmeric, stir, then bring to a boil. Lower the heat and simmer, uncovered, for 10 minutes, then drain, discarding the liquid. Cut the pineapple into bite-sized pieces.
**2** Wash and dry the saucepan and return to heat with the oil. When moderately hot, add the onion, star anise, cardamom, cinnamon and cloves, and stir-fry over medium heat for 2 minutes. Add the garlic and ginger, and stir-fry over low-medium heat, 2 minutes. Add 1 cup (250 ml) water, salt and sugar. Bring to a boil and simmer, uncovered, for 2 minutes.
**3** Put in the pineapple and chili and simmer for 2 minutes. Taste and add more sugar, if desired. Serve hot with rice and other dishes.

# Laotian Grilled Eggplant

## *Yam makheua*

Eggplant, a rather neutral vegetable, is never dull in Southeast Asia. You can find variations of grilled eggplant salad in Cambodia and Thailand, but what gives this Laotian version its distinctive flavor is the roasted shallots, garlic and chilies. Combine these with the smoky flavor of the roasted eggplant and you get a really flavorful salad. It is easy for Lao cooks to grill the ingredients over hot coals, but you'll still get a good result using a gas or electric grill or dry-roasting in a wok.

**Serves 4**
**Preparation time:** 10 mins
**Cooking time:** 10–15 mins

2–3 (about 13 oz/375 g) slender Asian
   eggplants
3 shallots, unpeeled
3–4 cloves garlic, unpeeled
2–3 red finger-length chilies, preferably green
1/4 cup (12 g) coarsely chopped fresh coriander
   leaves (cilantro) or dill
1/4 cup (10 g) coarsely chopped mint leaves
1 green onion (scallion), thinly sliced
2–3 tablespoons fish sauce
3 tablespoons lime juice
2 teaspoons sugar
Salt, to taste

1 Prick the eggplants in several places with a fork, then cook over hot charcoal or under a very hot grill, turning until the skin has started to blacken and the eggplants are soft. Alternatively, you could set the eggplants on a rack directly over a gas flame or under a broiler and cook until done. Leave until cool enough to handle, then half lengthwise and scrape out the flesh with a spoon. Chop coarsely and put in a bowl.

2 Put the shallots, garlic and chilies on a fine mesh grill and cook over charcoal, a gas flame or under a broiler, turning until slightly blackened and soft; you could cook these at the same time as the eggplants. Alternatively, put them all in a heavy dry wok and cook, turning several times, until they darken and become soft; the chilies and garlic will be ready before the shallots. When cool enough to handle, cut off the stem end of the chilies and slice. Peel the shallots. Cut the rounded end off each garlic clove, then grab the skin of the pointed end and squeeze out the garlic. Pound or process the shallots, garlic and chilies in a spice grinder just until they turn into a coarse paste.

3 Put the eggplants in a bowl and stir in the shallot paste, herbs, fish sauce, lime juice and sugar. Taste and add a little salt, if desired. Serve with rice and other dishes.

# Stir-fried Tofu and Bean Sprouts

Isn't it nice when really healthy vegetable dishes also taste great? This recipe gives you the protein and phytoestrogens of tofu, together with the rich beta-carotene, iron and vitamin C content of the Chinese chives. The Chinese chives also add an earthy flavor, but if you can't find these, green onions work well. Fish sauce, sugar and black pepper give a Cambodian accent to this easy and deliciously healthy vegetable dish.

**Serves 4**
**Preparation time:** 20 mins
**Cooking time:** 4 mins

3 tablespoons oil
2 cloves garlic, finely sliced
1 cake pressed tofu, dried, cut into $^1/_2$-in
 (1-cm) dice
Bunch of garlic chives, or 6 green onions
 (scallions), cut into $1^1/_2$-in (4-cm) lengths
4 cups (200 g) bean sprouts, scraggly tail ends
 removed, washed and well-drained
3 tablespoons fish sauce
1 tablespoon sugar
$^1/_4$ teaspoon freshly ground black pepper

**1** Heat the oil in a wok for 30 seconds, then add the garlic and stir-fry for 5 seconds. Add the tofu and stir-fry over medium-high heat until crisp and golden all over, about 3 minutes. Add the garlic chives or green onions and stir-fry for 30 seconds, then add the bean sprouts and stir-fry for another 30 seconds.
**2** Sprinkle over the fish sauce, sugar and pepper and stir-fry for 30 seconds. Transfer to a serving dish and serve hot with rice.

# Red Curry and Tofu

*Tua fak yow tau hu*

It's amazing what a difference a little Thai red curry paste and Asian basil leaves makes to this simple combination of tofu and long beans. You can use either home-made or bought curry paste (page 15) for this tasty vegetable dish, which is ready in moments.

**Serves 4**
**Preparation time:** 10 mins
**Cooking time:** 10 mins

1/4 cup (60 ml) chicken stock or water
1 tablespoon fish sauce
1 teaspoon sugar
1/2 cup (125 ml) oil
1 cake pressed tofu, patted dry with paper towels
2 teaspoons minced garlic
2–3 teaspoons Thai Red Curry Paste (page 115)
13 oz (375 g) green beans, cut into 1¹/4-in (3-cm) lengths
1/4 cup (12 g) firmly packed sprigs of Asian basil leaves

1 Combine the stock or water, fish sauce and sugar in a small bowl, stirring to dissolve the sugar. Set aside.
2 Heat the oil in a wok, add the tofu and fry until golden brown and crisp on both sides. Drain well on paper towels, then cut into 1/2-in (1-cm) dice.
3 Discard all but 2 teaspoons of the oil. Reheat the oil, add the garlic and stir-fry over medium heat for a few seconds, then add the curry paste and stir for just 15 seconds. Add the green beans and stir-fry for 2 minutes.
4 Add the stock mixture, stir to mix well, then add the diced tofu. Stir-fry over medium heat until the beans are cooked, about 2 to 3 minutes. Add the basil leaves, stir and then transfer to a serving dish. Serve hot with rice and other dishes.

# Silken Tofu with Chinese Vegetables

## Tau hu sawam

The name of this elegant, Chinese-inspired Thai recipe translates as "heavenly tofu" and that's a pretty good description of its appearance and flavor. The feather-light texture and relatively neutral flavor of silken tofu is enhanced by a sauce and is a perfect foil for decorative pieces of carrot and mushroom, surrounded by *bok choy* cabbage. It's great for serving at a special dinner and tastes every bit as good as it looks.

**Serves 4**
**Preparation time:** 15 mins
**Cooking time:** 12 mins

2 rolls (250 g each) silken tofu, cut into bite-sized slices
1/2 small carrot, very thinly sliced, blanched in boiling water for 3 minutes
6–8 fresh or canned straw mushrooms, rinsed and drained, halved lengthwise
2 teaspoons cornstarch
1/2 cup (125 ml) chicken stock
2 teaspoons oyster sauce
1 teaspoon fish sauce
1/2 teaspoon sugar
1/4 teaspoon white pepper
2 teaspoons oil
1 teaspoon very finely minced garlic
4 baby *bok choy*, halved lengthwise, blanched in boiling water for 2 minutes, drained, or 1/2 lb (250 g) broccoli florets, blanched until just cooked

1 Put the tofu slices in a single layer in a shallow heat-proof bowl. Place 1 slice of carrot half on top of each piece of tofu, then arrange 1 mushroom half on top of the carrot.
2 Combine the cornstarch, stock, oyster sauce, fish sauce, sugar and pepper in a small bowl, stirring to dissolve the sugar. Set aside.
3 Heat the oil in a small saucepan and stir-fry the garlic over low heat until golden. Add the stock mixture, bring to a boil and stir until it thickens and clears, about 1 minute. Spoon over each piece of tofu.
4 Put the dish of tofu in a bamboo steamer or on a perforated rack set in a wok of rapidly boiling water. Cover and steam for 5 minutes. Remove the dish from the steamer. Dip the *bok choy* in boiling water to reheat, drain well and place around the tofu before serving.

# Fried Tofu with Tomato Sambal

*Tua hu sot cha*

This easy recipe consists of pressed tofu, pan-fried until crisp and golden outside, served with a tomato sauce. Sounds simple—and it is—but the flavor is even better than you might expect. The fresh tomato sauce is accented with a perfect balance of fish sauce, soy sauce, garlic, sugar and salt, another example of the delicacy and sophistication of the Vietnamese palate.

**Serves 4**
**Preparation time:** 10 mins
**Cooking time:** 10 mins

3 tablespoons oil
4 cakes pressed tofu (about 13 oz/375 g), dried with paper towels
Sprigs of fresh coriander leaves (cilantro), to garnish

Tomato Sambal
1 teaspoon oil
1 teaspoon finely minced garlic
2 medium ripe tomatoes, skinned and diced
1/4 cup (60 ml) water
4 teaspoons fish sauce
2 teaspoons soy sauce
2 teaspoons sugar
2 teaspoons tomato paste
1/4 teaspoon freshly ground black pepper

**1** Prepare the Tomato Sambal first by heating the oil in a medium saucepan. Add the garlic and stir-fry over medium heat until golden. Add the tomatoes and stir-fry until slightly softened, about 2 minutes. Add the water, fish sauce, soy sauce, sugar, tomato paste and pepper. Bring to a boil, lower the heat, cover and simmer for 3 minutes. Remove from the heat but keep warm.
**2** Heat the oil in a skillet until very hot. Add the tofu and fry until golden brown underneath, about 3 minutes. Turn and fry the other side, about 3 minutes. Drain on paper towels and transfer to a serving dish. Pour over the Tomato Sambal, garnish with coriander sprigs and serve with steamed rice and other dishes.

# Chapter 7

# Desserts

Even though meals in Southeast Asia are likely to end with fresh fruit, this doesn't mean that you can't find all kinds of irresistible cakes and sweet concoctions—it's just that they're more likely to be eaten as a between-meal snack. A common (and welcome) sight on the streets of Thailand in particular is a mobile vendor of sweetmeats. Dozens of intricate and often beautifully colored or decorated cakes, some of them nestling in tiny cups of banana leaf, prepared by specialist cooks allow everyone to indulge in their passion for something sweet without having to spend time cooking.

Bananas are probably the most widely grown fruit in Southeast Asia, so it's not surprising to find them appearing in many cakes or desserts. Bananas are often partnered with coconut milk, such as in the Vietnamese recipe for Banana and Sago Pudding (page 156). Malay and Indonesian cooks often add other ingredients to this combination, including pieces of ripe jackfruit, young coconut, or diced sweet potato and yam.

Glutinous or sticky rice is readily available in most of Southeast Asia, inexpensive and with a delicious flavor and texture. It's almost always transformed into desserts and you're sure to share the passion for this once you've tried Balinese Black Rice Pudding (page 157), the inimitable partnering of Thai Mangoes with Sweet Sesame Coconut Rice (page 151), or Cambodia's banana-leaf packets of Sweet New Year's Rice Cakes (page 148).

There are cooling, syrupy desserts too, such as Thai Red Rubies in Sweet Coconut Milk (page 155). And did you know you can find pancakes and crêpes in Southeast Asia? Try Burma's Rice Flour Crêpes with Sweet Cinnamon and Peanut (page 150) and Indonesia's quaintly named "bachelor in a blanket" (Coconut Pancakes, page 154).

# Sweet New Year's Rice Cakes

*Nom n'sahm chaek*

It's always exciting to buy banana-leaf wrapped packages in those parts of Southeast Asia where you don't speak enough of the local language to be certain what's inside. This Cambodian concoction was one of my more successful stabs in the dark, banana leaf filled with glutinous rice, coconut milk, banana and grated coconut. You can either steam or grill the cakes, which are always served during the Chaul Chham or Cambodian New Year. Aluminum foil could be used to replace banana leaf, although the flavor and texture won't be the same.

**Serves 4–8**
**Preparation time:** about 1 hour + 3–4 hours
    soaking
**Cooking time:** 35 mins

**1 cup (250 ml) coconut milk**
**¼ teaspoon salt**
**1¼ cups (250 g) uncooked glutinous rice,
    soaked 3–4 hours, drained**
**½ cup (50 g) freshly grated coconut, or ½ cup
    (40 g) desiccated coconut moistened in
    4 tablespoons milk**
**8 pieces of banana leaf, each about 9-in (23-cm)
    square, softened in a gas flame or hot water**
**8 very small finger bananas (about 3½ in/
    9 cm long), or 2 large bananas, halved
    lengthwise, cut across into 3½-in (9-cm)
    lengths**

**1** Bring the coconut milk and salt slowly to a boil in a saucepan, stirring all the time. Add the drained rice, lower the heat and cook over low heat, stirring constantly, until all the coconut milk has been absorbed and the rice has started to form a dry sticky mass, 4 to 5 minutes.
**2** Transfer to a bowl, stir in the grated coconut and leave until cool enough to handle. (Check the sweetness of the bananas; if not using the really sweet ladies' fingers, you may want to add about 1 tablespoon of caster sugar to the rice mixture.)
**3** Put the banana leaf pieces, darker side down, on a bench or table top. Add one-eighth of the rice to each leaf, spreading it to make a thin rectangle a little wider than the banana. Put a whole banana or a banana quarter down the center of the rice. Moisten your hands with water, lift the sides and ends of the banana leaf up and use them to help to push the rice over the top of the banana, molding the rice so that it completely encloses the banana. Use your hands, if necessary.
**4** Fold over the end of the banana leaf closest to you, tuck in the sides and roll up as firmly as possible so that the rice remains clinging around the banana; give the completed roll a gentle squeeze to make sure the rice is compressed. Put the packets in a steaming basket or on a perforated rack set well above the water level in a wok and steam over rapidly boiling water for 25 minutes. Leave to cool slightly while still wrapped in the banana leaf.
**5** If you prefer to grill the packets over charcoal, put over a moderate (not hot) fire, turning the packets a couple of times until the leaf starts to char slightly and the rice is cooked, 15 to 20 minutes. Check a roll to make sure the rice is translucent, which means it is cooked.
**6** Serve the packets either warm or at room temperature. They are normally eaten while holding onto the banana leaf wrapping (which keeps your fingers from getting sticky). If you want to be a little more elegant, you could put a roll in a bowl and drizzle the top of each with coconut cream, or sprinkle with some lightly toasted sesame seeds.

# Rice Flour Crêpes with Sweet Cinnamon and Peanut

*Ye mon*

Looking for an inexpensive and easily made dessert? Try this simple Burmese recipe, light and crispy rice flour crêpes filled with crunchy peanuts and sweetened with cinnamon sugar. Even if you haven't a thing in the house (naturally, I'm assuming everyone has rice flour and peanuts), you can make this delightful dessert or mid-afternoon snack in minutes.

**Serves 4–6**
**Preparation time:** 10 mins
**Cooking time:** 20 mins

2 cups (320 g) rice flour
1/4 teaspoon bicarbonate of soda (baking soda)
Pinch of salt
21/2 cups (625 ml) cold water
1/2 cup (125 g) caster sugar, or slightly less if preferred
1 teaspoon ground cinnamon
2 tablespoons oil
2–3 tablespoons butter
11/4 cups (190 g) dry-roasted peanuts, coarsely ground

1 Put the rice flour, baking soda and salt in a bowl and stir in the water to make a very thin batter. Combine the sugar and ground cinnamon in a small bowl and set near the stove with the peanuts and butter.
2 Heat 2 teaspoons of the oil in a 8-in (20-cm) skillet, preferably nonstick, swirling it to coat the sides and base. When hot, pour in 1/3 cup (85 ml) of batter, swirling the skillet so that the batter spreads evenly. Cook over medium-high heat until the top of the batter is set and the bottom turns golden brown, about 2 minutes.
3 Take about 1/2 to 1 teaspoon butter on the point of a knife and spread it over the top of the pancake so that it melts in. Sprinkle over 2 tablespoons of the peanuts and about 1 table-spoon of cinnamon sugar and cook for about 15 seconds.
4 Carefully fold the pancake in two, cook a few seconds longer, then transfer to a serving dish. Repeat until the batter is used up, adding 1 tea-spoon of oil to the pan each time, to make eight pancakes. Serve hot.

# Mangoes with Sweet Sesame Coconut Rice

## Mamuang khao niaw

This partnership of sweet ripe mangoes with glutinous white rice bathed in creamy coconut milk is deservedly a Thai classic and is the only exception to my conviction that serving ripe mangoes any way but plain and simple is gilding the lily. When mangoes are in season, buy a couple, follow this recipe and paradise will be yours.

**Serves 4**
**Preparation time:** 7 mins
**Cooking time:** 20–40 mins

1 cup (200 g) uncooked glutinous rice
2/3 cup (170 ml) thick coconut milk
1/4 cup (60 g) caster sugar, or more to taste
1/4 teaspoon salt
2 large ripe sweet mangoes
4 tablespoons coconut cream
2 teaspoons sesame seeds, for garnish
  (optional)

**1** Put the rice in a bowl and pour over enough boiling water to cover. Stand for 15 minutes, then drain.
**2** Spread a large clean piece of cheesecloth or tea towel inside a steamer, or over a perforated metal disk that fits in your wok. Spread the rice evenly over the cloth, cover the steamer with a lid and set in a wok over boiling water. Steam until the rice is tender, about 40 minutes, topping up the water in the steamer with additional boiling water every 10 minutes or so to ensure plenty of steam. When the rice is cooked, remove the steamer from the wok and leave the rice to cool slightly.
**3** Combine the coconut milk, sugar and salt in a bowl, stirring to dissolve the sugar. Add the warm rice, mix well and leave the rice for 30 minutes to absorb the coconut milk. Divide the rice between four serving plates.
**4** Cut each mango in half lengthwise, as close to the stone as possible. Cut each half into four lengthwise slices and scoop out the flesh from the skin with a spoon. Put four slices on each plate next to the rice and serve, spooning coconut cream over the top of each portion of rice.

> **NOTE:** Although mango is the best, you could try other fruit such as ripe papaya (pawpaw), canned or fresh jackfruit or even ripe bananas with the sticky rice. The Thais often add a sprinkle of lightly toasted sesame seeds or crushed dry-roasted peanuts to the top of the rice when serving.

# Water Chestnut and Sweet Corn Pudding

## *Tar kor haed*

You can use either fresh or canned water chestnuts, or sweet corn kernels, to give texture and flavor to these lovely creamy sweetmeats, which are particularly good after a meal of spicy food. Although normally served in tiny banana leaf cups, these are time consuming to make and since the cakes are not steamed (when the moisture of the banana leaves would be an important factor), it's more practical to use small bowls.

**Serves 4–6**
**Preparation time:** 10 mins
**Cooking time:** 8 mins

**5 pandanus leaves (about 12 in/30 cm in length), cut into 2-in (5-cm) lengths, or a few drops each of pandanus essence and green food coloring (only if using water chestnuts)**
**1³/4 cups (435 ml) water**
**Few drops jasmine or vanilla essence (only if using sweet corn)**
**1/2 cup (80 g) tapioca flour**
**1/3 cup (85 g) caster sugar**
**1/2 cup (about 100 g) finely diced fresh or canned water chestnuts, or 1/2 cup (60 g) drained canned sweet corn kernels**
**3 tablespoons rice flour**
**1¹/2 cups (375 ml) thick coconut milk**
**Large pinch of salt**

1 If you are using water chestnuts, put the pandanus leaves and ³/4 cup (185 ml) of the water into a blender and process until the leaves are finely pulverized and the water has turned bright green. Strain through a fine sieve, pressing down to obtain as much juice as possible. Combine the juice or a few drops of pandanus essence with the remaining water, tapioca flour and sugar in a medium saucepan. If using sweet corn, combine 1³/4 cups water (435 ml) and jasmine or vanilla essence with the tapioca flour and sugar.

2 Cook over low heat, stirring constantly with a wooden spoon, until the mixture becomes very thick and clear, leaving the side of the pan. If using fresh water chestnuts, blanch in boiling water for 1 minute. Drain and add the blanched or canned water chestnuts (or the sweet corn kernels if using) to the cooked mixture, reserving about 2 tablespoons for garnishing. Transfer the mixture to six or eight small glass dessert bowls, about 1/2 cup (125 ml) in capacity.

3 Combine the rice flour, coconut milk and salt in a small pan. Cook over low heat, stirring constantly, until the mixture has become very thick. Spoon the rice flour mixture over the top of each water chestnut mixture in the dessert bowls, spreading evenly. If using sweet corn, decorate the top of each portion with a few of the reserved kernels. Cool, then refrigerate until required.

Water Chestnut and Sweet Corn Pudding

# Sago Pearls with Sweet Coconut Cream   *Gula melaka*

An American friend, faced with this dessert for the first time, remarked unkindly that the sago looked like frog spawn. When I finally persuaded her to taste this soothing mixture of jelly-like sago, creamy coconut milk and sweet palm sugar syrup, she was ecstatic. This Malaysian dish used to be a great hit with the colonial British and was an essential item after a big curry tiffin. This is not difficult to make and can be prepared well in advance.

**Serves 4**
**Preparation time:** 10 mins
**Cooking time:** 15 mins

1 cup (180 g) dried pearl sago
8 cups (2 liters) water
1 tablespoon milk
1 cup (250 ml) thick coconut milk
Pinch of salt

**Palm Sugar Syrup**
3/4 cup (135 g) shaved palm sugar
3/4 cup (185 ml) water
1 pandanus leaf, raked with a fork and tied into a knot (optional)

**1** Put the sago in a sieve and shake over the sink to dislodge any loose starch. Bring the water to a boil in a large saucepan. Slowly pour in the sago, stirring constantly with a wooden spoon. Boil uncovered, stirring occasionally, until the sago balls turn transparent, about 15 minutes.
**2** Tip the sago into a large wire mesh sieve and hold under cold running water to wash away the starch, about 45 seconds. Shake the sieve until the liquid has gone, then stir in the milk, which will change the dull grey color of the cooked sago to a more appealing white. Transfer the sago to four glass serving dishes and when cool, refrigerate.
**3** Make the Palm Sugar Syrup by combining the sugar, water and pandanus leaf in a small saucepan. Bring to a boil, stirring until the sugar has dissolved. Simmer until the syrup has reduced to 1/2 cup (125 ml). Discard the pandanus leaf and leave to cool.
**4** Transfer the Palm Sugar Syrup and thick coconut milk to separate small jugs, adding salt to the thick coconut milk. Serve with chilled sago, each person adding the syrup and thick coconut milk to taste.

# Coconut Pancakes

## *Bujang dalam selimut*

I love the Indonesian name for these pancakes, which translates as "bachelor in a blanket." Known as *kuih dadar* in Malaysia, the pancakes are filled with freshly grated coconut and palm sugar, although if you have to use desiccated coconut, this also works well. These pancakes (one of my daughters' favorites when she was young) are usually a great hit with children. For a more sophisticated version, try the sauce as described in the Note.

**Serves 4–6**
**Makes about 12 pancakes**
**Preparation time:** 20 mins
**Cooking time:** 30 mins

1 cup (125 g) plain flour
Pinch of salt
1 egg, lightly beaten
1–1¹/4 cups (250–310 ml) milk
1–2 few drops green food coloring (optional)
1–3 few drops pandanus essence (optional)
3 tablespoons oil

**Filling**
¹/2 cup (90 g) shaved palm sugar
¹/3 cup (85 ml) cup water
1¹/2 cups (150 g) freshly grated coconut,
    or 1¹/4 cups (100 g) desiccated coconut
    moistened with 1 cup (250 ml) milk

**NOTE:** If fresh pandanus leaves are available, use these instead of green food coloring and pandanus essence; blend 4 pandanus leaves, chopped, with ¹/2 cup (125 ml) of the milk, then press through a sieve. Add the pandanus-flavored milk to the batter along with the rest of the milk. You could also make a coconut sauce to pour over the pancakes. Combine ¹/2 cup (125 ml) coconut cream, ¹/2 cup (125 ml) water, 1 teaspoon sugar, 1 teaspoon cornstarch and, if desired, a few drops of pandanus essence. Cook over low heat, stirring constantly, until the sauce thickens and clears, 2 to 3 minutes. Serve at room temperature.

1  Sift the flour and salt into a medium bowl. Make a well in the center and add the egg and 1 cup (250 ml) of the milk. Mix to make a smooth thin batter, adding more milk, if necessary. Add the food coloring and pandanus essence, if using.
2  Prepare the Filling by putting the palm sugar and water in a small saucepan. Heat gently, stirring until dissolved, then add the coconut. Stir over low heat for 1 minute. Spread out a plate to cool.
3  Heat a small nonstick skillet (about 6 in or 15 cm in diameter) with about ¹/2 teaspoon of the oil, swirling to cover the bottom of the pan. Pour out any excess oil. Heat until moderately hot. Add almost ¹/4 cup (60 ml) of the pancake batter, swirling to spread over the bottom of the pan. Cook until set underneath, about 45 seconds, then turn and cook another 30 to 45 seconds. Stack on a plate and continue until the batter is used up.
4  When the pancakes are cool, put 3 tablespoons of the Filling in the center of each pancake. Roll up the end closest to you, tuck in the sides, then roll up to enclose the Filling firmly. Serve at room temperature.

**Coconut Pancakes**

# Thai Red Rubies in Sweet Coconut Milk

## *Tub tim krob*

Which would you prefer: a bowl of rubies or of sapphires for dessert? You can use either fresh or canned water chestnuts for this attractive Thai recipe, where a little red food coloring transforms them into rubies, or blue coloring produces sapphires, which are served floating in chilled sweetened coconut milk.

**Serves 4–6**
**Preparation time:** 35 mins
**Cooking time:** 8 mins

1 cup (250 ml) water
1¹/4 cups (250 g) sugar
Few drops of red or blue food coloring
¹/4 cup (40 g) tapioca flour
30 water chestnuts, peeled and finely diced
2¹/2 cups (625 ml) coconut milk
Rose or jasmine essence, to taste

**1** Bring the water and sugar to a boil, stirring to dissolve the sugar. Boil uncovered for 1 minute, then cool and refrigerate.
**2** Bring a large saucepan of water to a boil and add enough food coloring to color the water. Put the tapioca flour in a plastic bag and add the diced water chestnuts. Hold the top of the bag closed and shake to coat the water chestnuts. Transfer the water chestnuts to a sieve or colander and shake to dislodge any excess flour.
**3** Put the floured water chestnuts in the saucepan of boiling water and simmer, uncovered, for 2 minutes. Tip them into a colander and drain, then transfer to a bowl of iced water to cool. (The water chestnut pieces will be covered with a pale red or blue jelly-like coating.)
**4** Just before serving, combine the chilled sugar syrup, coconut milk and flavoring essence. Divide the rubies (or sapphires) between four to six bowls and add the flavored coconut milk to each bowl. Add an ice-cube or two to each serving, if desired, and serve immediately.

# Banana and Sago Pudding

*Che chuoi*

Variations on this banana and coconut milk theme are found throughout Southeast Asia. Nonya cooks in Malaysia may add diced sweet potato or yam to the basic mix, creating the delightfully named *bubor cha cha* (which sounds to me like a South American dance), while other cooks add ripe jackfruit or pieces of jelly-like young coconut meat. This Vietnamese version is very simple: bananas, sago and coconut milk, sweetened with palm sugar and sprinkled with sesame seeds.

**Serves 4–6**
**Preparation time:** 25 mins
**Cooking time:** 10 mins

3 tablespoons dried pearl sago, soaked in cold water for 10 minutes, drained
4 cups (1 liter) coconut milk
4 tablespoons shaved palm sugar, or more to taste
Pinch of salt
8 very small finger bananas, or 4 ripe but firm medium bananas, cut diagonally into 3/4-in (2-cm) slices
2 tablespoons sesame seeds, toasted until golden brown

1 Put the sago in a sieve and shake over the sink to dislodge any loose starch. Put in a saucepan and add the coconut milk, palm sugar and salt. Bring slowly to a boil, stirring occasionally, then lower the heat and simmer, uncovered, until the sago balls are starting to turn transparent, about 10 minutes.
2 Add the banana slices and simmer for 5 minutes. Transfer to four to six serving bowls and serve warm or at room temperature, sprinkling with the sesame seeds just before serving.

**Banana and Sago Pudding**

# Balinese Black Rice Pudding   *Bubor pulot hitam*

Just about everyone who tries this delicious nutty-tasting dish while traveling in Indonesia or Malaysia falls in love with it. Some cooks combine white and black glutinous rice, while Nonya cooks often add dried longans for a smoky flavor, but the basics of brownish-black glutinous rice (which turns a deep purple brown when cooked), palm sugar and coconut milk remain constant. This can be enjoyed any time, for breakfast, as a between-meal snack or as a dessert.

**Serves 4**
**Preparation time:** 10 mins
**Cooking time:** 1 hour

1 cup (200 g) uncooked glutinous black rice, washed in several changes of water, drained
6 cups (1.5 liters) water
2 pandanus leaves, raked with a fork, tied into a knot
2 tablespoons shaved palm sugar
1 cup (250 ml) coconut milk
1–2 tablespoons sugar, or more to taste
1 cup (250 ml) coconut cream
Pinch of salt

1 Bring the rice and water to a boil in a large saucepan, stirring occasionally. Cover, lower the heat and simmer for 30 minutes.
2 Add the pandanus leaves, palm sugar and coconut milk. Return to a boil, stirring to dissolve the sugar, then lower the heat and simmer, uncovered, stirring from time to time, until the rice is soft and swollen, 20 to 25 minutes. Remove and discard the pandanus leaves.
3 Taste and add white sugar, if desired. Divide the rice between four bowls.
4 Combine the coconut cream and salt, then pour 2 tablespoons into the center of each serving. Put the remaining coconut cream in a jug for adding to taste. Serve warm or at room temperature.

# Index

**A**

Anchovies
    about, 12
    Malaysian Coconut Rice, 91

**B**

Bamboo shoots
    about, 12
    Thai Red Beef Curry, 115
Banana leaves
    about, 12
    working with, 22
Banana(s)
    and Sago Pudding, 156
    Sweet New Year's Rice Cakes, 148
Basic recipes. *See also* Dips
    All-purpose Dippers, 26
    Burmese Crispy Dried Shrimp
        Sprinkle, 30
    Cucumber and Pineapple Salad, 25
    Daikon and Carrot, 30
    Red Bell Pepper Relish, 29
    Roasted Thai Chili Paste, 31
    Salted Soybean, Pork and Peanut
        Sauce, 31
    Vietnamese Bean Sprout Pickles,
        29
    Vinegared Cucumber Salad, 25
Basil (Thai)
    about, 12
    Chicken, Thai, 98
    and Green Curry Paste, Chicken
        with, 99
    and Red Curry, Fish Mousse with,
        128
Beans. *See also* Soybean(s), Salted
    Red Curry and Tofu, 143
Bean Sprout(s)
    about, 12
    Pickles, Vietnamese, 29
    Singapore Hokkien Noodles, 82
    and Tofu, Stir-fried, 142
Beef
    and Broccoli, Thai River Noodles
        with, 84
    Classic Indonesian Fried Rice, 88
    Curry, Thai Red, 115
    Grilled, Salad, Thai, 110
    Ground, Spicy Laotian, 119
    Jerky, Laotian Spiced, 46
    Lemongrass, with Peanuts, 109
    Noodle Soup, Vietnamese, 63

Satay, Extraordinary, 34
Soup, Spicy Thai, 51
Southern Thai Beefball Soup, 52
Stew, Laotian, with Asian Herbs,
    118
Bok choy, about, 13
Breads. *See* Pancakes
Broccoli
    and Beef, Thai River Noodles with,
        84
    Vegetarian Noodles with Chinese
        Mushrooms, 83

**C**

Cabbage
    about, 13
    Braised in Creamy Coconut Milk,
        137
    Salad, Crunchy Burmese, 69
    Vietnamese Chicken Salad, 73
Calamansi limes, about, 13
Candlenuts, about, 13
Cardamom, about, 13
Carrot and Daikon, 30
Cashews
    Barbecued Pork Salad with Thai
        Herbs, 70
    and Mango, Chicken with, 106
    Thai Green Mango Salad with, 67
Chayote, about, 13
Chicken
    Basil, Thai, 98
    Burmese Noodles in Coconut
        Broth, 76
    Coconut Soup, Fragrant, 55
    Fragrant Cambodian, 97
    Green Curry, 101
    with Green Curry Paste and Basil,
        99
    Indonesian Grilled, 104
    Laotian, with Onions and
        Tomatoes, 102
    with Mango and Cashews, 106
    Mild Javanese, Bathed in Coconut
        Milk, 103
    Noodle Soup, Madurese, 64
    or Pork, Thai Rice Soup with, 59
    Pork, and Shrimp, "Big Salad"
        with, 71
    Salad, Vietnamese, 73
    Spicy Tamarind, with Lemongrass,
        107

Stock, Basic, 23
Thai Barbecued, 100
Vietnamese Honey-glazed, 96
Vietnamese Mixed Coconut Rice,
    90
Wings, Fragrant Cambodian, 44
Chili(es)
    Crab, Famous Singapore, 127
    and Dried Shrimp Paste Dip,
        Malaysian, 28
    and Fish Sauce Dip, Simple Thai, 27
    Roasted, Paste, Thai, 31
    Thai Green Curry Paste, 101
    Thai Red Curry Paste, 115
    types of, 14
Chinese celery, about, 13
Chinese rice wine, about, 13
Cinnamon, about, 13
Coconut
    about, 14
    Balinese Seafood Satays, 47
    Chicken Soup, Fragrant, 55
    grated, dry-roasting, 22
    Pancakes, 154
    Pumpkin Soup, Fragrant, 56
    Toasted, Nonya Rice Noodles
        with, 77
    Toasted, Thai Rice Salad with, 86
Coconut Milk
    about, 14
    Banana and Sago Pudding, 156
    Burmese Noodles in Coconut
        Broth, 76
    Creamy, Cabbage Braised in, 137
    Fish Mousse with Basil and Red
        Curry, 128
    Green Curry Chicken, 101
    Malaysian Coconut Rice, 91
    Mangoes with Sweet Sesame
        Coconut Rice, 151
    Mild Javanese Chicken Bathed
        in, 103
    Sago Pearls with Sweet Coconut
        Cream, 153
    Singapore-style Laksa Noodle
        Soup, 60
    Sweet, Thai Red Rubies in, 155
    Sweet New Year's Rice Cakes, 148
    Thai Red Beef Curry, 115
    Vietnamese Mixed Coconut Rice,
        90
Coriander leaves (cilantro), about, 15

Corn
    Fritters, Southern Thai, 41
    and Spinach, Clear Soup with, 53
    Sweet, and Water Chestnut
        Pudding, 152
Crab
    Famous Singapore Chili, 127
    Vietnamese Spring Rolls, 36
Crêpes, Rice Flour, with Sweet Cinnamon
    and Peanut, 150
Cucumber
    and Pineapple Salad, 25
    Salad, Vinegared, 25
Curry
    Beef, Thai Red, 115
    Green, Chicken, 101
    Lamb, Malaysian, 111
    Paste, Green, and Basil, Chicken,
        99
    Paste, Green, Thai, 101
    Paste, Thai Red, 115
    Red, and Tofu, 143
Curry powder, about, 15

**D**

Daikon and Carrot, 30
Daikon radish, about, 15
Desserts
    Balinese Black Rice Pudding, 157
    Banana and Sago Pudding, 156
    Coconut Pancakes, 154
    Mangoes with Sweet Sesame
        Coconut Rice, 151
    Rice Flour Crêpes with Sweet
        Cinnamon and Peanut, 150
    Sago Pearls with Sweet Coconut
        Cream, 153
    Sweet New Year's Rice Cakes, 148
    Thai Red Rubies in Sweet Coconut
        Milk, 155
    Water Chestnut and Sweet Corn
        Pudding, 152
Dips
    Chili and Dried Shrimp Paste,
        Malaysian, 28
    Fish Sauce, Vietnamese, 27
    Salt, Lime and Black Pepper,
        Cambodian, 27
    Shrimp Paste and Lime, Thai, 28
    Tangy Tomato, 26
    Thai Fish Sauce and Chili, Simple,
        27

Duck, Roast, on a Bed of Crispy Noodles, 105

**E**

Eggplant
    about, 15
    Laotian Beef Stew with Asian Herbs, 118
    Laotian Grilled, 141
    Spicy Sambal, 138

Eggs
    Classic Indonesian Fried Rice, 88
    Scrambled, with Chinese Sausages, 116
    Simple Thai Pork Omelet, 113

**F**

Fish
    anchovies, about, 12
    Balinese Seafood Satays, 47
    Cakes, Fragrant Grilled, 132
    Fried, Thai, with Ginger Sauce, 129
    Grilled, with Sweet Soy Dip, 133
    Malaysian Coconut Rice, 91
    Mousse with Basil and Red Curry, 128
    or Shrimp Cakes, Tasty Thai, 35
    Penang Nonya Laksa Noodle Soup, 58
    preserved, about, 15
    salted, about, 19
    Smoked, and Green Mango Salad, 72
    Soup, Cambodian Sweet and Sour, 57
    with Sweet Tamarind Sauce, 130
    Tangy Marinated, 42
    Thai Tuna Carpaccio, 37
    Whole Sambal, Grilled, 131

Fish Sauce
    about, 16
    and Chili Dip, Simple Thai, 27
    Dip, Vietnamese, 27

Five spice powder, about, 16
Fritters, Southern Thai Corn, 41
Fruit. *See also specific fruits*
    Salad, Tropical, with Palm Sugar Dressing, 68

**G**

Galangal, about, 16
Garlic, crisp-frying, 22
Garlic chives, about, 16
Garlic-flavored oil, preparing, 22
Ginger, pickled, about, 18
Ginger buds, about, 16
Ginger Sauce, Thai Fried Fish with, 129
Green onions (scallions), about, 16

Green Papaya Salad, Sweet and Spicy, 66

**J**

Jicama, about, 16

**K**

Kaffir limes, about, 16

**L**

Laksa leaf, about, 20
Lamb Curry, Malaysian, 111
Lemongrass
    about, 17–18
    Beef with Peanuts, 109
    Soup, Thai, with Mushrooms, 65
    Spicy Tamarind Chicken with, 107

Lime(s)
    calamansi, about, 13
    kaffir, about, 16
    Salt, and Black Pepper Dip, Cambodian, 27

**M**

Mango(es)
    and Cashews, Chicken with, 106
    green, about, 16
    Green, and Smoked Fish Salad, 72
    Green, Pork, 117
    Green, Salad, Thai, with Cashews, 67
    with Sweet Sesame Coconut Rice, 151

Meat. *See* Beef; Lamb; Pork
Meatballs, Grilled Vietnamese, 43
Mint, Vietnamese, about, 20
Mousse, Fish, with Basil and Red Curry, 128
Mushrooms
    black Chinese, about, 12
    Chinese, Vegetarian Noodles with, 83
    Thai Lemongrass Soup with, 65

Mussels, Fragrant Steamed, 126

**N**

Noodle(s)
    Beef Soup, Vietnamese, 63
    'Birthday,' with Pork and Shrimp, 79
    Burmese, in Coconut Broth, 76
    Chicken Soup, Madurese, 64
    Crispy, a Bed of, Roast Duck on, 105
    Laksa, Soup, Penang Nonya, 58
    Laksa, Soup, Singapore-style, 60
    Rice, Classic Pad Thai, 78
    Rice, Malay, in Sweet Tamarind Gravy, 81
    Rice, Nonya, with Toasted Coconut, 77

Rice, Soup, Cambodian, 89
Singapore Fried Kway Teow, 85
Singapore Hokkien, 82
Thai River, with Beef and Broccoli, 84
types of, 17
Vegetarian, with Chinese Mushrooms, 83
Vietnamese Spring Rolls, 36

Nuts. *See also* Cashews; Peanut(s)
    candlenuts, about, 13

**O**

Omelet, Pork, Simple Thai, 113
Oyster sauce, about, 18

**P**

Pad Thai Rice Noodles, Classic, 78
Palm sugar, about, 18
Pancakes
    Coconut, 154
    Lacy Malay, 93
    Saigon Shrimp and Pork, 39

Pandanus leaf, about, 18
Papaya, Green, Salad, Sweet and Spicy, 66
Peanut(s)
    and Cinnamon, Rice Flour Crêpes with, 150
    dry-roasting, 23
    Lemongrass Beef with, 109
    Northern Thai Leaf Cup Nibbles, 40
    Salted Soybean, and Pork Sauce, 31

Pearl sago. *See* Sago Pearls
Pepper. *See also* Chili(es)
    Red Bell, Relish, 29

Pickles, Vietnamese Bean Sprout, 29
Pineapple
    Cambodian Sweet and Sour Fish Soup, 57
    and Cucumber Salad, 25
    Fragrant Spiced, 140

Pork. *See also* Sausages
    Barbecued, Salad with Thai Herbs, 70
    Cambodian Garlic, 108
    Cambodian Rice Noodle Soup, 89
    Chicken, and Shrimp, "Big Salad" with, 71
    Classic Pad Thai Rice Noodles, 78
    Crunchy Thai Stuffed Shrimp, 122
    Fresh Summer Rolls, 45
    Green Mango, 117
    Grilled Vietnamese Meatballs, 43
    Omelet, Simple Thai, 113
    or Chicken, Thai Rice Soup with, 59
    Salted Soybean, and Peanut Sauce, 31

and Shrimp, 'Birthday Noodles' with, 79
and Shrimp, Thai Fried Rice with, 92
and Shrimp Pancakes, Saigon, 39
Singapore Fried Kway Teow, 85
Singapore Hokkien Noodles, 82
Soy Braised, Nonya, 112
Stock, Basic, 23
Sweet Soy Balinese, 114
Vietnamese Mixed Coconut Rice, 90
Vietnamese Spring Rolls, 36

Poultry. *See* Chicken; Duck
Puddings
    Balinese Black Rice, 157
    Banana and Sago, 156
    Water Chestnut and Sweet Corn, 152

Pumpkin
    Coconut Soup, Fragrant, 56
    and Snowpeas, Stir-fried, 139

**R**

Relish
    Daikon and Carrot, 30
    Red Bell Pepper, 29

Rice
    Black, Pudding, Balinese, 157
    Cakes, Sweet New Year's, 148
    Fried, Classic Indonesian, 88
    Malaysian Coconut, 91
    Salad, Thai, with Toasted Coconut, 86
    Soup, Thai, with Pork or Chicken, 59
    Sweet Sesame Coconut, Mangoes with, 151
    Thai Fried, with Shrimp and Pork, 92
    Vietnamese Mixed Coconut, 90

Rice flour, about, 18
Rice paddy herb, about, 18
Rice paper wrappers, about, 18
Rice powder, roasting, 22
Rice vinegar, about, 18

**S**

Sago Pearls
    about, 18
    Banana and Sago Pudding, 156
    with Sweet Coconut Cream, 153

Salads
    Barbecued Pork, with Thai Herbs, 70
    "Big," with Chicken, Pork and Shrimp, 71
    Cabbage, Crunchy Burmese, 69
    Chicken, Vietnamese, 73
    Cucumber and Pineapple, 25

Green Mango, Thai, with Cashews, 67
Green Papaya, Sweet and Spicy, 66
Grilled Beef, Thai, 110
Rice, Thai, with Toasted Coconut, 86
Smoked Fish and Green Mango, 72
Tropical Fruit, with Palm Sugar Dressing, 68
Vinegared Cucumber, 25
Salam leaf, about, 19
Sauce, Salted Soybean, Pork and Peanut, 31
Sausages
    Chinese, Scrambled Eggs with, 116
    dried Chinese, about, 15
Saw-tooth coriander, about, 19
Seafood. See Fish; Shellfish
Sesame oil, about, 19
Sesame seeds, about, 19
Shallots
    about, 19
    crisp-frying, 22
    flavoring oil with, 22
Shellfish. See also Shrimp
    Delicate Squid with Thai Herbs, 125
    Famous Singapore Chili Crab, 127
    Fragrant Steamed Mussels, 126
    Singapore Fried Kway Teow, 85
    Squid with Garlic and Black Pepper, 124
Shrimp
    Balinese Seafood Satays, 47
    Chicken, and Pork, "Big Salad" with, 71
    Classic Pad Thai Rice Noodles, 78
    Crispy Dried, Sprinkle, Burmese, 30
    dried, about, 15
    Fresh Summer Rolls, 45
    Malay Rice Noodles in Sweet Tamarind Gravy, 81
    Northern Thai Leaf Cup Nibbles, 40
    or Fish Cakes, Tasty Thai, 35
    and Pork, 'Birthday Noodles' with, 79
    and Pork, Thai Fried Rice with, 92
    and Pork Pancakes, Saigon, 39
    Singapore Fried Kway Teow, 85
    Singapore Hokkien Noodles, 82
    Singapore-style Laksa Noodle Soup, 60
    Skewers, Marinated, 123
    Soup, Classic Tom Yam, 54

Thai Stuffed, Crunchy, 122
Vietnamese Spring Rolls, 36
Shrimp crackers, about, 19
Shrimp Paste, Dried
    about, 19
    and Chili Dip, Malaysian, 28
    and Lime Dip, Thai, 28
    toasting, 22
Snowpeas and Pumpkin, Stir-fried, 139
Soups
    Beef, Spicy Thai, 51
    Beefball, Southern Thai, 52
    Beef Noodle, Vietnamese, 63
    Chicken Noodle, Madurese, 64
    Clear, with Spinach and Corn, 53
    Coconut Chicken, Fragrant, 55
    Coconut Pumpkin, Fragrant, 56
    Fish, Cambodian Sweet and Sour, 57
    Laksa Noodle, Penang Nonya, 58
    Laksa Noodle, Singapore-style, 60
    Lemongrass, Thai, with Mushrooms, 65
    Rice, Thai, with Pork or Chicken, 59
    Rice Noodle, Cambodian, 89
    Tamarind Vegetable, Javanese, 50
    Tom Yam Shrimp, Classic, 54
Southeast Asian cuisine
    essential ingredients, 12–21
    flavors of, 8–11
    tips and techniques, 22–23
Soybean(s), Salted
    about, 19
    Pork, and Peanut Sauce, 31
Soy sauce, about, 20
Spices, working with, 23
Spinach and Corn, Clear Soup with, 53
Spring Rolls, Vietnamese, 36
Squid
    Delicate, with Thai Herbs, 125
    with Garlic and Black Pepper, 124
    Singapore Fried Kway Teow, 85
Star anise, about, 20
Starters and snacks
    Balinese Seafood Satays, 47
    Extraordinary Beef Satay, 34
    Fragrant Cambodian Chicken Wings, 44
    Fresh Summer Rolls, 45
    Grilled Vietnamese Meatballs, 43
    Laotian Spiced Beef Jerky, 46
    Northern Thai Leaf Cup Nibbles, 40
    Saigon Shrimp and Pork Pancakes, 39
    Southern Thai Corn Fritters, 41
    Tangy Marinated Fish, 42
    Tasty Thai Shrimp or Fish Cakes, 35

Thai Tuna Carpaccio, 37
Vietnamese Spring Rolls, 36
Stew, Laotian Beef, with Asian Herbs, 118
Stock, Basic Chicken or Pork, 23
Summer Rolls, Fresh, 45

T
Tamarind
    about, 20
    Chicken, Spicy, with Lemongrass, 107
    Gravy, Sweet, Malay Rice Noodles in, 81
    Sauce, Sweet, Fish with, 130
    Vegetable Soup, Javanese, 50
Tapioca, about, 20
Tofu
    and Bean Sprouts, Stir-fried, 142
    Fried, with Tomato Sambal, 145
    Malay Rice Noodles in Sweet Tamarind Gravy, 81
    Red Curry and, 143
    Silken, with Chinese Vegetables, 144
    Singapore-style Laksa Noodle Soup, 60
    types of, 21
    Vegetarian Noodles with Chinese Mushrooms, 83
Tomato(es)
    Dip, Tangy, 26
    and Onions, Laotian Chicken with, 102
    Sambal, Fried Tofu with, 145
Tom Yam Shrimp Soup, Classic, 54
Tuna Carpaccio, Thai, 37
Turmeric, about, 20

V
Vegetable(s). See also specific vegetables
    Chinese, Silken Tofu with, 144
    Stir-fried, with Oyster Sauce, 136
    Tamarind Soup, Javanese, 50
Vietnamese mint, about, 20

W
Water Chestnut(s)
    about, 20
    and Sweet Corn Pudding, 152
    Thai Red Rubies in Sweet Coconut Milk, 155
Water spinach, about, 20–21
White fungus, about, 21
Wild pepper leaves, about, 21
Winged bean, about, 21
Woodear fungus, about, 21

Published by Tuttle Publishing, an imprint of Periplus Editions (HK) Ltd.

www.tuttlepublishing.com

Text copyright © 2010 Wendy Hutton
Photographs © Periplus Editions (HK) Ltd

ISBN: 978-0-8048-4166-5
(Previously published as Green Mangoes and Lemon Grass)

Book design by the Periplus Design Team

Distributed by

North America, Latin America & Europe
Tuttle Publishing
364 Innovation Drive
North Clarendon, VT 05759-9436 U.S.A.
Tel: 1 (802) 773-8930;
Fax: 1 (802) 773-6993
info@tuttlepublishing.com
www.tuttlepublishing.com

Japan
Tuttle Publishing
Yaekari Building, 3rd Floor
5-4-12 Osaki; Shinagawa-ku;
Tokyo 141 0032
Tel: (81) 3 5437-0171;
Fax: (81) 3 5437-0755
www.tuttle.co.jp

Asia Pacific
Berkeley Books Pte. Ltd.
61 Tai Seng Avenue, #02-12,
Singapore 534167
Tel: (65) 6280-1330; Fax: (65) 6280-6290
inquiries@periplus.com.sg
www.periplus.com

12 11 10
8 7 6 5 4 3 2 1

Printed in Singapore